Another Global City

Another Global City

Historical Explorations into the Transnational Municipal Moment, 1850–2000

Edited by Pierre-Yves Saunier and Shane Ewen

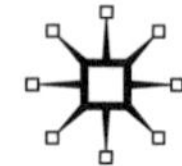

ANOTHER GLOBAL CITY

First published in 2008 by
PALGRAVE MACMILLAN™
175 Fifth Avenue, New York, N.Y. 10010 and
Houndmills, Basingstoke, Hampshire, England RG21 6XS.
Companies and representatives throughout the world.

PALGRAVE MACMILLAN is the global academic imprint of the Palgrave
Macmillan division of St. Martin's Press, LLC and of Palgrave Macmillan Ltd.
Macmillan® is a registered trademark in the United States, United Kingdom
and other countries. Palgrave is a registered trademark in the European
Union and other countries.

ISBN-13: 978-0-230-60663-0
ISBN-10: 0-230-60663-6

Library of Congress Cataloging-in-Publication Data

Another global city : historical explorations into the transnational municipal
    moment, 1850–2000 / edited by Pierre-Yves Saunier and Shane Ewen.
       p. cm.
    Includes bibliographical references and index.
    ISBN 0-230-60663-6
    1. Municipal government—History—19th century. 2. Municipal
    government—History—20th century. 3. Globalization—Political aspects.
    4. International relations and culture. I. Saunier, Pierre-Yves. II. Ewen, Shane.

JS66.A66 2008
307.76072'2—dc22   2007050074

A catalogue record of the book is available from the British Library.

Design by Scribe Inc.

First edition: August 2008

10 9 8 7 6 5 4 3 2 1

Printed in the United States of America.

Contents

Preface

Writing the history of cities has been an exercise in paradox: we historians, from Henri Pirenne to Fernand Braudel, have viewed the generic city within the long-term flows of social and economic forces, and stressed its nature as being a "crossroad." At the same time, the overwhelming number of theses, articles, and books have dealt with the history of particular cities, often through urban biographies. From here, we recognize a discrepancy and a gap: a discrepancy between our claims and our endeavors, and a gap between the riches of what we know about the idiosyncrasies of specific cities and the scarce amount we understand about the contribution of these histories to the history of the wider world. The time is ripe for mending the discrepancy and bridging the gap. As historians begin to study the global history of our world—ostensibly by historicizing globalization—urban historians have an important part to play.

The historical study of cities as sites and actors for the flows that have connected and disconnected the globe is clearly a promising field. Consider the kind of flows identified by anthropologist Arjun Appadurai as creating major disjunctures in our modern world: ethnoscapes (the flows of people and their impact), mediascapes (for information), technoscapes (technologies), financescapes (capital), and ideoscapes (ideas, ideals, and ideologies).[1] We think that urban historians can contribute here by explaining how cities—as platforms, hubs, and sites for these different temporal and spatial flows—have often been places where disjuncture was created. Taking ethnoscapes as an example, urban historians can historicize Appadurai's assertion that the global movement of people is an essential feature of the world today, which affects national policies and international relations "to a hitherto unprecedented degree." They can point to thirteenth-century Venice, sixteenth-century Mexico or Goa, early modern Constantinople, or late nineteenth-century New York City and demonstrate how urban authorities and societies have so often had to face the question of transcultural urban landscapes and polyglot societies. They did find some of their solutions in the observation of cities across borders and oceans, as in the extreme case of racial segregation.[2]

Cities have also been sites for temporary migrations, such as those generated by pilgrims or tourists. There again, urban historians can trace the historic nuances of these migrations by showing how much the impact and responses to these momentous eruptions have transformed Mecca, Rome, Benares, or cities on the European Riviera and the Southeast Asian seashore over centuries. Similar suggestions could be made for each of Appadurai's "scapes." Consider briefly how values such as freedom and identity have been assembled and maintained in urban settings. Local newspapers and, more recently, mass media have historically lived off a diet of city news, while a host of technologies have emerged, spread, and organized for and between urban sites: mediascapes have a long urban track record.

In all these fields, and others, there is room for urban historians to examine how global forces have shaped cities' evolutions well before the last decades of the twentieth century as well as to explore the contribution of city life, technologies, and actors in shaping these global forces. This exploration of cities as sites and actors of globalization is the fundamental question facing historians who want to prove that cities matter and chart their contribution to world history. This book is only a glimpse in that direction, with its focus on the connections and circulations among municipal urban governments in the modern age. But there are clues that other historians are moving in a similar direction.

Shane Ewen and Pierre-Yves Saunier

Notes on the Contributors

Andrew Brown-May is a senior lecturer in Australian history at the University of Melbourne (Australia), and co-editor of *The Encyclopedia of Melbourne* (Cambridge University Press, 2005). ajbm@unimelb.edu.au

Shane Ewen is a senior lecturer in social and cultural history at Leeds Metropolitan University (Great Britain). He has written extensively on British municipal history, especially in relation to fire services and urban networks. s.ewen@leedsmet.ac.uk

Jeffrey Hanes is a professor of history and Director of the Center for Asian and Pacific Studies at the University of Oregon (United States). A specialist of modern urban Japan, he is now working on a manuscript that examines the production and consumption of urban space in modern Osaka. hanes @oregon.uoregon.edu

Yon Hsu is a research fellow at Centre for Broadcasting Studies, Concordia University, Montreal (Canada). She completed her doctoral dissertation on Montreal's urban diplomacy. She is currently writing a manuscript on the transnational networks of antagonism, affinity, ignorance, and cooperation between Taipei and Shanghai. yonhsu@yahoo.ca

Nancy Kwak is an assistant professor of history at Polytechnic University, New York (United States). She received her PhD from Columbia University in 2006 for her thesis on "A Citizen's Right to Decent Shelter: Public Housing in New York, London, and Singapore, 1945 to 1970." kwak161 @gmail.com

Nora Lafi is a researcher at the Zentrum Moderner Orient in Berlin (Germany). Her research deals with the dynamics of the Ottoman urban reforms. She has recently edited *Municipalités méditerranéennes: les réformes urbaines ottomanes au miroir d'une histoire comparée* (K. Schwarz, 2005). nora.lafi@rz .hu-berlin.de

Renaud Payre is an associate professor of political sciences at the Université of Lyon (France). He has written *Une science communale? Réseaux réformateurs et municipalité providence (CNRS Editions, 2007)*. He is now researching contemporary European networks of cities and municipal internationalization policies. Renaud.payre@wanadoo.fr

Silvia Robin is a professor of political science at Rosario National University (Argentina). She dedicates her research to civil society and political parties and to the analysis of the local political scene. silviarobin@gmail.com

Pierre-Yves Saunier is a researcher at the Environnement Ville Société team (CNRS/Université de Lyon, France). His current research attempts to reconstruct the history of nursing circulations and connections in the modern age. Pierre-yves.saunier@wanadoo.fr

Jonathan Soffer is an associate professor of history at Polytechnic University, New York (United States). He is currently writing a biography of New York Mayor Edward I. Koch. jsoffer@poly.edu

Sébastien Velut is a researcher at the French Research Institute for Development (IRD). His work deals with the spatial effects of globalization, particularly local and regional development issues in Argentina and Chile. He edited, with Jérôme Lombard and Evelyne Mesclier, *La mondialisation côté Sud* (Editions de l'IRD, 2006). sebastien.velut@ens.fr

Marjatta Hietala is a professor of history at the University of Tampere (Finland). She has studied extensively the diffusion of innovations and the long-term urban development. Her publications include *Services and Urbanisation at the Turn of the Century: The Diffusion of Innovations* (Finnish Historical Society, 1987) and (with co-author Marjatta Bell) *Helsinki the Innovative City: Historical Perspectives* (Finnish Literature Society, 2002). Marjatta.hietala@uta.fi

CHAPTER 1

Introduction

Global City, Take 2:
A View from Urban History

Pierre-Yves Saunier

Since the 1960s, when it emerged as a distinctive subdiscipline, urban history has attracted endless questions about the autonomy of its realm—both among its followers and its critics—not least over whether the city was a dependent or an independent variable.[1] Much of this energy derived from the fact that there was a clear connection between the intellectual agenda of the discussion (Was there an order of facts that can be labeled as specifically "urban"?) and its academic focus (Was it possible to create a new field with its apparatus of chairs, research funds, and dedicated organisations?). One of the cleavages that emerged from this discussion was the distinction between those who claimed that cities were cohesive and active social bodies, and those who insisted that they were a node in systems of cities that were fueled by exogenous economic and social processes. The frailty of such debates has been pinpointed by outsiders such as Charles Tilly, who once admonished urban historians to leave their bailiwick and stop oscillating between "the time space particularism of local history and grand timeless, spaceless processes, causes and effects."[2]

The diagnosis was interesting, but Tilly's cure for this disease was to exhort urban historians to admit that their turf was quintessentially social history and to turn back to interpreting "the ways that global social process articulate with small-scale social life."[3] The problem is that this suggestion was not foreign to the discussions that had fathomed the futility of the cleavages he had singled out: the overlap or distinction between urban and social history had always been at the heart of the debate, notably between the supporters of the "new urban history" and the followers of the British historian H. J. Dyos.[4] The Gordian knot was hard to cut, especially when it took a form that was so close to the debate between agency and structure, which has harnessed so much of the energy of the social sciences and humanities, for a very meager return if we consider that there is no possible winner in such a badly arranged show.

For those interested in cities throughout history, new possibilities nevertheless lurk, which ought not to muddy these lingering discussions. As is often the case, it is a shift into the landscape of a discipline that creates the opportunity to make former frontlines less absorbing. This also seems to be true with the urban dimensions of human societies, and it is from here that this volume takes its cue. There are ways not to hit a middle ground between two competing definitions of a subdiscipline but rather to go beyond and show how urban history contributes to an understanding of one of the most salient anxieties of today's world. We begin by appreciating the place and contribution of history to studies of globalization.

In through the Back Door: Globalization and the Discipline of History

When studies of globalization took off in the late 1980s, the choir began by stressing the novelty of interdependencies, interconnections, and awareness of global movements. Globalization, it sang, had its roots in the 1960s and 1970s, but it did not develop fully until the 1980s and 1990s. This short horizon was shared by those who celebrated globalization's achievements and those who lamented its impacts,[5] as well as by those who stressed the economic aspects of globalization, its governance, or its cultural aspects.[6] It was not only that the history of interconnections and interdependencies was forgotten: even for those who claimed to build from historical elements, history was considered a liability. Arjun Appadurai, despite stressing his interest in writing genealogies of today's cultural cosmopolitanisms, concludes by suggesting that we "cut into the problem through the historical present," and he insists on the unprecedented nature of this present.[7] When summoned to pronounce the current intensity and future of globalization, it seems there was no time left to scrutinize the past. But history came through the back door while discussions about economic globalization raged.

Political scientists, geographers, sociologists, and anthropologists who had embarked on the globalization train began to question the historical nature of globalization and to wonder how new were the different phenomena that were encapsulated within it.[8] Part of this debate revolved around the question of periodization: "how old was the current world economic system?" This question triggered interesting discussions, which took on the heritage of the world-system theory elaborated by Fernand Braudel and Immanuel

Wallerstein.[9] The interest for global civil society protagonists also forced social scientists to solicit the works of historians to contextualize their own research.[10] But this was quite tangential to historians themselves. Explicit engagements with globalization were scarce outside the sphere of economic historians.[11] For sure, historians of the nineteenth and twentieth centuries had investigated numerous interconnections and interdependencies across nations for some time. But they had adhered to asking questions that were relevant to their own discipline or field. American historians developed their ideas of a "transnational history" that stretched across U.S. borders, mostly to fight against prevailing views about American exceptionalism;[12] women's historians explored the crossnational bonds of informal and organized sisterhood to explain feminist pasts;[13] while historians of the Black Atlantic tried to extract the substance of antislavery and liberation movements to challenge the racial lines of their national histories.[14]

This began to change toward the end of the twentieth century, or so it seemed. The historical gaze now contributed to debunk several assumptions about the youthfulness of late twentieth-century interconnections. A powerful example, recounted by Ewa Morawska, concerns the contribution of migration historians to the sociology of current migration in the United States.[15] Alejandro Portes, one of the most influential scholars in immigration sociology, identified "transnational communities" as one of "the themes for a new century," putting transnationalism on the agenda in sociology and the anthropology of immigration.[16] Historians of migration, themselves long aware of crossover identities and practices in the nineteenth and early twentieth centuries, disagreed on the claims that this was a novel phenomenon. To paraphrase Morawska, they pinpointed the historical inaccuracies of such claims, established similarities between past and present transnational involvements, and acknowledged their differences. Conversely, they also gained some stimulating comparative views of their own field. The result was a more balanced account of continuity and change in this enduring phenomenon, and a renewed interest in collaboration and exchange between historians and social scientists.[17]

Similar attempts by historians to engage with globalization scholarship have recently emerged. Manifestos and recommendations were one form of this engagement, confronting globalization studies with their chronological blindness and using history to stress some of their analytical weaknesses.[18] New disciplinary proposals, and revivals of former fields, have flourished.[19] National blinkers half opened onto a wider perspective.[20] Moreover, historians reshuffled their questions to examine past links, aspirations, and projects that witness the historical nature of interconnections and interdependencies. Medieval and early modern historians, with their tradition of being less dependent on the iron cages of national histories, were the quickest to kick off—as suggested by the breadth of Sanjay Subrahmanyam's suggestions for "connected histories"[21] or Serge Gruzinski's exploration of the Spanish monarchy's attempt to dominate the "four parts of the world" between 1580 and 1640.[22] Others were also ready to march. In 2002 Anthony G. Hopkins led a collective charge in proposing a periodization of specific forms, projects, and practices of globalization since the fourteenth century, and he deepened his quest by directing a collective investigation of the interactions between the universal and the local in 2006.[23] One of the contributors to the first collection, Christopher A. Bayly, soon strode onto center stage with a very clear message: historians are now willing to investigate the connections and circulations through which interconnectedness and interdependencies have increased and recessed over time, including the modern age.[24] Conferences, workshops, projects, and publications have emerged at a high rate over recent years.[25] The result has been an increased historical awareness among globalization scholars[26] and the emergence of an interdisciplinary dialogue where first-hand historical research is used to deepen our understanding of globalization.[27] The growing interest for this transnational perspective in modern history—that is, the study of circulations and connections across different national contexts—is partly a result of this motivation to engage globalization as a historical object.[28] This is the kind of contribution we would like to make in our own field.

Global Cities: The Irrelevance of History?

Though our historical interest in connections and circulations among and about municipal urban government was born from our explorations into the municipal archives of two cities—Birmingham (Great Britain) and Lyon (France)[29]—we have never felt that we should limit our interest to these two cities or to the historical period we were studying. At first sight, an interest in the organizational or technical know-how that municipal governments used to create and maintain fledgling policies of housing, planning, firefighting, or public health seems quite parochial. But the fact that this know-how, from the last decades of the nineteenth century, was circulated across borders by municipal officials, technicians, firms, scholars, and reformers took us well beyond our favorite cities. On the one hand, these very connections and circulations demanded an attempt to follow their deployment and to place the activity of a given city into a wider exchange of knowledge, ideas, technologies, or regulations with its own cartography and chronology. On the other hand—both within the current policy making of our chosen cities and among urban geographers, sociologists, and planners—the buzz words of the 1990s were "benchmarking," "internationalization," and "networking," while cities competed to find a niche and become a place on the economic map, especially in Europe. This *Zeitgeist* is probably why we followed, regularly though not assiduously, the development of three threads of scholarship that never failed to intrigue us, for they all seem both close and distant.

In other districts of the social sciences and the humanities, our colleagues were at work analyzing the importance of cities as places in the new international division of labor (the world city / global city thread), the development of the international activities of municipal urban governments (the internationalization of cities), and the fortune of local authorities' networking (multilevel governance). These sociologists, geographers, and economists seemed to be very different creatures. Some of them were flying from Singapore to Seoul, where local authorities were listening to their advice about how to rise to the rank of "global city"; others were pronouncing the rebirth of cities in an age of transnational governance and obsolescence of the nation-state; while many pursued softer versions of these gleaming activities. All of them surfed the globalization wave, claiming that this new international political economy had given a renewed importance to the study of cities. Despite not really being at ease with such entrepreneurial and prophetic skills, we learned a lot from what they wrote.

The insistence of world cities' scholars on hierarchies led us to wonder about the polarities of our own circulations and connections; the very detailed analysis of what specific municipal governments could gain from contemporary networking propeled our curiosity for the costs and benefits of "transnational municipalism" decades earlier; and current municipal policies to attract foreign investment and market cities' image on the regional or global scene led us to question what was at stake in intermunicipal cooperation and competition throughout the modern era. Bits of what they said sounded familiar to us: the interchange of urban policy recipes and methods was a basic ingredient of the municipal scene in the nineteenth century, local-authority networking was on the map from the early twentieth century, and, more generally, some cities were commanding places in the organization of the world economy for centuries. In fact, we could not help but think that we had something in common and that the interrelations between the cities we were studying had some sort of connection with their narratives of competition, networks, hierarchy, and command.[30]

The reverse was obviously not true, at least from our perspective: few of these scholars had much interest in what municipal urban governments did across borders from the mid-nineteenth century to the last decades of the twentieth. There were one or two exceptions. Jeffrey Sellers, for example, has considered that the current international activities of municipal urban governments, especially in terms of creating links with one another across borders, had some historical precedents not only in the celebrated Hanseatic League but also in circuits that took shape during the nineteenth century.[31] But that was the extent of it.

At its best, history is used as a heuristic tool to explain variations in the fate of specific global cities and to account for their accumulation of global characteristics. Janet Abu-Lughod's historical examination of America's global cities, as well as Neil Brenner's reflection on her volume, blatantly illustrate this limited teleological use of history.[32] Despite Abu-Lughod's insistence that "history matters," her historical explorations are limited to tunneling through the past to unveil the "roots" of current global cities, with a focus on current characteristics such as those established by global-and world-city scholarship (notably the impact of global economic flows and cycles on the city's position and social space). As she writes, "explaining the developments during [the] most recent cycle of urban development constitutes the ultimate goal of this book."[33] John Rennie Short, too, did not live up to his claim that the *longue durée* matters. Though he repeats that globalization is far from new and that cities have not suddenly globalized but rather have de- and re-globalized, he remains wedded to the contemporary process of "globalizing" cities, showing no interest in the historical contributions that cities have made to this uneven and unlinear globalization process.[34] One of the most recent projects to have been launched by the Globalization and World Cities (GaWc) research network, "Cities in Economic Expansion and Current Crisis of the Modern World-System," calls for "empirical geo-historical description and analysis," but this empiricism does not include first-hand historical research as it launches for extensive collection of quantitative data.[35] All in all, Anthony King's repeated caveats of the present-mindedness and economic-centeredness of global/world cities' scholarship seem to have remained unheeded.[36]

This neglect has been especially clear in our sphere of interest, that is, the role of municipal urban governments in fostering interconnections and interdependencies among cities in the nineteenth and twentieth centuries. World city scholars have for some time not been interested in the role of city governments as global actors or globalizing actors for their cities.[37] There are some clues for such an interest in the recent agenda of world city scholarship, which explores second and third tier cities with a claim to reconcile market- and agency-based approaches to global cities.[38] The role of local political practices in constructing and conquering global city status is now a case in point, and Saskia Sassen stresses that this is an underdeveloped subject.[39] But this has not yet led to any consideration of the past contribution that "local political practices" in their most visible form—the municipal urban governments—have made to the story of global connections. More generally, there is a lack of interest in what municipal governments did between the nineteenth century and the 1980s, as if they had been wiped off the connections map by the construction of nation-states.

With the emergence of a state-centered political and economic world order from the Westphalia treaties to the late twentieth century, cities, as political units, became irrelevant for world city scholars according to P. J. Taylor: "Cities became nationalized, mere components of nation states, cogs in national economies."[40] Exit municipal urban governments and rest in peace; as the pendulum of history swung in favor of nation-states, it was as if cities had become nonentities as sites or protagonists of the intense crossnational, regional, and global economic flows of the nineteenth and twentieth centuries. It would be only at the favor of a new political and economic order, the globalization moment of the late twentieth century, that they would resurface to benefit from the attention of world city scholarship.

The growing literature on the internationalization of cities and the changes to urban governance exhibits a similar historical ambivalence. While most world city scholars engage with world system theories and their medieval and early modern avatars, most scholars of the internationalization of cities bluntly confine their interest to the last three or four decades.[41] According to most, the new world economic and political order was born "yesterday," and it was only following the cue that municipal urban governments adjusted their governance structure and policies to develop their investment appeal. Even Patrick Le Galès, who actively considers the historical development of urban governance in Europe and stresses the agency of cities in claiming international status from the 1980s, concludes that the nineteenth and twentieth centuries mark the eclipse of European municipal governments as significant actors.[42] Integrated within the national economy and polity, it was only from the 1980s, with the strengthening of the European Union (EU) and the retrenchment of the state, that municipalities found a window of opportunity to return as significant political and economic agents.[43]

Shifting toward the third stream of social science studies that we have followed, Le Galès acknowledges the long history of formal municipal networks similar to those that blossomed in Europe during the 1980s. He fares better than the bulk of scholarship, which surveys the emergence of multilevel governance in two contexts. For those focussing on the forms and impacts of European integration, in particular stressing the growing role of policy networks, the associations and networks of municipal urban governments, which lobbied the EU and tried to shape a supranational urban policy, were an interesting case in point. But the hypothesis and empirical studies that were derived from this interest were limited to the 1980s.[44] Another set of scholars were interested in world-size municipal networks, as one of the clues that witnessed the recent strengthening of a "global civil society," which contributed to framing and answering issues beyond the national domain. This literature on social movements, and issue and advocacy networks, has elected a few central themes: social contention, human rights, women's rights, and the environment, among others.[45] It is in this context that empirical investigations of municipal networks within climate protection have developed.[46] Here again, it was not even considered possible that municipalities had done anything to consider these environmental questions before recent decades, and some preliminary statement that the history of transnational municipal networks began in the 1980s is a clear indication of the chronological horizon of these studies.[47] Even a cursory reading of the recent urban historical literature would have revealed a more complex and long-term narrative of managing the urban environment and natural resources.[48]

This contention that the history of cities was not relevant was another reason why we were fascinated by the scholarship on world cities, the internationalization of cities, and transnational networking. We did not blame any of these authors for doing so, firstly, due to the benefits we derived from their achievements and, secondly, because we do not think that anyone should be taken to task for having paid tribute to the disciplinary division of labor. Clearly, their agendas and projects were only foreign to those of us who prefer to consider historical context. Nevertheless, we were left with this contrast between a sense of familiarity on our part and an estrangement from history on behalf of this impressive mass of scholarship.

Explorations into the Transnational Municipal Moment

On the one hand, historians are beginning to historicize globalization—understood here as the uneven pulse of interconnecting bonds between regions, cultures, religions, linguistic worlds, and nations. On the other hand, the urban side of globalization studies dismisses one section of the history of cities—the nineteenth and twentieth centuries—as irrelevant. Even an urban theorist like Michael Smith, who we believe has hit the right buttons in his criticisms of global/world city theory,[49] does not see the history of cities as a way to "historicize the global city."[50] Smith's wider political and historical context historicizes the criss-crossing of social spaces across borders and between localities but excludes the history of cities as a possible resource. However, his call for localized studies of transnational urbanism and his concern for transnational practices make us believe that there is a passage to be explored here. Briefly put, this is how this volume has emerged: a proposal to make urban history one of the avenues to historicize globalization and its urban sides, as well as a proposal for the crossfertilization between the history of cities and urban studies in the globalization test tube.

While there are many possible urban ways to contribute historical depth to the study of globalization (as briefly hinted in the Preface in this volume), we have chosen to focus on a very specific one in this book. It just seemed to be most appropriate to open a conversation with current scholarship on global cities, on the internationalization of cities, and on city networks and their contribution to multilevel governance. The point of departure for this ambition is to reverse two postulates made by our colleagues who work on more recent decades. One is the role of cities as mere sites for the flows that have made and unmade the world. The other is the oblivion into which the moment between the beginning of the nineteenth century and the end of the twentieth century has fallen. We want, instead, to insist on a "transnational municipal moment," which came into existence at the very moment when the state crystallized in its national form. To do so, we have chosen to focus on the role of municipal urban governments as one embodiment of urban agency, in its most institutional form, and to explore the "transnational municipal moment" through a range of contributions that explore its different chronological, geographical, and thematic manifestations.

However, we do not believe that municipal urban governments impersonate cities, and it is clear to us and the other contributors to this volume that many other protagonists participated in the establishment, operation, and maintenance of those durable structures, which are increasingly studied under the umbrella concept of "governance."[51] But what municipal urban governments have to offer are a range of first-hand archival opportunities to study how policies, knowledge, regulations, and know-how were exchanged by discrete protagonists who recorded their activities in reports, correspondence, budgets, and regulations across time and space. It is to these records, stored in municipal archives, that we turned our attention, since we believe that the historical contribution to the study of globalization must be based on first-hand original scholarship, not merely on an assemblage of second-hand materials. Municipalities are, then, an appropriate target for scholars who want to revisit the global city in historical time.

We contend that from the mid-nineteenth century there emerged enduring protagonists and durable structures, cultures, legal, and organizational frameworks, which facilitated the transnational activities of municipal urban governments, patterned on long-lasting circulatory regimes and spaces, which still contribute to frame the activities of cities on the world scene. We share a set of hypotheses that support this contention.

Firstly, we observe the definition of perceived convergences across different nations during the nineteenth century: although a sense of difference never yielded abruptly to a discourse of similarity, there was nevertheless an increasing discourse of "transnational municipalism," which insisted on the existence of a common horizon for cities in Europe and the North Atlantic, but also outside the "industrial west."[52] The common growth of cities was the result of major economic, social, and cultural change through which a number of "issues" were established around a sense that common problems were faced by urban dwellers and leaders from Glasgow to Mumbai. Secondly, we accept the idea that municipalities were a matrix in the development and implementation of policies aimed at regulating the social domain that emerged from this changing economic, social, and cultural order—the space between the individual and the state, between the private and the public—especially in Europe between the late nineteenth century and the 1930s. This encompassed unemployment, housing, public health, transportation, and education. The nationalization of these functions and the emergence of the welfare state often extrapolated from these municipal experiments and the personnel that was involved in their operation.[53]

Thirdly, we argue that throughout the modern age, from 1850 to 2000, these municipal policies were eagerly observed and exchanged across national borders, to be rejected or emulated, through the different communities in which municipal technicians and elected officials participated. Municipal officials, as well as city dwellers, lived on daily comparisons with foreign experiences to decide on the major questions faced by urban municipal governments. Fourthly, we think that the different communities that took part in this market of municipal knowledge operated in shifting frames that enabled them to sift, winnow, and claim specific ideas and know-how. Intermunicipal circulatory regimes—those sets of long-term patterns and relatively stable interactions between mutually identifiable protagonists in a given geopolitical and geographical framework—have operated since the second half of the nineteenth century, and their impact is still felt in current trends like the internationalization of cities or local authority networking.

All these are not idiosyncratic isolated statements. They rely on a body of scholarship that has been churned out by various sections of the social sciences and humanities, which turned their attention to these leftovers of modern history: urban governments.[54] We now turn to put some of these results in context while we scrutinize the two intertwined processes, which developed from the nineteenth century and made the transnational municipal moment possible. They are the "municipalization of the world"—that is, the common rules and conventions that urban municipal governments came to live by across the globe—and the establishment of a "world of municipalities"—or the connections and circulations that these municipalities created to cope with this situation and the problems urban governments have faced.

The Municipalization of the World

To continue the crossdisciplinary dialogue, we are capturing cities at the very moment they disappear off the radar screen of world city scholars—that is, at the beginning of the nineteenth century. In fact, we take the integration of cities into the national states' apparatus to be a necessary condition for transnational intermunicipal relations to take place. This integration has so far been largely treated according to its economic dimension, the expansion of markets, and the new order of production, which have been seen as the causes for integrating urban economies into national markets. Politically, if we follow Charles Tilly,[55] the rise of the modern state had already strangled urban political autonomy in Europe by the fifteenth century, and the state's invention of local authorities as cogs in the machine was the cherry on the cake. But the establishment of this order, precisely because it was a by-product of the consolidation of the national state, also created the conditions for a common landscape of resentment and aspirations among municipal officers and the urban elite in different countries. The juridical battles that raged at different points in nineteenth-century Europe about the respective importance and nature of state and municipal sovereignty showed that such an integration was not accepted flatly. That these discussions used references and precedents across national borders bears witness to a sense of a common, though unhappy, fate for municipal governments in the Europe of national states.[56] The perception of shared subaltern legal conditions by protagonists of municipal life was a crucial incentive to pay attention to municipal life across national boundaries.

In spite of obvious differences as to the domain that they granted to municipalities, national laws granting legal status to city government were approved in discrete sequences between the late eighteenth and mid-nineteenth centuries. Without considering the numerous revisions and modifications, there is a sense of rhythm from a rapid enumeration of the municipalization of the European city: France established a common mold for local communities with its decree of December 14, 1789; Prussia forged a municipal legislation in 1807; England created an incorporation standard with the Municipal Corporations Act of 1835; Belgium gave municipalities their national status in 1836; Norway enacted a municipal status in 1837; a later sequence involved Denmark in 1857, Sweden in 1862, and Italy in 1865. This did not mean that national homogeneity was obtained, and the case of imperial Germany, with its many different municipal legislations, is testimony of the diversity of municipal status inside a single nation-state. But the municipal condition—that is, the relative position of the urban government within a national institutional framework—became a common situation in Europe during the first two-thirds of the nineteenth century.

The municipalization of the world, in this foundational wave, was more than a roll call of national legislations, though. There were several moments where municipalities were "reinvented" and the municipalization of the world revamped, following the shifts in jurisprudence or legislation often triggered by the efforts of municipalities to expand their domain. Several of these moments are discernible throughout the modern age. Among the most salient episodes were the late nineteenth and early twentieth centuries, when municipalities on both sides of the Atlantic opened a conversation where foreign experiments and examples were used to justify municipal intervention in the fields of housing, transportation, lighting, water provision, and public health. The transatlantic debate on municipal trading was the highlight of this time, an episode we are quite familiar with thanks to the studies of a number of scholars.[57] Another important occurrence was the remunicipalization that came in Germany, Japan, and Italy after World War II, when the rebuilding of municipal governments was seen as one of the keys to re-educate these countries in the values and privileges of democracy, especially in the U.S. and British zones in Germany.[58] But the pattern was not limited to such extreme situations, and the prospects of English local government reorganization simultaneously served as a lesson for American political scientists interested in postwar reform under more centralized urban governments.[59]

Yet this was the municipalization of the world, not just Europe. Some of the frames that established municipalities as surrogates of the national government were not confined within the limits of a given country. The French framework that put the *commune* at the bottom of the political and administrative pyramid traveled in the wagons of the revolutionary and imperial armies throughout Europe. It was taken even further when the French colonial adventure began, first in Algeria and later in sub-Saharan Africa and Asia. Meanwhile, the British formula, which established municipal corporations as part of the unitary tradition established by parliament, migrated across the ocean to North America, South East Asia, and Australia. Similarly, Dutch, Belgian, Spanish, and Portuguese municipal legislations made their mark in their respective overseas projections. Though municipal government was not deemed the appropriate form of government for native populations in any European empire, there was eventually an establishment of municipal urban governments—with a touch of electoral legitimacy, if only because the colonial powers were anxious to find a tax basis to contribute to the expanding costs of urban infrastructures.[60] Municipal councils appeared—as in British-controlled Shanghai in 1854—while municipal legislation developed—as with the Indian Municipal Act of 1874 and the Nigeria Townships Ordinance of 1917.

There is much that remains to be uncovered about these migrations and the adaptations and inventions they fostered, and it is clear that we cannot just confidently map, for example, the spread of the English or French "models" as homogeneous and conflicting blocks. First, because the intensive cross-observation between the two countries from the end of the eighteenth century—notwithstanding, or because of, their fiery antagonism—quite likely included their respective municipal legislation.[61] The anglophile French liberals who made the French municipal law of 1837, and the cautious French-mongers who established the Municipal Corporations Act of 1835, might have had an eye on each other's system. Second, the municipalization of the world did not simply involve the steady export of European-invented municipal government to faraway lands. On the one hand, there existed institutional structures of accountable urban governance whereby inhabitants were associated to city government before "national" legislations made their mark. In Macao, Manilla, and Havana, municipal government designed in Spain and Portugal had to downsize existing authorities, which had been established in the course of centuries of urban life. Though there are hints that the urban government system was weak in China, the growth of the municipal government "made in the West" after the 1911 Revolution did not take place in a vacuum,[62] and structures of urban government have been identified from Korea to Kyrgyzstan via Sri Lanka. On the other hand, it was from their agency that some non-European countries like Japan or empires like that of the Ottomans designed reform projects through an observation of European municipal institutions. This could be a very painstaking process that included surveying European municipalities and even, as with Istanbul, the creation of two pilot municipalities in Beyoghlu and Galata, and a linguistic and functional translation of the European vocabulary, beginning with that of "municipality" (*belediyye*).[63] On the whole, recent research into this process suggests that new municipal institutions did not simply erase previous structures: in Beirut, Tunis, and Damas, scholars have found a strong connection between premunicipal institutions and the municipalities.[64] The process was not merely about "importing" European-made municipal urban government.

If there is still a lot to learn about this first wave of municipalization, we are really at a loss with the second wave, which followed World War II. As former colonial possessions gained autonomy, they adopted the nation-state framework of their former metropolises. One aspect involved the implementation of municipal legislations, creating a common subaltern status for urban governments and expanding the status of municipalities that had often been hitherto reserved to a select number of urban sites—as in French controlled Africa. Between 1940 and 1960, the municipal condition became the common lot of cities throughout the world. There is much to be learned about this second wave, especially the references that were used by the newly independent countries to shape their municipal legislations or practices. At first sight, it would seem that colonial frameworks were discarded, but some aspects of them certainly remained in place while other references and experiments were sought or provided by multilateral or bilateral cooperation. The UN's (United Nations) division of technical assistance and its public administration branch sent their technical advisors into the municipal field as well. What kind of advice may have been given and taken by and from the U.S. Agency for International Development and Point IV program advisors, or by Soviet and Soviet-trained administrators, and later by Chinese- or Cuban-trained personnel, is an area that offers interesting research opportunities in the near future.

A third wave of municipalization has been taking place since the 1980s. It has been mostly studied by political scientists, especially on the European level. They stress that European integration and the redefinition of capitalist mechanisms on a world plane opened up possibilities for European municipalities to act as organizers and regulators of local societies, as well as protagonists in the economic re-arrangement of the world order.[65] In many European countries, this triggered municipalities to seize on new competencies and re-assert their presence. For some, this was a remunicipalization of Europe, another episode in the long feud between city and state, where the former was soaring again, casting off the yoke of the latter as national states retrenched. Yet, this third and more recent wave was not limited to Europe. In Latin America, the transition from authoritarian to democratic regimes, often gave way to a new status and role for municipal governments, all the more since it took place in a context where the national governments were compelled to retrench their activities and expenses under pressure from multilateral and foreign loaners. Across the world, similar opportunities also flourished, while international organizations like the UN and its agencies were anxious to open direct channels with municipal and other local governments, especially in order to promote policy initiatives in the domain of the environment and human settlement.[66] There is more in this recent trend than the mere perpetuation of a European showdown with the rest of the world.

We think that there is a lot to be gained from connecting these different moments together. As a transnational circulation, the municipal condition participates in making an interconnected and interdependent world, creating a common culture among urban governments on a world scale. Charting and mapping its developments would be a significant contribution toward historicizing globalization. The debates about the subaltern condition of municipalities within nation-states—as exemplified by past debates, such as the one on municipal trading; by the fights of the 1950s around the European charter of self-government; or by the current discussions for the establishment of a world charter of local self-government—also signify that this is a transnational arena. Last, but not least, there are interesting comparisons to be made between the three beats that give its rhythm to the municipalization of the world. At the turn of the nineteenth and twentieth centuries—like that of the twentieth and twenty-first centuries—opportunities were seized by municipal governments to raise their profile and step forward in new spheres (i.e., housing or services yesterday, economic governance and international relations today, social cohesion and urban renewal in both cases). In both contexts, there was a similar component of liberal laissez-faire in the mainstream definition of national states' competencies, which left urban governments to face the matters that the growth of urban populations, the importance of inner-city poverty, or the huge demand for infrastructure confronted them with. Another common feature in this long-term history is that, from the late nineteenth century, urban governments built worlds of their own from their perception of common status, fate, and problems, where they could compare situations, exchange experiments, define problems, and adapt solutions.

The World of Municipalities

From the last decades of the nineteenth century, and sometimes in contravention of their respective national governments, municipalities engaged in cross-border conversations. These were carried out by municipalities but also by the individuals who were connected to, or interested in, municipal government as a career, a field of study, or a market. The history of this world of municipalities, which Marjatta Hietala was the first to unearth in the 1980s,[67] has been steadily developing.[68] We think that it is relevant, unto its very specific details, to the current study of globalization and the place of cities within it. Another reason why it is relevant is that the three regimes, which have ordered the world of municipalities for more than 150 years, are still more or less in operation today, and they continue to shape what urban municipal governments think and do, individually and collectively. Our purpose is to accordingly identify the regimes and configurations of intermunicipal exchange, those long-term patterns and relatively stable interactions between mutually identified protagonists. Specific cities moved in and opted out of the structures and channels that ruled these regimes, according to the tactics and strategies of their governing and administrative leadership. They still knew they were out there, though, and there are few lines of municipal work that were not affected one way or another by the symbolic, practical, technical and political resources that ran though the world of municipalities.

The first regime is one of informal international transfers dating from the late nineteenth and early twentieth centuries. Selective borrowing or imperial imposition were the most frequently observable processes of exchange. As they often took place between two or more geographically defined points, transfers provide a convenient, though approximate, way to define the flows that developed under this regime. Originally, this regime was developed in Europe and the North Atlantic, but it quickly expanded toward Latin America, North Africa, Australia, and the Middle East, most often following imperial tracks. The selling of services, the exchange of know-how, as well as the definition of urban problems and municipal government canons has ever since been pulsing through the channels that have opened in and around changing cores and contested geographies. The paradigm of this regime, its social and cultural engine, was emulation to cope with current urban problems as a "modern metropolis" should, and its actors were mostly municipal technicians, elected officials, and those who had to define and tackle urban affairs nationally. Its impact was felt through the traveling of technologies, regulations, and designs; it was organized and maintained by peer-to-peer contact.

The second regime is one of structured transnational organization. Sketched on the eve of World War I, it took an enduring form during the 1920s. Under its spell, the field was formalized with dedicated long-lasting institutions, which acted as stages and stagers of the interchange in municipal matters. These transatlantic clearing houses, specialized institutions and individuals, contributed to create, orient, and feed webs through which information was selected, winnowed, changed, translated, adapted, and selected. Members of municipal governments were one of the hard-gamers in these networks but also strove to control them alongside an increased number of protagonists. Intergovernmental organizations and philanthropic foundations played a major role in setting up the regime itself,[69] while the emphasis placed on technical and administrative aspects of municipal urban government renewed or opened avenues for technicians and social scientists to embark on new journeys as experts.

The organizations of municipalities spearheaded this regime, in a thicker and thicker fabric where the hegemony of the International Union of Local Authorities (created in 1913) was disputed after World War II by new organizations that adopted a different stance, defined a new circulatory space, or introduced a different political creed.[70] Under this regime, the definition and diffusion of "one-best-way" solutions tended to substitute for the variety of ad hoc imitations, borrowings, and impositions. What is at stake is a definition of universal tools, words, ideas, professionals, and policies to cope with the city as a regional and global fact. In this regime, the interplay between the different municipal organizations on the one hand, and the world order on the other, is a crucial one. Indeed, one of the major stakes that the municipal organizations have contested is to be recognized as the voice of municipalities in the world, and to sit at debates that had previously been the exclusive domain of the national governments. The creation, in 2004, of a new intermunicipal organization called "United Cities and Local Governments" is clearly the expression of this ambition to make the voice of cities heard by the UN and other intergovernmental organizations such as the World Bank. It is also the result of the insistent invitation by these intergovernmental organizations for municipal associations to provide them with a single partner, one that could provide both easily identifiable partnerships, and opportunities to shunt national governments on subjects that they would not be keen to commit themselves to, such as the Kyoto protocols.

The third regime we label the global and regional competition maze. Its growth in the 1980s took place in conjunction with major changes to the political world order, in the international political economy, and in urban governance in several national and regional settings. The result was explicit research of economic competitiveness by individual cities, which resorted to collective strategies to achieve this goal.[71] In Europe alone, more than forty thematic networks have been created to band municipalities together by issues, public-policy sector, size, regions, and features.[72] These networks often include firms and regional governments side by side with cities. Often tailored for a specific aim and very much concerned with lobbying those political institutions located in Brussels, they have thrived on a market-oriented discourse of competition, including competition among their members and between the networks. Mayors feature prominently in their activities, while the administrative or technical branches of municipal governments are mostly sidekicks that provide backstage logistics or expertise. These European features are roughly valid for other regional scenes and also for the global arena. The variety of partners that have bet on cities to develop their strategies (e.g., utilities firms, regional and global intergovernmental organizations) still fuels the development and operation of this regime.

These three regimes are not strictly temporal; they intertwine rather than succeed one another; their protagonists and features can recess in the background or resurface in an uneven manner. There are, of course, continuities of discourse, practice, and personnel that we will not examine here, though the enmeshment areas between the different regimes are of special interest. Our point is that those regimes are all in operation today, with their actors, structures, and values rooted in time. They need to be considered together with economic globalization or governance changes to appreciate the current internationalization of cities. They may also provide a key to finding the urban variable—the specific contribution of cities to the making of the modern world, so deceptively pursued by urban historians since the 1970s. These are the guidelines we briefly sketched when we invited a group of scholars with different perspectives to join us in this pursuit, and we hope readers will find their contributions as useful as we have.

CHAPTER 2

In the Precincts of the Global City

The Transnational Network of Municipal Affairs in Melbourne, Australia, at the End of the Nineteenth Century

Andrew Brown-May

The Victoria Room is a time capsule at the heart of old empire.[1] It is situated in the town hall of Melbourne—named in 1837 for the British monarch of the day—in the state of Victoria.[2] The corner stone of the Melbourne town hall was laid by Queen Victoria's second son, Prince Alfred, Duke of Edinburgh, in 1867. Shoulder to shoulder with his fellow loyal Melburnians, journalist and author Marcus Clarke had "bunting on the brain" as he cheered and shouted, baked on veranda tops, was deafened by brass bands, and had his toes trodden on during the duke's visit, which was the first by British royalty to Australian shores.[3] Here Melbourne's municipal authority was ensconced, at the heart of civic power, at the height of an imperial age. Once the office of the deputy town clerk, the Victoria Room's polished cedar bookcases climb giddily up to fanlight level on the east and south walls. Carved consoles supporting a continuous timber cornice separate the cases into sections, the shelves bowing under the weight of the corporation's former professional library.[4] For a hundred years after E. G. FitzGibbon commenced his thirty-five-year reign as town clerk of the city christened "Marvellous Melbourne" by George Augustus Sala, the walls of the Victoria Room and its adjacent corridors and offices echoed to the command of only four town clerks, those "chief instruments of local power."[5]

Asa Briggs brought Melbourne to the attention of urban scholars in the 1960s as a city that, despite nuances of social texture (for example, in relation to the comparative absence of destitution, contempt for authority, and passion for sport), was a predominantly British species of metropolis.[6] But as

David Cannadine has reminded the postimperial historian, the decorations have long since been taken down. Briggs's chapter on Melbourne in *Victorian Cities*, published four decades ago, was noted by Cannadine as a lone attempt by a British historian to contextualise the burgeoning global urban network of that "vast interconnected world."[7] While Cannadine's point—speaking solely from a British imperial perspective—may now be rejected in the context of a proliferation of postimperial geographies and literatures,[8] his urging of historians to investigate what this empire looked like and to explain how it was imagined and constructed is still timely. Such an agenda is consonant with current interest in imperial connections and urban geographies of empire. It is also part of a reconsideration of the currency of ideas, mentalities, and commodities that produced hybridized or homogenized physical and social spaces. For this volume we might seek interconnections and affinities, rather than separation and otherness, to challenge simplistic understandings of the metropolis/periphery binary. In *Imperial Cities*, geographers Felix Driver and David Gilbert have cogently observed that while the hybridity of architectural, ceremonial, and other symbolic landscapes has come under the scrutiny of scholars of the imperial domain, historians are yet to turn adequate attention to the living spaces of the imperial or networked city.[9] Postcolonial notions of hybridity, diaspora, or transculturation, as applied to the contact zones of colonization, have more effectively been endorsed by cultural geographers such as Jane M. Jacobs, and more recent understandings of urban globalization have been prefigured and explored by A. D. King and others.[10] Technology transfer has featured as a preoccupation of historians interested in the subject of diffusion—by way, for example, of comparative analysis of urban utilities, such as transit, sanitation, and power-supply networks.[11] David Hamer's *New Towns in the New World* is a distinguished example of scholarship on comparative frontier and urban life across continents, while Driver and Gilbert's collection has given sharper focus to the "overlapping territories and intertwined histories of modern imperialism."[12]

Doreen Massey's assertion, cited by Driver and Gilbert, that "the identity of places in the modern world is constituted as much by their relation with other places as by anything intrinsic to their location"[13] brings me neatly back to the town clerk's library, where Albert Shaw's 1895 work on *Municipal Government in Great Britain* sits gathering dust, practically and symbolically. The subtitle of Briggs's chapter on Melbourne in *Victorian Cities* was "a Victorian city overseas," and it is all too easy to simplistically conflate the city's British nomenclatures with a narrow understanding of the sources of reform influence. Shaw was of a different opinion:

> It requires no peculiar discernment on the part of the traveler to discover that large towns are becoming alike the world over. There is something to be

regretted in the loss of picturesqueness, quaintness, and distinctive flavor. But if our observer be public-spirited and humane, the spread of modern improvements will not greatly vex him. . . . He will sympathise with the efforts of the present generation of Italians to make Rome, Naples, and many another historic city the fit abiding-place of hopeful communities whose gaze is forward rather than backward. . . . He will be impressed and gratified as he notes the renovation and development, on the scientific lines of modern city-making, of Athens and Bucharest, Belgrade and Sofia.[14]

Melbourne's municipal governance may well have been established in the British tradition,[15] and it certainly felt the ripple effect of systematic urban reform programs in Great Britain from the 1830s,[16] but it is clear that Melbourne's municipal supervisors followed trends that transcended continents, hemispheres, and empires. The concern of this chapter is to suggest that much more specificity is required—for a study of urban governance in general, and the social character of towns in particular—in determining the nature and chronology of imperial influence, cultural networks, institutional lineages, and localized parameters. The process of tracking the vectors of those values that informed and legitimized the creation of civic mindedness and urban thought-worlds, reveals sets of problem-solving practices that historicize the notion of the global city.

The transformation of public use of the street forms the focus of this chapter, with reference to the provision of street amenities and the development of by-laws governing certain public behaviors. This process broadly characterized as municipalization[17]—the desire of urban authorities to improve the lives of their inhabitants, to change their behaviors, and to exercise more control over the provision of services—was effected by responses to localized exigencies, by changing social protocols and somatic behaviors, and by sets of ordinances influenced by exogenous factors. The importance of analyzing imperial connections and more broadly globalized urban geographies is increasingly noted by urban historians, though again hermetic local studies predominate at the expense of detailed explorations of linkages and relationships. Networked transformations in municipal regulatory frameworks might, for example, be tracked through exchanges of municipal intelligence, whereby sets of by-laws, model regulations, annual reports, minutes, and accounts were circulated among authorities in Australia, New Zealand, Great Britain, continental Europe, North America, India, and South Africa. A study of municipal interchange and the agents of urban concepts and tools, with examples from the period during the 1860s–1920s, can not only explain the affinities and aberrations, the correlations and differences, of this or that city. It also, importantly, belies the range of exceptionalist tropes of distance, isolation, parochialism, innovation, or incipience that variously mark the urban self-identity as well as the historiography of towns and cities across the globe. Analysis of transitional periods of municipal regulation—the enforcement of new laws dealing with previously accepted behaviors, now legally proscribed; the adoption or adaptation in the face of local contingencies of generic or exotic regulations—may usefully inform our understanding of the city-making process.

In analyzing changes in municipal regulations, the local and global factors of influence, and the networks of information exchange, this chapter is preoccupied with the chronology, context, and methodology of intermunicipal exchange. It is along these lines that individual city histories can be refreshed, not in terms of looking simplistically for globally homogenizing tendencies but rather in exploring the multiple identities of place-as-process. Placing city history in a transnational context exposes urban problems as generic entities, while at the same time enabling the drawing of specific cultural distinctions. If the precinct, borough, or ward boundaries of a municipality can be seen as permeable rather than enclosing frames, then the identity of individual places might indeed be uniquely differentiated.[18]

The Town Clerk as "Boss Panjandrum"

Seeing the colonial city through imported glasses could be a declaration of hope for what it might become in terms of a true tally of the here-and-now. The streets within its new-world grid took on the associations of their mainly London counterparts, as they were related by physical, cultural, or functional equivalence. Although the character of Melbourne in the mind of its observers paralleled Cape Town, Birmingham, London, or Nottingham, popular equivalence saw Collins Street as a colonial Regent or Bond street, Elizabeth Street as Oxford Street, Bourke Street as Cheapside, and Stephen or Little Bourke streets as an antipodean St. Giles. Elizabeth, Collins, and Bourke streets might be as crowded as the Strand—Little Collins Street scarcely as wide as Cornhill—while street buildings in general reminded the Londoner of Pall Mall and St. James streets. But the connectivity between Melbourne and the cities and towns of the "Old World" was more than metaphorical. The daily practicalities of its municipalization were enjoined back at the Melbourne town hall, where municipal bureaucracy placed the town clerk at the center of institutional structure: mastermind of committee agendas, keeper of by-laws, doyen of corporate memory, and conduit of the correspondence, which for the years 1842–1983 now sits in over a thousand boxes at the Victoria Public Record Office.[19]

Across the expanding municipal web in metropolitan and regional cities and towns Australia-wide,[20] the reign of town clerks was often marked by longevity and influence disproportionate to their apparent status. William Bold, town clerk of Perth in Western Australia from 1901 to 1944, was said to have "comported himself like the boss Panjandrum," and many of his fellow office bearers across the nation could equally have been described as being "the real mayor," with the mayor "merely his easy going factotum."[21] Matching the longevity of Melbourne's city officials, Adelaide in South Australia had four town clerks between 1869 and 1937.[22] Of the nineteen nineteenth-century Australian town clerks with an entry in the *Australian Dictionary of Biography*, seven were Scottish-born, five English, two Irish, one Welsh, and four local-born. While some had backgrounds as journalists, accountants, auctioneers, architects, drapers, or chemists, just as many were jacks-of-all-trades, having perhaps turned their hand to a series of jobs as goldminers, farmers, merchants, or teachers. Many of Victoria's nineteenth-century town clerks migrated as young men to the goldfields of the early 1850s. Although no detailed prosopographical survey has been undertaken, their career paths in a more mobile settler-society were guided less by the parameters of, for example, internal promotion or lifelong appointment than might have affected their British or European counterparts. Compared to their confreres in Glasgow or the Paris regional towns, though able to create themselves as indispensable administrative keystones, they were less likely to be managerial specialists until professionalization in the twentieth century.[23]

In the minutiae of the town clerk's daily correspondence, one gets a clear and immediate sense of the interchanges of information and the vectors of knowledge crisscrossing continent and globe: all of the advertisements and catalogs, prospectuses and blueprints, schemes and inquiries, tenders, letterheads, sketches, and handbills that formed the daily diet of municipal intelligence. The arresting design of trade catalogues—with their sophisticated artwork, elaborate embossing, and fancy foilwork—put into circulation for an eager audience, particular versions of modernization, visions of modernity, and mechanisms of efficiency.[24] The artifacts, machines, and mechanisms of civic improvement and public amenity—police sentry boxes, cab shelters, dust carts, letter pillars, stamp vending machines, street watering carts, fire alarm pillars, water fountains, horse troughs, public toilets, bollards, ventilator columns, ticket machines, and hitching posts—were reviewed and compared, tried and tested on paper before they became everyday features of the footpath. Well-traveled citizens or visitors were ever-ready to draw the attention of the corporation to international comparators by way of material culture of public life as well as sets of values about amenity, aesthetics, and the protocols of civic life.

In 1915 the Sydney city council was reviewing the regulation of the sale of fruit from wheelbarrows in city streets, and as was common practice by this time, the Sydney Town Clerk T. H. Nesbitt wrote to his Melbourne counterpart, John Clayton, requesting "that you will be good enough to forward a copy of the By-Law under which such action is taken." Clayton noted in reply that although his council had not yet adopted such a by-law, the matter was dealt with under an act of parliament administered by the Department of Agriculture, and a copy of which he enclosed.[25] By this time, it is clear that as well as interchange on a case-by-case basis, circular letters requesting copies of yearly publications such as by-laws, annual reports, minutes, and accounts were dispatched from Melbourne to as many as seventy municipalities in Great Britain, North America, India, New Zealand, South Africa, and continental Europe. Addressees include municipalities in England and Wales (Leeds, Liverpool, Manchester, Nottingham, Cardiff, Bristol, Birmingham, Sheffield, Bradford, Walsall); Scotland (Edinburgh, Glasgow, Dundee, Aberdeen); Ireland (Dublin, Belfast); North America (Quebec, Toronto, Ottawa, Montreal; Washington, DC, New York, Philadelphia, Boston, San Francisco, Buffalo); South Africa (Johannesburg, Durban, Capetown, Pretoria, East London); India (Calcutta, Bombay, Madras, Delhi); and New Zealand (Wellington, Auckland, Dunedin, Christchurch).[26]

The shelves in the Victoria Room betray more than a simplistic imperial relationship between core and periphery. Certainly one can consult, *ex libris* the town clerk's office, the manuals, yearbooks, proceedings, and annual accounts of British civic administration, as well as engineering, architectural, and legal periodicals.[27] But just as prominent are volumes from Bombay, Dunedin, or Toronto. Of interest also on these shelves is a constellation of treatises and sourcebooks, many published in North America between about 1890 and 1910, on such subjects as sanitation, refuse disposal, food inspection, and traffic engineering, as well legal primers relating, for example, to nuisances, light, the police offences acts, and motor cars.[28] In their midst, Shaw's *Municipal Government* presaged the imminent explosion of this "science and art of modern city government," propounding certain fundamental principles distilled from administrative, statistical, engineering, technological, sanitary, educational, social, and moral science: "The problems to be solved are so similar . . . regardless of national distinctions, that they afford an important field of comparative study both descriptive and critical."[29] Although Shaw articulated the coalescing of a modern and universalist municipal ideal at century's end, municipal interchanges had a longer history dating from an earlier period of colonial city-making.

Communicating the World-in-Between

Increasingly over the latter half of the nineteenth century, a more deliberate attempt was being made to subscribe to an organized and increasingly professionalized municipal network. Correspondence dating from at least the 1860s reveals detailed exchanges of copies of by-laws between Melbourne and other regional, intercolonial, and international centers including Hobart, Sydney, Dunedin, Wellington, Brisbane, Geelong, and Adelaide. Relevant by-laws were requested when specific regulations were being contemplated elsewhere: awnings in Geelong (Victoria), hawkers in Ballarat (Victoria), and internal municipal management in Lyttelton (New Zealand).[30] Irish-born FitzGibbon embarked on a world tour in 1876 to see for himself the progress of the municipal idea. In Birmingham, Manchester, Paris, Rome, and Bombay, "the philanthropic, beneficent, and enlightened spirit which animates the great corporate Councils, is shown, by their interests and activity in all that affects the physical and moral well-being of their districts."[31] Other corporation officers regularly followed in his footsteps.

Irene Maver has elaborated on the travels of Glasgow's civic officials in the immediate pre–World War I years, as they provided technical expertise to their counterparts, from Chicago to Bombay and Sao Paulo.[32] Pierre-Yves Saunier reiterates that tracking "the journeyings of municipal technicians, the enquiries of enlightened amateurs, the official delegations of town councillors . . . was not bound by a simple centre-periphery relationship."[33] The Western world that they combed "for experiments which could be adapted for home use," however, does not appear to have included Melbourne, nor indeed any Australasian or Asian cities at all, and although Saunier is correct in observing the constraints of geography, politics, and language on the traveling habit of northern hemisphere city officials, it seemed less of a shackle on the worldview of antipodean municipalists.

Melbourne's nineteenth-century city officials had some pre-existing knowledge of British experiences gleaned from their formative years prior to emigration, and they undertook further reconnaissance of municipal affairs across the globe. Although they were exceptionally well informed of the international progress on municipal matters—their files bursting with patterns and precedents—the extent to which their northern hemisphere brethren had any reciprocal cognizance of their own progressive undertakings is less certain. But it might be assumed that the personal reporting of FitzGibbon and his ilk on their overseas trips might have kept overseas municipalities somewhat informed of Melbourne's achievements.

From matters of public toilets and pedestrians, to street paving and lighting, personal and official correspondence reveals the fluency and extent of the circulation of ideas and information about urban concerns. In the 1880s a traveler versed in both cities could compare the inadequacies of Melbourne with the convenient and ubiquitous provisioning of Glasgow with public urinals. The obvious solution to the distaste occasioned by the visibility of public toilets on city streets was to build them underground, and as early as 1895 the Melbourne town clerk and city surveyor were in possession of details of underground toilets in Aberdeen, London, Leeds, and Bournemouth and looked forward to the completion of Melbourne's sewage system before introducing the first underground toilet in 1902.[34]

French-born Justin Drouhet, an engineer, railway draftsman, and painter who came to Melbourne in the early 1860s, had brought the city council's attention in 1864 to the latest in enameled street name-plates, as used in Paris: "very strong . . . always perfectly clean and easy to read from a distance, also in the dark are a beautiful ornament."[35] A special committee reported in March 1866 on the formation of Melbourne's streets and on available systems of street repair, considering the arguments for and against the John Loudon McAdam and Thomas Telford systems.[36] By 1870 test portions of asphalt had been laid on footpaths in Elizabeth Street. The latest paving technologies were being reported from Glasgow, Bombay, Paris, and Rome. The Val de Travers Asphalt Paving Company, which first laid asphalt in London's Threadneedle Streets in 1869, petitioned the city council with the advantages of their product: easily cleaned, conducive to good health, noiseless, unaffected by heat or cold, fireproof, durable, smooth, and easily repaired.[37]

A suggestion was put forward for the 1867 royal visit that Melbourne pedestrians should adopt the English practice of keeping to the right hand side of footways. A decade later the system was again put before the city council: "It must be obvious to all traversing the streets the inconvenience of walking all over the path way there being no system laid down to guide foot passengers similar to that in London & other large towns."[38] The suggestion was put in 1888 that placards be set up as in London, requiring pedestrians to keep to the right. In 1921 the city engineer toured abroad to study the relief of traffic congestion in the United States, England, and Europe. By this time it was considered that pedestrians should no longer have their backs to the traffic, since during busy traffic periods they inevitably and dangerously spilled onto the roadway. In 1922, while authorities in London and Perth felt that it would be difficult to alter traditional habits, the system of keeping to the left was working in Sydney. Victoria police supported the change: "The traffic in Melbourne has 'speeded up' and will 'get faster' to such a degree that it will not be safe for pedestrians to step off footpaths on to roadways with their backs to the traffic as in times past."[39] In the early 1920s safety zones were constructed at central intersections, while jaywalking (noted as an American term) and the habit of pedestrians standing on the roadway waiting for trams were formally discouraged. Mechanical traffic lights were already in use in some American cities, but in Melbourne the white-gloved hand signals of the traffic police were favored for their ability to react to the contingencies of street traffic flow. By 1925 the rule of the footpath had been changed to "keep to the left," with white lines painted down the middle of footpaths. Where it had been customary for a gentleman in the 1880s to accompany a lady on her left-hand side—thus exposing her to the road but shielding her from fellow pedestrians—the change in the rule of the footpath by the 1920s might be further explained by a reversal of hazards from the crowd to the car.

The impact of "the gospel of electricity" and new plate-glass technology for shopfronts heralded a new era in the art of shop-window design and illumination, which was informed by Melbourne's electrical engineer's first-hand observation of the lighting of shop windows in Berlin and New York. In 1911 City Electrical Engineer H. R. Harper toured Europe, the United States, and Canada, studying the technology and provision of lighting in principal cities. Noting the introduction of the metal filament lamp, which had significantly cut lighting costs and enabled advances in artistic illumination, Harper considered that the lighting of British provincial towns was inferior to Melbourne. Berlin was considered to be the best-lighted city, although most European cities were lit with electric arc lamps of the obsolete "open" type. These did not compare to the "modern" flame arc used in London, Berlin, and for about eight years in Australia. The United States favored the "enclosed" arc lamp, and Harper was struck by the impressive lighting of open spaces in Chicago and the almost excessive illumination of New York.[40] Melbourne in 1915 boasted 177 miles of lighted streets, but nothing could compare with the shining "White Ways" Harper had seen in the United States. Lighting was now not simply a practical aid to the pedestrians avoiding this ditch or that muddy pool, nor was it merely a symbol of status; it had become an integral feature of urban capitalist consumption.[41]

The relatively expensive and time-consuming intercontinental visits of municipal employees were perhaps a sideline in the trading of ideas. They were just one of a broader set of strategies, of which direct and targeted correspondence was the most effective means of transmitting knowledge. Informants could be citizens or municipal officers, tourists or technicians. Information could be gleaned as the result of official request or incidental observation. The summary effect was a veritable storehouse of knowledge, regularly plundered for patterns and precedents, which municipal operatives could then apply to their local situation, either in anticipation of future requirements or as a reaction to existing conditions. The fashioning of such knowledge was naturally undertaken within a local milieu of specific legal frameworks, administrative practices, and cultural attitudes.

As has already been suggested, the axes of internationalization in Melbourne's case extended well beyond narrow imperial pathways. The establishment of a city morgue in Melbourne[42]—before any British counterpart—was based both on specific local conditions (population explosion on the back of the gold rush decade of the 1850s and extreme summer temperatures) as well as information furnished in 1868 by the chief commissioner of police on the Paris precedent, "now the most complete structure of the kind."[43]

The books on the Victoria Room shelves date from the 1880s through to the 1910s, a period of increased internationalization and codification of networks and technologies of governance. In the Australian context, bodies such as the Municipal Association of Victoria (formed 1879; incorporated 1907) and the Victorian Town Planning and Parks Association (formed 1914) reflected both a nascent political concern to consolidate and lobby for the interests of municipal government in the context of other spheres of government, as well as burgeoning international consciousness about the efficiency and quality of life of the modern city.[44] In order to explore in more detail the mechanisms of municipalization in transitional periods, this chapter now turns its attention to an examination of the process of municipal interchange in the particular context of the regulation of public nuisances in Melbourne.

The Suppression of Nuisances: Problems and Patterns

The power vested in Melbourne's municipal government to prevent and suppress public nuisances "for the good rule and government of the town,"[45] however constrained within broader legal parameters, might be seen to balance ideal notions of the public good with an agenda set by ratepayers and commercial interests who petitioned and comprised its membership. The desire to clean up public space was applied to a set of behaviors regarded as immoral, threatening, annoying, and dangerous. Why were the citizens complaining in one particular place and at one particular time? Christopher Hamlin posed these questions in a Scottish context, in relation to Edinburgh's fetid irrigation controversy of 1839–40, and concluded that such ruptures and environmental controversies might be nested in broader issues—for example, of private interests setting the agenda for public action, or of constructions of social order, obligation, and responsibility.[46] This is not to say, of course, that the currency of ideas and the circulation of new knowledge—in this case, theories of disease causation—were not important ingredients of social change. When public behavior that yesterday was taken for granted as normal becomes unacceptable today, regulatory modifications or innovations might also be analyzed in the context of the web of municipal intelligence.[47]

Early twentieth-century Melbourne was alarmed, for example, by the proportions of the expectoration nuisance, which first reared its head locally in August 1901. Children, it seems, were learning improper manners not only from intemperate and working-class men but from a broader male population (even an ex-mayor was seen spitting) who thought it "manly" to spit. The nuisance was exaggerated by growing awareness of the spread of contagious diseases, and Robert Koch's theories on consumption were cited as evidence that spitting needed to be stamped out.

In January 1902 it was reported in *The Australian Woman's Sphere* that the Board of Health[48] acknowledged growing municipal attempts to suppress the spitting nuisance, suggesting that control should also be exercised over women wearing long trailing dresses, acting "as scavengers . . . [carrying] refuse and filth into their homes." In April a visitor from Tasmania, lecturing on the germ theory of disease, professed his astonishment and disgust "at the condition of the footways at street corners in the city, caused by expectoration by pedestrians."[49] An antispitting by-law was passed in 1903, and active measures were subsequently taken to discourage the now illegal activity. Justified by public-health concerns, spitting was now classified an urban nuisance par excellence. Breaches of the by-law were pursued by the city health inspector, and many cautions were issued for spitting in the streets. The corners of Swanston and Bourke streets were a major locus of the spitting nuisance; when this corner was specifically kept free of loiterers by police on "move on" duty, the spitting nuisance noticeably abated. Regular prosecutions continued through the decade, declining into the 1920s.[50]

In the mid-nineteenth century, spitting in public was a relatively unnoticed natural function; at least, little comment on it may be found in social discourse. By the late 1870s spitting was noted as part of the lout's antisocial repertoire, "converting the pavement into a beastly puddle of expectoration in the midst of which they practice the breakdowns, the quicksteps, the double shuffle, which appear to be the highest of their achievements."[51] Regulations against spitting were as much a means of controlling perceived social threats and antisocial behavior as stemming the spread of disease. In Melbourne's case, the rise of spitting as a definite public nuisance after the turn of the twentieth century and the introduction of prohibitive laws superseded a period where spitting, although never an unproblematic natural function, could at least be ignored in the public sphere.

The 1903 spitting by-law was facilitated by a growing concern to combat contagion and a transformed sensibility as to the nature of spitting as a publicly indecent act. At this juncture in the transformation of attitudes, "apparently decent men" as well as loiterers and louts could engage in a grossly offensive act. Although the development of spitting as a manifest public nuisance coincides with increased medical knowledge as to disease causation, as Norbert Elias suggests, this may not be the essential cause in the shift in social sensibility; hygienic reasons are only very belatedly proposed after centuries of changes in attitudes toward the act. By the 1920s behavior that had once at worst provoked social discomfort and demanded simple avoidance and was at best excused on the basis of the poor health of the spitter, or as the prerogative of the smoker, was now anathema in the modern city; regulation had indeed played a part in the transformation of thresholds of the tolerable, as "the tendency to spit" became a superfluous public act. But the medical justifications may have been merely secondary gains from the prohibition, the primary intent being to add to the raft of discretionary laws controlling "undesirable" bodies in public space.[52]

Knowledge of interstate and overseas regulations was a vital exogenous factor. While Melbourne was contemplating antispitting laws in 1901, Sydney had already enacted a by-law, while Bendigo (in regional Victoria) had notices against public spitting. By July 1902 the city council was erecting notices against spitting, though the introduction of strict regulations, as in some American cities, was deemed by some a more appropriate measure to allay the evil. From Robert Koch's 1882 discovery of the tubercle bacillus, one might track the diffusion of regulatory frameworks and subsequent changes in thresholds of tolerance: from an 1886 French hygiene council public order against spitting, through subsequent municipal ordinances—for example, in New York (1896), Boston (1896), San Francisco (1897), Sydney (1900), Melbourne (1903), and Virginia (1906). A paper by Elmer B. Borland, professor of hygiene and dietetics at the Western University of Pennsylvania, was published in the *Journal of the American Medical Association* in 1900. Borland had been reviewing progress of municipal regulation of spitting since he had read a paper on the matter five years previously to the Allegheny County Medical Society. Half of the twenty-two cities with whom Borland had been in communication had enacted special laws and another quarter regulated spitting under their general nuisance acts. By 1916, over 90 percent of American cities with populations over 25,000 had enforced spitting laws.[53] The preoccupation of the historian, of course, should not be with obsessive comparative attention to simplistic regulatory chronologies but rather to the ways in which laws are nested both in global and local traditions.

Although it is unclear whether Borland's piece was directly consulted by Melbourne's decision makers, it is certain that they were specifically informed by knowledge of other national and international measures. Generally, newspapers and journals reported comparative progress on the matter, directly connecting the city council to a catalog of meriting healthy cities: "Other cities in other lands have passed by-laws, which are rigidly enforced, prohibiting expectoration in any public place, and why cannot Melbourne follow suit?"[54] But more particularly, San Francisco had introduced regulations in 1897 prohibiting expectoration in public buildings, street railway cars, or on sidewalks, while allowing for provision of spittoons; copies of its orders were lodged in the Melbourne town clerk's correspondence files.[55] Correspondence from Sydney's town clerk in September 1901 included copies of that city's 1900 "By-Law for Regulating the use of Streets, &c., in the City of Sydney," with a note that "it is worthy of mention that, with the assistance of the Police, a number of convictions have been obtained under this by-law, with an appreciably beneficial result in checking the nuisance."[56]

In the framing and enacting of by-laws as regulatory frameworks, and in their relationship to retrospective or subsequent social change, we might perceive a spectrum of endogenous and exogenous factors that are equally instructive in understanding the city-making process. Immanent or inventive local responses addressed local accidents[57] or exigencies. After a baby was speared through the eye, for example, Melbourne's By-Law of April 1913 followed the lead shown by regulations in Sydney and Adelaide in 1912 in banning hatpins, which sometimes protruded up to three inches from the crown of ladies' narrow brimmed hats.

Other species of ordinances either rejected novelty outright or imposed new conceptions of progress and order onto existing conditions. Under an 1862 by-law introduced to regulate overhanging signs and flags, the traditional iconographic shop signs of the pawnbroker's balls, the barber's pole, the pestle and mortar, or the ubiquitous large suspended imitation objects were now classified as objectionable, obstructive, and inimical to street architecture. The traditional pillar veranda had by the turn of the twentieth century become synonymous with the "Veranda Post Evil," its replacement by cantilever technology justified by the unsightliness and obstruction of the former structures but also importantly by their anachronism and association with the congregating idler.

Broader patterns of diffusion, adaptation, and adoption—the selective contact change brought about through intercontinental flows and crosscultural exchanges—are also observable in municipal rule-making. Melbourne's town clerks, and their equivalents across the globe, were parochial guardians, sensitive to the specificities of their local domains and more or less attentive to the petitioning of local lobby groups. Largely due to the efforts of medical societies and women's political groups, Melbourne's first underground toilet for women was opened in 1902—the year Australian women gained federal suffrage. Men's street urinals, by comparison, had been introduced in the 1850s. But these municipal officers were also the vectors of planned and codified external change agencies and ideologies. In Melbourne's case, the lineages of regulation and innovation do not align with crude center/periphery models; by the turn of the twentieth century they derived as much from North American civic ideologies and actions as from British ones (where, it should be noted, it seems that spitting was not regulated).

Conclusion

The instruments of modernity in the second half of the nineteenth century are by now well rehearsed: internal and global migration and mobility, the spread of railways, increasing literacy, and mass circulation newspapers. Historians can, however, still marvel and puzzle over the alacrity with which knowledge of the 1851 discovery of gold in Victoria penetrated hamlets and communities across the globe. More broadly, colonial and international exhibitions brought an empire's productions to one's doorstep, while cultural institutions were early established as the outriders of civilization and civic betterment. An enduring leitmotif of Australian history has been that distance and isolation have been the greatest forces in shaping the continent's fortunes. But Geoffrey Blainey qualified the isolation thesis in *The Tyranny of Distance*. Isolation equally led to invention, adaptation, and innovation such as James Harrison's pioneering of refrigeration technology in the 1850s. Anaesthetics invented in Boston were being used within a year or so in Launceston and Adelaide. For people and commodities, according to Blainey, the cost of distance is high, "but for ideas the freight has often been cheap."[58]

Students of the city should be particularly concerned with ways in which urban history might refresh its methodologies using the more sophisticated local analyses now at our disposal across the globe. Rather than thinking even of the metropolitan/periphery model of diffusion, the idea of a more enmeshed "world in-between" is most useful. Having completed a ten-year project to produce an *Encyclopedia of Melbourne*, I am concerned that such endeavours should be the beginning rather than the end point of urban analysis. Though the city encyclopedia has become a favored genre of urban historians—perhaps based on the supposition that the "city is much too vast for any single historian to embrace"[59]—this chapter has sought to locate "Marvellous Melbourne" as a precinct of the global city. Local studies can tend toward parochialism, an accumulation of innovations, adaptations, and claiming primacy. Getting the "facts" right is important. So too is appreciating that "firsts" have a much more interesting history beyond the bald facts. As Daves Rossell has asserted, "the original first becomes a marginally important fact in itself, but each of the firsts is important as part of a tradition of claiming primacy, and as part of individual efforts to distinguish themselves in a unique manner. . . . Having a first is not like winning a race but rather like being part of a far more general exultation in innovation and novelty."[60] The historian's role is not only to document the past, but to add value to the "facts," and in the cases of technological firsts or municipal innovations, the most relevant framework is often transnational. Tracing such broader patterns of influence may have particular resonance in the Australian context, not just to obviate parochialism and the problems of isolation that can mar national histories.[61] Sensitivity to connections can reveal both the penetration of transnational municipal ideas into local contexts, as well as the ways in which these ideas are tested, adapted, and brokered, and themselves feed back into reformulated understandings of macro processes.[62]

Despite its British nomenclature, Melbourne is not a British city; its citizens are perhaps less neo-British than denizens of a new world-in-between. In another context, Graeme Davison has suggested cognizance of the European continental city ("as much an object of imagination and desire as a dimension of lived experience") as a counterpoint to Englishness as the overbearing reference point for Australian urban development.[63] While the Victoria Room in the Melbourne town hall is a metonym of Anglo-centricity, an analysis of municipal connections can extend the view beyond narrow imperial geographies to reveal more universal influences in the endeavors of Melbourne's municipal officers to make the city what Albert Shaw envisioned as a "fit abiding-place of hopeful communities."[64] If we pursue the metaphor and regard each distinct urban settlement as a precinct or ward of the global city, we historicize our nuanced understandings of globalization, while also "avoiding a hierarchical opposition between the global and the local."[65] The vectors of official and unofficial communications continue to be the subject of much interest for Australian historians—efficient communication is the *sine qua non* of effective government.[66]

In scholarship on the global scale, the subjects of spitting, street signs, toilets and hatpins may almost seem inconsequential, but in the preoccupation with overarching networks and webs of influence, the urban historian should never lose sight of the individual everyday lived experience of the city dweller across time and space. If urban historians truly concur that towns and cities are "constituted by their relationship with other places . . . connected to them by discursive flows of information, knowledge and belief, as well as by more material flows of capital, commodities and labour,"[67] then an exciting and demanding research agenda lies in front of us. In a globalized world, we also must surely have the capacity to transcend geography, politics, and language in ways our municipal forebears could not—by traveling north and south of the equator in equal measure and welcoming all manner of interested strangers to our city gates.

CHAPTER 3

Mediterranean Connections

The Circulation of Municipal Knowledge and Practices during the Ottoman Reforms, c.1830–1910

Nora Lafi

The question of the circulation of municipal knowledge has benefited in recent years from renewed historiographical attention.[1] The result of this new tendency in reading municipal history between Europe and North America is not only a new perception of the interactions between municipalities and urban societies but also a renewed consideration of the diffusion of a local democratic governance and of the relationship between a bureaucratic apparatus and urban space and society. The main methodological achievement is in the illustration of new ways of practicing crossed history and of new paths toward a common global history of cities. But this globalized urban history also has to confront the world in its spatial extension in order to question conventional wisdom about circulatory patterns, models, influences, and most of all, its relationship to modernity, conceived here as a passage from old-regime structures to something representing democracy. If discussions remain centered within the limits of the Western world as it is generally perceived,[2] and the circulation of urban knowledge is read through the lens of a limited geographical horizon, there can be no true global history.

Confronting these new trends in urban history, with the dominant discourses on the so-called non-Western world, opens up the Ottoman Empire as one of the new frontiers for research. The Ottoman Empire provides the experimental conditions to go beyond interpretations centered

This research was made possible thanks to the support of the Deutsche Forschung Gemeinschaft (DFG).

on a Westernized "imported" model and invent a truly globalized urban history, one which integrates complex considerations of this long-held "fuzzy" periphery into its historiography. The aim of this chapter is to, thus, re-assess the conventional wisdom that municipal reforms in the Ottoman Empire were only the sole result of imported ideas and techniques from Western Europe.[3]

This dynamic integration of the peripheries into global history, a program that responds to converging suggestions in current research, is not only a way to study "subaltern" areas with new instruments but also a new trajectory in constructing the global paradigm.[4] It is no longer necessary for discussions on universal history—like at the time of Croce or Meineke—or even for chronological journeys through the conceptual minefield of world economy. But surely it is time for the insertion of these peripheral spaces into this nascent global analysis.[5] This ongoing *aggiornamento*, mainly based upon a new vision of China, India, and the Islamic world might, of course, contest the very core of the founding paradigms, but it is the only way to go beyond the ideological ambiguities carried by world history and defied by global history. Geographical enthusiasm is insufficient to invent new theoretical grounds, though. Global history is global only when its methods allow the pursuit of a comparative approach that goes beyond conventional prejudices. It requires less a simple universal explanation of the function of all human societies, than a comparative methodology.[6]

The stake here is mainly to reconsider our perception of the circulation of ideas and reforms that enabled or constrained the modernization of Mediterranean societies during the course of the nineteenth and twentieth centuries. The subliminal starting point (although sometimes enounced very explicitly) is that such circulations traveled from north to south and west to east. The "Mediterranean Crossings" hypothesis I will explore in this chapter, illustrated with the case of the urban reforms in the Ottoman Empire, is that circulations were more complex than this orthodox donor (Western)–recipient (Eastern) relationship, whereas modernity, even when imported in its exact form, dynamically interacted with societies in which processes of change were already evident.

The study of Mediterranean circulations is a minefield. It provides opportunities not only to understand the circulation of ideas between different cultures but also to confront the impact of colonialism and imperialism. The very vision of modernity being prejudiced by these issues, the stake of promoting a renewed global history involves reconsidering two centuries of unequal circulations and, ultimately, a different reading of the fate of modernity in "subaltern" societies. The study of the Ottoman Empire demonstrates how circulations amounted to more than a simple translation of knowledge from export to import societies.

The Ottoman Empire is particularly adapted to such a historiographical program. On the one hand, the concept of empire has recently aroused new developments in global and imperial history.[7] These have revisited the canonical empires, or developed comparative imperial questions among the Russian, the Habsburg, and the Ottoman empires, bringing about new insights into the treatment of local characters, the dynamics of integration and assimilation, the importance of circulation as a social glue for imperial constructions, and the governance of diversity. In the Ottoman case, a whole new generation of scholars is especially keen to discuss the complex interactions between local and global, and to reach beyond the nation and religion as the central paradigms.[8] This is not to suggest that these notions are irrelevant, but as they turn our eyes to specificities and peculiarities, they sometimes mask the dynamics of the circulation of ideas associated with modernity.[9] This insistence on cultural specificities also contributed to the conceptual isolation of the Ottoman region, despite Franz Rosenthal's proposals for a firm inscription of Muslim societies into the study of world history as early as 1952.[10]

This conceptual isolation forms a very effective sidekick to the "decline theory." Certainly, the Ottoman Empire's difficulties provided a significant opportunity for Western European powers to export their conception of modernity, together with their geopolitical domination. However, this alleged "Ottoman decline" has for too long been seen as masking European imperialism. In 1910, in spite of important territorial losses under the appetite of some European powers, the empire's sudden disappearance was not envisaged. It is blunt teleology to read the history of the empire in the light of its sudden disappearance triggered by World War I. This has led to a disparaging view of the empire's modernization program—the *Tanzimat* process—enacted between 1830 and 1910. On the contrary, this modernization program provides an important occasion for the historian to integrate a periphery, marked by its convergence with the main industrial West, into a more complex vision of the circulation of the modernity paradigm. The very vision of modernity might be reopened by such a perspective, which proceeds on the hypothesis that several competing visions interacted coterminously.

The conjunction of these different views has resulted in an emerging paradigm that maintains the Ottoman city as irreducible by essence to any other reality. This has prevented specialists from the Arab imperial provinces from confronting other historiographies. The city was Ottoman *in se* and met modernity by importing particular European characteristics. Even important works, such as Elden, Goffman, and Masters's *The Ottoman City between East and West*, struggle to disentangle Ottoman urban history from the conventional burden of the East-West dichotomy.[11] A way to better understand modernity is to know what came before. In the case of the Ottoman Empire, though, the characterization of what presaged modernity is unclear. Until recently, no one seemed to accept using concepts elaborated elsewhere to describe the Ottoman "old-regime." However, its study provides a better understanding of the rhetoric of belonging in the empire, the modalities of both central and local governance, the role of the notables and the customization of imperial power to rule plurality and diversity.[12]

Ottoman municipal reforms have something to deliver here, as a moment when an established regime of urban governance interacted with reformist impulses coming from Istanbul, but including a detour by municipal experiments in foreign lands. This process, itself complex and not reducible to a one-way journey, induced a change in the urban system—the analysis of which requires a multiscale focus on the effects of the circulation of reformist ideas. Accordingly, this chapter focuses not only on circulations between the empire and the rest of the world but also within the empire. In reference to different case studies, crossing from North Africa to the Middle East, I will focus on the local implementation of Ottoman reformist impulses and their dynamic relationship with previous forms of urban government. Paying attention to the urban civic sphere further avoids complacency in merely focusing on the unequal import-export relationship between the East and the West.

The Ottoman Municipal Reforms in Historical Context

The *Tanzimat* period, beginning in the 1830s, is a key age in the study of the Ottoman Empire. Paradoxically seen as a last desperate attempt to salvage bits and pieces from the wreckage, or as a true reformation movement aiming at administrative modernity, the *Tanzimat* are generally considered an importation into the Ottoman Empire of European administrative and bureaucratic solutions.[13] But the *Tanzimat* can also be read in a more strictly Ottoman chronology: they came after both the reformist impulses, mainly in the military organization, of the *nizan-i-cedid* (new order) period, during the reign of Sultan Selim III (1789–1807); and also the troubled period at the beginning Mahmud II's reign (1808–39), which was riven with constant clashes between conservatives and reformers. The *Tanzimat* continued a trend in Ottoman history and need to be read in the empire's historical context, rather than as an imitation of external influences. Although some of their features came externally, they initially emerged from an internal demand. There again, one must not fall under the spell of "decline theory" and read the entire Ottoman history in the light of its final moments, where external pressures might have been much stronger than any internal logic. Be it in the military domain, with the creation of artillery schools; in the economy, with important fiscal reforms; or in the central administration, with its ministerial reorganization, the European installation is generally underlined. The urban reforms are also conventionally read in this intellectual frame. The objective here is not to deny their European aspects but to provide a dynamic reading of the so-called receptive societies to complete the analysis of the journeys of possible "models."

Before the *Tanzimat* reforms, towns were ruled according to an old-regime schema characterized by the existence of privileges, the dominant role of traditional notables, and the powers of the confessional communities and guilds. All Ottoman towns were provided with an old-regime style of urban government, generally in the hands of the mercantile notability and the most powerful guilds, which met in a civic assembly, at the head of which was a "chief of town" (*shaykh al-bilad, shaykh al-madina, naqib al-ashraf*). This urban administration was responsible for public order, markets and building supervision, taxation, and also symbolically represented the civic corps before the representative of the central imperial power.

This scheme had many different forms according to the specific place.[14] But the gist was that the individual was defined according to his sense of belonging to certain units: the confessional, professional, familial, and sometimes tribal. His place in, and relation to, society depended on this sense of belonging. Both local traditions and the strata of imperial recognition of local situations conferred different privileges to certain professions, families, confessional communities, and cities. These private laws (that is, laws which were not universal but were designed to differentiate between individuals according to specific criteria) constituted the core of the old-regime corpus of rules for urban government. This corpus was the result of an accumulative logic and did not bear marks of a search for a rational division of tasks and competences on a uniform basis. In fact, the competences of the various instances were sometimes contradictory, as they might be found to take their cue from specific conflicts and agreements that took place decades or even centuries ago. Typically, in this old-regime urban scheme, a specific guild might have been granted a fiscal, professional, or civic privilege during the seventeenth century and still retain it in the nineteenth.

In every provincial capital, a governor represented the imperial power and dealt with this scheme according to Istanbul's instructions and to the tradition of mediation and negotiation with the local elite. There was no uniform urban administration at the imperial scale, and the empire adapted to every local situation according to a logic of negotiation with local bodies. This does not mean that there was no organization, just that it was framed under a specific urban governance regime. It was in this context that the *Tanzimat* reforms were implemented. They were part of the Ottoman state's effort to introduce a new rationality into its administration. One can read the whole movement as a passage from old-regime to administrative modernity in the introduction of general rules instead of specific privileges.

The *Tanzimat* reforms began as early as the 1830s with reforms to the military, under the reign of Sultan Mahmud II. Indeed, this was a period in which very few European states had enacted, or were enacting, similarly profound changes to their institutional and administrative structures. Sultan Abdul-Majid I's *Gülhane Hatt I Sharif* edict of 1839, for example, contained important measures that contributed toward social and religious equality. The *Hatt I Humayun* edict of 1856, which allowed non-Muslims to become civil servants,[15] and the *Dustur* (constitution) of 1876 enacted by Sultan Abdul-Hamid II were similar milestones on the *Tanzimat* trail. Soon thereafter, though, the constitution was suspended and the empire experienced several decades of inertia in implementing a new administrative scheme. The initial impulses—themselves still ambiguous in the constitution of an administrative modernity and a new definition of the self in its relation to religious, professional, and family belonging—were contrasted by a politics of reaction. In interpreting this period the conventional wisdom, shared by several generations of historians, is that the reforms were the product of external influences.[16] Generally, the phenomenon is seen as a top-down one, with reformist impulses coming from Europe, irrigating the central administration in Istanbul and then various parts of the empire.

A new generation of Turkish scholars has introduced new variables into this discourse, proposing a richer vision of the Ottoman society before and during the reforms.[17] They have made it possible to contextualize Ottoman municipal reforms, by studying the administrative and social evolution of the empire.[18] We are now more familiar with the roots of the Ottoman reforms, a key point in the journey of Ottoman modernity.[19] In this context, the analysis of municipal reforms can sketch new directions.

Questioning the Reformist Narrative

Turkish historiography has accepted the reading of the Ottoman urban reforms through the prism of an imported European style of municipal government. Though such an explanation clearly challenged Turkish nationalism, most of the existing Turkish literature illustrates the *Tanzimat* as the application into the Empire of "Made-in-Europe" measures. Ilber Ortaylı, one of the most authoritative Turkish historians, insists on the importance of Istanbul as an Ottoman laboratory for the implementation of

European-style municipal reforms, which were then to be spread throughout the empire.[20] The narrative is very effective. Firstly, an experimental phase took place in Istanbul's Galata district, starting in 1857 after three years of study by a reform commission. This phase is universally described as the application of municipal reforms on a European model to a very particular corner of the empire, mostly populated by non-Turks.[21] Secondly, an experimental phase was devolved to a series of test cities during the 1860s and early 1870s. Thirdly, the reforms were diffused across the whole empire through the 1864 Provincial Law and the 1877 Municipal Law.[22] The latter created the urban municipalities, with a municipal council elected by male tax-paying Ottoman landowners, a mayor, and a fiscal system. Municipalities were granted important powers, from building rights to hygiene, and from water distribution to education.[23]

This chronology of the different steps of the local reforms corresponds to important phases in the implementation of the municipal reforms, and more generally, in the modernization of the structure of Ottoman urban administration. Legally, it accounts for most of the main measures, but its basic assumptions can be challenged, beginning with the alleged existence of a European model that served as the matrix for Ottoman municipal reform. Yet Europe was not a homogeneity of municipal structures; indeed, no generic European "model" existed during the 1850s. There were many frames of reference on which the Ottomans could base municipal reform. These included the dominance of the modernizing prefect over the submissive Parisian and several other French municipalities; the broad range of German regional legislations; and the quasi-liberal fiefdom of the British corporations. Elsewhere, the Italian municipalities were in a confused state, marked by the dismantling of many of the institutional reforms that had been passed in 1848.[24] As for local democracy, the persistence of the property qualification for electors illustrates the difficulties of implementing reform across the continent. On the other hand, the fact that the Galata quarter contained a large Greek and "European" population was not such an exception in the empire. Europe was not a block of exportable modernity, and the empire was not a block of "indigenous" homogeneity in the outback, with islands of diversity where modernity could be tested.

This does not mean that no "European" knowledge was used in the empire, though—far from it; municipal European knowledge did indeed circulate, as did publications and experts. The Ottoman government of 1854 was also fascinated with Haussmann's Paris, just as so many other governments were throughout the world.[25] But once this fascination is attested, there remains the question of how it was turned into material to be used in the Ottoman context.

During the reform period, Ottomans did indeed send many fact finding missions to Europe. The organization of the Prussian army, for example, was studied carefully, from the time of Azmi Efendi—Ottoman Ambassador in Berlin (1790–92)—to the middle of the nineteenth century.[26] Many European experts were also invited to teach in the newly created artillery schools, or hired as Ottoman army officers. The Ottomans also collected information on European cities, particularly their administrative and fiscal systems. For example, Mehmet Said, one of the early nineteenth-century Ottoman travelers, took in the German city-states and the remnants of their Hanseatic heritage.[27] During the *Tanzimat*, several fact-finding parties were sent to Europe, while ambassadors were required to write reports about urban reforms so that their memos could be read by Istanbul's reform-commission members. European experts and technicians were also hired to work in many of the empire's cities. The figure of the French or Italian engineer working in an Ottoman city is a classic image of the age. Public works, cartography, cadastral surveys, medicine, and education were the main domains of this collaboration. The mapping of Ottoman cities was often commissioned to French or Italian cartographers. As for water and sewage, it was common to hire French engineers from the *Ponts et Chaussées* to serve in Ottoman cities during the second half of the nineteenth century. More generally, many European engineers worked privately in the empire, proposing public-works projects or submitting proposals to obtain the concession of a public service.[28]

Europeans were not only looking at the empire as a market. Indigenous reform texts were translated into European languages and discussed in specialized European journals. George Young's or Démétrius Aristarchi's efforts to collect comprehensive data on the Ottoman legislation during the final third of the nineteenth century were part of this process, just like the many accounts of the Ottoman reforms published throughout Europe.[29] In his *Letters on Turkey* (1856), the French-speaking writer Jean Henri Abdolonyme Ubicini provided a detailed account of the Ottoman modernization effort, covering subjects ranging from fiscal to education policy. He was very keen to describe the progress of urban reforms and gave credit to the Ottoman government for a rational modernity effort of the old urban governance scheme.[30] In France, Germany, Great Britain, and Italy, great attention was paid to what was happening in the empire's cities. In the best colonial science fashion, Ottoman urban knowledge was crucial for European powers because of their aspirations to command and conquer the region. When Laurent-Charles Féraud wrote a detailed account on Tripoli during the 1880s, he acted as much as an informant of the military secret service as a historian and erudite.[31] The logic was the same for Italian geographers in Asia Minor. A case study investigation of this subject still has to be done, but there are clues for how the Ottoman urban governance experience has been an inspiration in newly conquered European Mediterranean colonies.[32]

This two-way circulation bore strong ambiguities: it was rarely a circulation between equal partners, though the commissioning of a foreign expert for a precise task cannot be seen as a surrender to domination. Sometimes, too, in remote Arab provinces of the Maghreb or the Middle East, when European consuls were a factor in the implementation of urban government reforms, these ambiguities were even stronger. The reforms they promoted were not necessarily modern but were meant to reinforce the influence of European expatriates on the urban scene. Indeed, while Ottoman administrative modernization was mainly meant to preserve these provinces from European imperial encroachment, European consuls resisted them and promoted the persistence of the old-regime organization to retain their patronage network intact and effective. In Tunis, the modernization drive was Ottoman, and the support for the old regime was indeed European.[33] The attempt to create a reformed municipality was clearly fought by the French consul, who tried to maintain the old-regime system in order to deepen his influence and patronage over the local nobility. Hence, the reforms were not fully applied in Tunis: the mayor did not wholly succeed the *shaykh-al-madina* from the old regime.

For all of these connections, the circulation of urban-government reform experiments and results not only occurred between Western Europe and the Ottoman Empire. There were also interesting circulations of urban knowledge (including the type of municipal administration and the organization of the municipal bureaus) between the empire and newly independent or autonomous countries in its periphery. The tradition of nationalist historiographies has limited the growth of comparative studies in this field. Notwithstanding such methodological obstacles, there is a tie between the definition of municipal urban government in Greece after independence and the Ottoman municipal reform experience. Greek notables in Istanbul were the key point of contact in this dual circulation.[34] There was also a definite link between Istanbul and the Egyptian reforms of the mid-nineteenth century, at a time when Egypt gained relative autonomy.[35] Greek and Egyptian urban notables both had strong Ottoman urban cultures and were conversant with debates in Istanbul. Throughout the empire, the leaders of urban communities also kept an eye on discussions about urban government in Greece, even after the loss of the Greek provinces. The mere presence of Ottoman Greek notables in almost every city of the empire reinforced this potential for connections, just like the content of almanacs, newspapers, and the existence of Greek handbooks on Ottoman administration.

There were also more intriguing connections. Shortly after the beginning of the Meiji reforms in Japan in 1868, several delegations of Japanese observers were sent to Istanbul; they were searching for their own way to shove their old regime into modernity.[36] The Japanese saw the Ottoman reforms as a model of good practice, and the urban aspect of this question, including municipal affairs, was seen as an example of the passage from traditional institution to administrative modernity. In return, Sultan Abdülhamid II sent a party of Ottoman administrators and scientists to Japan in 1889. The wreckage of their frigate *Ertugrul* on the shores of Wakayama in 1890 left most of the Ottoman representatives dead, but the existence of the mission is a clue that the empire was looking for insights well beyond the Mediterranean rim.[37]

If Europe was a component of Ottoman urban-government reforms, it was thus in a far more complex way than has been hitherto suggested. On the one hand, documentation on what was happening elsewhere was part of the Ottoman governance, and it was included in a circulatory scheme that is not adequately described by the account of imported European experiments. On the other hand, urban reforms were genuine re-forms, which involved the revamping of something already existing and not the creation, *ex-nihilo*, of something new. They came in the context of an articulated tradition of urban governance. The question of the Ottoman municipal reforms during the period 1854–77 cannot be regarded as an example of a mere importation of a "Western" governing technique into an "Oriental" context. More satisfactorily, it was an attempt to impose a modernist reform (based upon a new definition of the individual and of civic rights) onto an old-regime frame. Reforms were in no way imported into a vacuum but rather were adapted by local notables to suit local circumstances, as the following section will make clear.

The Ottoman Path to Urban Modernity: Case Studies

The reason for the Ottoman modernization effort was mainly to resist European domination. At a time when, from Tunis to Damascus, from the Balkans to Asia Minor, pushy European consuls tried to reinforce their dominance over urban communities (through such traditional ways as consular protection or the granting of "private laws," exemptions, and privileges), Ottoman reforms attempted to counter this trend. Be it with a degree of European influence in the shaping of administrative solutions, these reforms were part of a truly Ottoman process. This assertion does not mean that the Ottoman Empire was homogeneous (it was even in its very nature not so), but rather that there was a political agenda in Istanbul for reinforcing the empire's coherence by granting the fidelity of local notables against attempts by European consuls to attract them into the net of foreign patronage. A new definition of local autonomy was the solution, in order to confirm the competences of local elites in running their cities and also to reinforce the Ottoman character of such autonomy. It was also an occasion to clarify the relationship between the instances of local autonomy and the central state, represented locally by the governor. This process occurred in the century-old frame of mediation between the central power and the local elite but introduced new organizational and political principles in the pattern. The main aim of the municipal reforms might thus have been to grant urban notables throughout the Empire with renewed civic prerogatives, in exchange for a renewal of their allegiance to the empire. This is why the Ottoman municipal reforms have to be read as a negotiation between the center and the periphery. The 1877 law was just the end of the process, crowning more than two decades of mediation, experimentation, conflict, and negotiation. It was the result of these mechanisms through which Ottoman administrators and governors dealt with very different local situations.

In this process, the circulation of knowledge about urban governance inside the empire was crucial. The first step was to survey the local declensions of the Ottoman old-regime urban governance.[38] Such documentation journeys were organized in the Balkans in the 1860s. As Tetsuya reports, "After the Crimean War, the reformists felt a necessity for effective local administration. In 1860, a special delegation, headed by the Grand Vezir, Kıbrıslı Mehmet Pasha, embarked on a four-month round trip to supervise the provincial reforms in the Balkans. In 1863, with the same purpose, special supervisors of local affairs were dispatched. They were charged with duties to implement improved measures requested by the local populace."[39] A similar process was followed in the various provinces of the empire, from the Middle East to North Africa. Not only was reform never implemented in a city without a previous documentation of local traditions, but the 1877 law was the result of two decades of crossed circulations between reformers (a group of statesmen close to the Sultan and a generation of governors), local notables, and Istanbul legislators. This was quite logical: if the problem was how to retain the provinces' tacit support, the solution was to negotiate a program for implementing a local declension of administrative modernity with urban notables; so they could identify it as a way to preserve and reinforce their prerogatives as notables, merchants, and land owners. It was crucial to give them some guarantees that, in the best fashion, reform was more cosmetic than substantial: since old-regime notables were city rulers because of their belonging to a particular family, guild, or community, they had to be convinced that they would still be city rulers under the reformed system—though henceforth it would be because of their belonging to a fiscal class. In this process, the locality had as much redesigned the center as the center had done so to the locality.

The imperial circulation of facts and figures about urban government also took place through the movement of technicians, administrators, and governors. The official gazette of the empire was distributed to all provinces and translated into local languages. In every city, local almanacs (*salname*) followed every step in the reforms, keeping lists of notables up-to-date and explaining the content of the reforms.[40] But urban notables were also anxious to send and collect their own information. They did not hesitate to write petitions to Istanbul when they felt that their prerogatives were under threat nor to send representatives to the capital city to make their claims in the appropriate way.[41] There was also an important peer-to-peer circulation of urban knowledge in the empire. From city to city, notables wrote to each other to share information and coordinate their actions.[42]

Local and imperial archives show that the implementation of municipal reforms in Tripoli, located in Ottoman North Africa, resulted from a complex interaction between local and imperial actors.[43] The governor, Alî Pasha al-Jazayrî—the son of an Algiers urban notable in exile in Istanbul after the French occupation—was sent into the city by the Ottoman imperial ministry of provincial affairs, first to study the old regime form of urban government[44] and then to negotiate the creation of a reformed municipality with the local notables. The aim for the imperial administrator was to reinforce the empire's presence in a region coveted by the French,[45] the English,[46] and the Italians. Signaling the vitality of the old regime, the *shaykh al-balad* became mayor of the new municipality in 1867. More than an importation, Ottoman modernity in Tripoli was first a confirmation and adaptation of the old regime. After a series of conflicts, which were part of the mediation process for the accommodation of a modern administrative solution within a traditional frame (and during which time Istanbul was pressed for decisions by provincial notables), the new municipality was formed. Predating the 1877 law, Tripoli's municipalization was a central part of a dynamic process in which the Ottoman path toward modernity was reflected through a combination of mediation, conflict, and negotiation.

The reason for the initial dispute in Tripoli was that Istanbul wanted to impose not only the administrative scheme but also its preferred choice as *shaykh al-balad*. Following tense conflict and mediation, Tripoli's notables accepted the new administrative structure on the condition that they selected its chief officer.[47] The Ottomans thus retained the city's loyalty for another fifty years, until the Italian occupation of 1911–12. Most significantly, though, the modern administrative system was the result of a negotiated reform between Istanbul and the traditional local leaders. It was not the product of an imported foreign model, which was why it succeeded.

Success was not to be met in Tunis, though. There, most urban notables were already in the net of the consular clientele. The modern Ottoman municipality did not succeed the old-regime structure, and both cohabitated: the *shaykh al-madina* (chief of the town's "old-regime" administration) and the *raïs al-baladiyya* (president of the reformed municipality). The persistence of the old regime signaled the Ottomans' failure to effectively negotiate the passage toward administrative modernity, as the colonization of the province was already under way.[48] Modernity had already been checked by imperialism. This example illustrates the importance of local characteristics in implementing reforms, as transimperial connections interfered with local conditions. But most of all, it illustrates Europe's ambiguity.

The European origins of the urban government reforms in Tunis are, at best, muddled, since the reformist impulse was the result of a transimperial negotiation process on the basis of local forms of urban autonomy. Indeed, the European influence in Tunis between 1850 and 1880 was more clearly expressed in the wish to increase consular rule and seize colonial territories. European consuls clearly chose to contrast the Ottoman municipal reforms with the old-regime governance scheme and plumped to play the *status quo* card, since this suited their wish to detach local notables from any Ottoman loyalty. This explains the partial implementation of the municipal reforms in Tunis. There was a batch of other reasons as well, such as the difficulties that derived from the break of confessional balances when the definition of civic rights of the individuals was to take place outside of their religious affiliation. However, the pressure of European imperialism remained a crucial mitigating factor in explaining how urban-government reforms were sometimes only partially applied throughout the empire.

In other cities of the empire, local situations tended to veer between these two extremes of a complete absorption of the old regime in Tripoli and a failed mediation in Tunis.[49] There generally existed an early implementation of the municipal reforms, long before the 1877 law, which was the result of a negotiation among local notables within their old-regime institutions. The new administrative framework generally confirmed their prerogatives: petitions, trips to Istanbul, pressure to replace a centralizing governor, and requests from other cities for advice or solidarity. The whole process exhibited a high degree of circulation, both between the center and the periphery as well as peer-to–peer—for example, from Beirut to Damascus and from Aleppo to Jeddah. The Ottoman municipal modernity definitely reflected the result of these interactions rather than a simple importation.

Conclusion

The study of the Ottoman municipal reform is a reflection of the very essence of the Ottoman Empire. The discussion of the "importation" thesis enables a reassessment of the European influence over so-called peripheries and also a deeper understanding of the very nature of Ottoman imperial governance itself. The prestige of European cities and governments played a role in framing the administrative reforms, but the empire was not a virgin field, ripe for an imported modernity. Modernity was definitely a two-way journey. In the Ottoman case, it was also negotiated in every city with the local notables in order to fit the existing social frame. Administrative modernity was the result of a complex process of interaction rather than the implementation of a prewritten codex. The 1877 law was passed only after two decades of local experimentation and negotiation. Indeed, the old regime had itself been negotiated on a similar basis, that of a dynamic relationship between the urban elite and the center. What was new with modernity was a dynamic relationship between universal principles, such as individual urban citizenship, and local situations. From the outset, the universal principle was weak and only directed negotiations. Ultimately, though, it grew stronger and allowed the Ottomans to retain their domination over a large part of the Mediterranean—from North Africa to the Balkans—for another five decades. Everything was in the process. The new principle was that urban governance was in the hands of a landowning notability, which fit socially with the old regime's merchant notability. Modernity was, therefore, defined by a change in the definition of the notable rather than a change in the composition of the notability, merchants having enough properties to be granted access to municipal power through the new institutional mechanisms.

The Ottoman municipal modernity failed to confront certain issues, however, which ultimately proved critical. The first of these was the persistence of the old regime where it had proven impossible to negotiate reform. Cities such as Tunis were almost already lost, though. The second, and more important, problem was that Ottoman modernity often failed to address the diverse nature of cities in the empire, with their many religious, national, or linguistic communities. The old-regime privileges, exemptions, and rules were unsustainable in a modern administrative environment. Where initial negotiations were unsuccessful in implementing a durable balance, the situation often proved difficult a few decades later. Indeed, the Ottoman municipal law, for the very reason of its modernity, was not ductile enough to fit the situation. The Ottoman Empire, in the end, did not find the right fit for adjusting modern administrative tools and methods with the arcane cities it had to manage. The advantage of the old regime was that it allowed greater flexibility in the treatment of the question and in the governance of diversity. Yet it also allowed a deepening of the European influence, and therefore it was chosen to reform it. Municipal government, conversely, allowed the empire to maintain control temporarily but ultimately failed to foster a new commonality and loyalty at the city scale. The modern urban citizen never really emerged from the reform to meet the definition of the municipal notable.

In the Ottoman Empire, modernity brought a great deal of ambiguity in its treatment of certain local specifications but also in its relationship with Europe. This ambiguity was later reinforced when former Ottoman cities were seized by the Europeans. It was already the case in Algiers, conquered in 1830, at a time when it was "normal" to have an old-regime situation and where "modernity" was later wholly colonial and fundamentally prejudiced by the unequal treatment of individuals according to their identity. This was the case in Beirut, Damascus, Tripoli, Rhodes, and Aleppo after World War I, where their modern municipalities were transformed by the colonial powers in ways that did not reflect true modernity—including the unequal treatment of individuals (both settlers and locals) and the political use of the communal bias. One consequence of the developing scholarship on old-regime imperial urban governance is the emergence of a more accurate view of this moment. This second generation of "Mediterranean crossings," which took place in the 1920s and 1930s, can be seen under a new light. In most cities, a modernized Ottoman municipality pre-existed the European colonial reforms and even the national reforms. Moreover, in many cases the municipal solutions enacted through colonialism were a setback—in spite of all the limits of the Ottoman reforms—in the evolution toward a local and democratic municipal-inspired modernity.

For Ottoman history, the study of municipal reform reveals a functioning of the imperial apparatus, which includes modernization processes to conventional old-regime procedures. From the perspective of comparative global history, the Ottoman case illustrates the existence of a variety of complex interests and actors involved in the circulation process.[50] Most of all, the case demands a reassessment of studies on the so-called reception societies themselves. Simple ideas on circulations often derive from simple ideas on reception. At the end of the nineteenth century, many Ottoman cities were genuine local societies, with their dedicated organization and interaction with Istanbul, other Ottoman cities, and cities in Europe and beyond. Rather than being a passive receiver of European ideas, the empire teemed with projects and tensions, which were developed within a dynamic web of circulations that sifted and winnowed foreign experiments. Modernity, even in peripheral environments, arrived in a rich and articulated reality. Not only does the image of the Ottoman city, as shown in the tradition of *Orientalism*, need to be corrected but our search for a way to place cities in the narrative of global, crossed, or transnational history is transformed by taking these environments into account. The Ottoman city is taken here as being much richer than simply the product of external Western reform impulses. It was also a city with a rich social and institutional history, which entered into a new age of communication during the nineteenth century. The Ottoman city interacted with Western cities on a number of scales and levels, rather than one of a simple donor-recipient relationship. It was not a mere scene where modernization designs were sketched, tested, or implemented but rather one aspect of a transnational conversation about the making of the modern city.

CHAPTER 4

Pacific Crossings?

Urban Progressivism in Modern Japan

Jeffrey Hanes

One of the most storied Japanese examples of the "transnational municipal moment" took place in the wake of the Great Kanto Earthquake of September 1, 1923. This unprecedented disaster, which killed an estimated 140,000 people, reduced Tokyo and Yokohoma to rubble. Somewhat surprisingly, the first international plea for assistance was addressed to the famed American municipal progressive Charles A. Beard. On September 7, after some delay, Beard received the following cable from Viscount Gotô Shimpei, the mayor of Tokyo: "Earthquake and fire destroyed the greater part of Tokyo. Thoroughgoing reconstruction needed. Please come immediately if possible, even for a short stay."[1] Why did the mayor of Tokyo turn first to an American municipal progressive for counsel as he began to contemplate the future of Japan's capital?

Gotô's request did not come completely out of the blue. As it happens, Beard had recently returned from a six-month-long lecture and study tour of Tokyo at the invitation of Gotô himself. In his reminiscences, Beard offers some clues regarding Gotô's position. Central among the tasks assigned to him, writes Beard, was to "help in arousing a deeper interest in municipal government and public administration among college and university students and among the citizens of the leading Japanese cities."[2] On a practical level, Gotô asked Beard to accomplish this by lecturing to Japanese audiences on the American approach to municipal problems and by assisting in the organization of the newly formed Tokyo Institute for Municipal Research. But Gotô did not stop there; he explicitly challenged Beard to suspend disbelief and to approach his job in Japan as if he were the mayor of Tokyo himself.[3]

On the surface, Gotô's instruction might appear to be a simple gesture of hospitality toward a distinguished authority on municipal affairs. But it was much more than this. If the relationship between Gotô and Beard was about the professional and personal bond between two prominent municipal progressives, it was not formed to facilitate dialogue but rather to elicit a monologue. Gotô humbly downplayed his own significance as a municipal policy maker, stepping smoothly into the role of facilitator, and pointedly placed Beard on a pedestal. Whether or not Beard knew it, Gotô's gracious gesture masked a reflexive Japanese tendency toward humility in the face of Western knowledge and expertise that dated from the Meiji era (1868–1912). In the belief that all nations progressed along the same developmental trajectory—and that Japan remained relatively backward compared to the West—the Japanese had identified modernization with Westernization and initiated the facile practice of "cultural borrowing."

The Japanese tendency toward Western emulation, as Beard well understood, had led to the imposition of an alien system of municipal administration adopted from Germany. The German model was consistent with the goal of the Meiji leaders to establish a "unitary" nation-state, as opposed to a "federal" one such as the United States, with a strong bias toward "uniform policy."[4] What emerged was a state-centered "vertically split administration,"[5] which gave most cities limited autonomy, but placed the largest—Tokyo, Osaka, and Kyoto—under the direct jurisdiction of prefectural governors as "special cities."

This imported "city system" gave the central government control not merely over urban administration but over urban growth as well—by restricting local decision making as well as local taxation. The "special city" designation was especially onerous for Osaka. This vibrant port city, which had served as the commercial entrepôt of the Tokugawa shogunate, had a long history of political autonomy. Not to be outdone by the myopic Meiji leadership, Osaka's entrepreneurial elite attempted to modernize Osaka on their own in the late nineteenth century. By dint of their energy and capital, the city was transformed into an industrial metropolis by the turn of the twentieth century. Yet this dramatic change did not result in an equivalently dramatic alteration of Japan's city system, as hoped, but only served to highlight its inadequacy. Unsurprisingly, Osaka soon witnessed the rise of a local movement for greater urban autonomy.

Although Osaka's local leadership made political inroads in the early twentieth century, not until Seki Hajime (1873–1935) took office as mayor of Osaka in the mid-1920s did this movement for urban autonomy gather momentum. Noting that urban industrialization had transformed Osaka into a sprawling metropolis that desperately needed to be acknowledged as such, both geographically and administratively, Seki called on the central government to grant Osaka "metropolitan autonomy" (*daitoshi jichi*). By

1925, he had achieved his first objective: a dramatic expansion of the city's administrative boundary, which effectively confirmed its metropolitan identity as Greater Osaka (Dai Osaka).[6] The second objective, however, remained more elusive. In order to realize true metropolitan autonomy for Osaka—or, as Seki envisioned it, Greater Osaka's ascension to the regional administrative standing of a prefecture—Seki needed to trigger a comprehensive overhaul of Japan's city system.

Interestingly, while Seki's argument against the old administrative framework hinged on the criticism that the Meiji leaders had inappropriately projected a Western model of urban administration onto Japan, his argument for a new administrative framework also drew on Western experience. But rather than slavishly reciting lessons learned from the West, as the earlier generation of Meiji modernizers had, Seki approached the business of cultural borrowing in an entirely new way. He engaged the issues critically and comparatively, with an eye toward adopting and adapting ideas and policies to meet the specific challenges facing Japan. What enabled him to make this methodological leap was the new ideological faith of progressivism that he and many other reform-minded Japanese had come to embrace.

Seki Hajime came to progressivism as a young man, after embarking on a career as a state-centered academic economist committed to the goal of transforming Japan into an "advanced" nation-state. During a three-year sojourn in Europe at the turn of the twentieth century—during which he studied with some of the world's foremost political and social economists— Seki underwent a transformation of his own. Converting to progressivism, Seki joined a movement that was spreading like wildfire across the modern world. Simply put, progressives acknowledged the sorry fact that urban industrialization had bred endemic social problems but also embraced the firm belief that these problems could be overcome through proactive social reform. As described by Daniel T. Rodgers in his trailblazing book, *Atlantic Crossings*,[7] the most astounding thing about progressivism was its international reach. Its adherents on both sides of the Atlantic, having acknowledged the parallel development of industrial capitalism in Europe and North America, had formed a transnational fellowship of true believers committed to the crossfertilization of reformist ideas and policies designed to address the social problems industrial capitalism had spawned.

If mutual exchanges between progressives reached across the Atlantic, the same was not true of the Pacific—though not entirely due to distance and prejudice, as one might assume. While it is true that the West viewed early twentieth-century Japan through a warped ethnic and cultural lens that depreciated its significance as a modern nation-state, the Japanese themselves were complicit in the perpetuation of a leader-follower dynamic. As

Beard's exotic encounter with Japan in 1923 illustrates, old habits die hard. Although Gotô himself was a tried-and-true municipal progressive, readily recognized by Beard as a fellow traveler, he was prone nonetheless to an earlier, more obsequious, Japanese habit of cultural borrowing that was hardly conducive to the sort of transnational interchange that might be described as Pacific Crossings.

By contrast, Seki Hajime pushed the limits of transnational exchange by embracing the ideal of intellectual interchange. Rather than imitatively reproducing Western ideas in Japan, or passively soliciting the expert commentary of Westerners, he envisioned a dialogue between East and West. If he failed to achieve true transnational interchange—in the sense of sparking the sort of dialogue that Beard tried to strike up in Japan—it was not for lack of trying. In the absence of significant transnational progressive traffic to Osaka, Seki offered readers and listeners the next best thing: a dialectic method that brought foreign ideas to bear on Japan and brought Japan to bear on those same ideas. Seki's example tells us a great deal about the vagaries of interchange during the "transnational municipal moment," and it also demonstrates the enduring value of exchanging urban ideas and policies.

Progress before Progressivism

In the waning years of the Tokugawa Era (1600–1868), as the Japanese were drawn into the wider world after two hundred years of relative reclusion, their notions of time and space underwent profound change. For centuries, they had imagined history as a series of whorls through time. In times of crisis, they hearkened back to a "golden age," when the cosmic order of the social world was in harmony with nature. Rather than peering into the future toward the dawn of a new age, they contemplated the past and its enduring relevance to the present. All this changed with the arrival of the West on Japan's doorstep in the mid-nineteenth century. The shock of watching the "barbarians" defile the sacred Japanese archipelago, with the arrival of the American Commodore Matthew Perry's "black ships," was followed by an extraordinary period of collective self-reflection. A vocal, forward-looking minority read the historical writing on the wall. Ostrich-like isolation, they soberly observed, was no longer a viable option: Japan had little choice but to confront the outside world.

Once the Japanese had scouted the West—a process that began under the Tokugawa shoguns with a touring embassy to Europe and the United States in 1860—their insular worldview collapsed. If the Japanese continued to view Westerners as barbarians, they also saw them in an entirely new light. How was it, they asked themselves, that barbarians had come into the possession of such technological marvels as mechanized factories, steamships, locomotives, dirigible balloons, and cameras? More pertinently, how was it that barbarians had managed to transform cities such as Paris, Vienna, Berlin, New York, and London into modern metropolises that legitimately counted as manmade wonders of the world?

In time, the allure of Western civilization, combined with the looming threat of Western imperialism, propelled Japan toward an accommodation with the outside world that led to the Meiji Restoration in 1868. Repudiating Japan's immediate past, the leaders of Japan's newly formed nation-state self-consciously turned their eyes toward the future. They embraced the Western notion of linear time, accepted "the normality of change" (Immanuel Wallerstein's evocative term), and set about "synchroniz[ing] Japan with the temporality of progress."[8]

Not only did the Western nations provide compelling evidence of the dramatic advancement of modern civilization, they offered the comforting explanation that this advancement was attributable to the universal laws of historical progress. Unsurprisingly, given the vulnerability of their new nation-state, the Japanese seized on the idea of progress with reckless abandon and embraced its most extreme iteration: the notion of unilinear progress. According to this deceptively simple dictum, the inexorable laws of historical change propel all nations forward toward perfection, along a unilinear trajectory of development—though on different national timetables.

The comforting notion of unilinear progress enabled the Japanese to indulge in what Albert C. Craig has memorably termed "teleological insight."[9] Simply put, the Japanese could project their own future based on the prior accomplishments of the (more) advanced Western nations. By this enticing logic, the Western nations were not intrinsically superior to Japan, only more historically advanced. Thus, progress simply involved catching up. In short, according to the logic of unilinear progress, the "advanced" West (a place) was synonymous with the "modern" Future (a time). By reflexively associating modernization with Westernization in this way, the Japanese leadership brought "new times" to Japan through the creation of new spaces.[10] Western-style buildings, railway stations, factories, and smokestacks became Japan's modern icons of progress, and the cities in which they were constructed became synonymous with modernity.

For Japan's largest and most important city, the new national capital of Tokyo, this exercise in emulation augured nothing short of an urban transformation. This city, originally known as Edo, had served as the capital of the Tokugawa shogunate right up to the Meiji Restoration. After some debate among the new leaders over the optimal location and identity of a national capital, Edo was declared the imperial capital and renamed Tokyo, or "the

Eastern Capital."[11] Over the following thirty years, guided by the facile formula of modernization as Westernization, the Meiji leaders embarked on an extended excursion into the exotic world of modern "capital planning" (*shuto keikaku*), in an effort to transform Tokyo into a modern imperial capital. This transformation can be first seen in the early 1870s, following a devastating fire that destroyed the downtown district of Ginza. Using this as a pretext to conduct an extreme makeover of a central part of the capital, Tokyo's prefectural governor called for the creation of a European-style mixed-use neighborhood on the site.

The government hired the British architect Thomas J. Waters to build what became known as Ginza Bricktown (Ginza Rengagai).[12] The newly built district, which consisted of one thousand "fireproof" brick buildings with pillared arcades, astride cobblestone streets and sidewalks lit by gas lamps, was envisaged as the launch pad of a modern urban journey, which would lead inexorably to Tokyo's transformation into a magnificent Western-looking capital. Yet, Tokyoites did not rush to follow the red brick road to modernity; and the Meiji leaders simply conjured new images of urban modernity and hatched new plans for Tokyo's imperial future.

The most enduring concept of modernity to capture the Japanese imagination was conjured directly from continental Europe: Tokyo as the Paris of the East. The "capital of modernity"[13] first captured the attention of the Meiji leadership following the Iwakura Mission, an official delegation sent to scout the West in the mid-1870s. To its members, Paris represented the prototypical modern capital.[14] By the 1880s, momentum was building among the Meiji leaders for the re-creation of Tokyo as a Paris of the East. The Meiji leaders hired two experienced European architects, Hermann Ende and Wilhelm Böckmann, to initiate the transformation, beginning with the design of a vast "capital district." Drawing on the Parisian design prototype, as well as their experience in modern Berlin, Ende and Böckmann produced a fittingly ambitious plan. Around a huge rectilinear plaza adjacent to the imperial palace—from which wide, Champs-Elysée-like boulevards were to radiate across the center of Tokyo—they planned a monumental Baroque-style complex of state ministry offices built from granite and marble. Yet, this modern pipe dream, too, soon evaporated. In the end, all that came from this major capital planning initiative were two lonely ministries.[15]

Other sweeping visions of Tokyo as a modern imperial capital similarly failed to achieve the extreme makeover that their inventors envisioned. Shibusawa Eiichi's plan to transform Tokyo into Japan's "commercial capital" (*shôto*) by developing it into an "international port" (*kokusaikô*), as well as Taguchi Ukichi's bold scheme to accomplish urban modernization by bringing Tokyo up to (Western) urban codes, went unrealized. Although bits and pieces of all the plans were executed, the master plans were all abandoned. Tokyo ended up a spatial patchwork quilt that witnessed the futility of imitation and emulation as an approach to urban modernity.[16]

Not only were the Meiji leaders slavishly wedded to the facile idea of modernization as Westernization, but they were myopically mired in capital visions that emphasized static symbolic space and entirely ignored the kinetic dimension of modern cities. Rather than envisioning a grand new capital encompassing the urban hinterlands, they drew a geographical boundary around Tokyo that actually replicated the old city limits of Edo.[17] In effect, they knew that the process of urbanization (*toshika*) was changing their city, but refused to acknowledge its existence.

Much as the Meiji leaders circumscribed the boundaries of the new imperial capital, they also circumscribed its political autonomy. In keeping with the highly centralized administrative structure that the conservative faction of the Meiji leadership designed for the new nation-state, the central government retained control over the capital itself. This, in turn, was consistent with the strictly hierarchical system of local administration implemented in 1889. Introduced prior to the promulgation of the Meiji Constitution, this administrative framework was intended to restrict local autonomy (*chihô jichi*) in the interest of national stability.[18] As justified later by its primary proponent, the Meiji leader Yamagata Aritomo, it was a necessary anchor for the new nation-state: "A sound administrative system for the cities, towns, and villages—one which will steer a middle course and produce good results—will not be affected by the political upheavals of the central government."[19]

As explained by Kurt Steiner, the framework of local administration that the Meiji leaders introduced was Napoleonic, with a German twist. Its primary architect was a Prussian advisor by the name of Albert Mosse, who was brought to Japan as a government consultant (*oyatoi*) in 1886. At the behest of Yamagata, Mosse drafted the Law of Cities, Towns, and Villages (*shichôson-hô*), which was enacted in 1889. The German-inspired guidelines accomplished two important outcomes. They created a local administrative system worthy of a highly centralized nation-state, establishing prefectures as regional "intermediate organs" of the central government with appointive governors who served Tokyo,[20] while also placing cities (*shi*), towns (*chô*), and villages (*son*) beneath these prefectures in a fixed administrative hierarchy.

While smaller cities were permitted to appoint mayors through indirect elections conducted by their city assemblies, this prerogative was not extended to Japan's three largest cities: Tokyo, Osaka, and Kyoto. Instead, a "Special Directive" (*tokurei*) gave the government direct control over these cities under the authority of appointive prefectural governors. The Meiji leadership's decision to retain direct control over the new and old imperial capitals, Tokyo and Kyoto, might reasonably be seen as a logical extension of nation-state building. But the designation of Osaka as a special case requires further explanation.

As the former commercial entrepôt of the Tokugawa shogunate, and Japan's second largest city during the Meiji Restoration, Osaka boasted a long history of regional dominance and autonomy.[21] For the Meiji leaders, Osaka was simply too strong and too important a city to be permitted significant autonomy under the new regime. The dubious designation of "special city" signaled their reluctance to grant autonomy to a city of singular importance, whose elite promised to be less pliable than others elsewhere.[22] Osaka's failed bid to become capital of the new nation-state only highlighted its danger to the authoritarian Meiji regime. As the unpredictable alter-ego of modernization, Osaka threatened the central government's calculated approach to modernization. By carefully circumscribing the city's autonomy, the Meiji regime expected to modernize Osaka on its own terms. The government sent this message loud and clear by inscribing national power directly onto local space. Not only did they seize control of Osaka's old castle grounds, transforming the site into military headquarters, they constructed a monumental prefectural office building directly opposite the Foreign Concession. The Meiji leaders thus created, literally and figuratively, two key vantage points that vividly represented the panoptic gaze of the state: one overlooking the city as a whole and the other watching over international trade.

Later, when city-planning initiatives were finally extended to Osaka and other cities, the Meiji leaders introduced urban plans that originated in Tokyo and reflected its unique identity and conditions.[23] But Osaka's elite devised plans of their own, aided initially by a hard-fought political victory in 1898. After nearly three decades of haranguing the Meiji leaders, Osaka's political elite pressured the central government into repealing the Special City Law. From 1898, Osaka's city council was permitted to appoint mayors as the city's chief executives—though they remained under the jurisdiction of Osaka's prefectural governor.[24] This gesture toward limited local autonomy, ironically, triggered independent municipal action on a grand scale. By the turn of the century, at great local public expense, Osaka embarked on a port-improvement project, which transformed the old commercial harbor into a modern port befitting the industrial metropolis that Osaka was rapidly becoming.

Despite securing a significant measure of local autonomy by the turn of the century, Osaka remained considerably constrained in its efforts to realize urban modernization. The central government's continuing control over taxation and planning often left city assemblymen and mayors alike hamstrung. Only by persuading prefectural and central authorities of the wisdom in their plans for city expansion, residential improvement, tax reform, and other forward-looking initiatives could they make the positive changes they envisioned. The stakes were high from the outset and were heightened immeasurably toward the turn of the century when urban industrialization wrought such dramatic changes in Osaka that it came to be known as the "Capital of Smoke" (*Kemuri no Miyako*). Osaka's rapid expansion, which was punctuated by pressing social issues, such as poverty, pollution, and substandard housing, captured the nervous attention of the Meiji leaders. After thirty years of confidently predicting the parallel progress of economy and society, the Meiji leaders were forced to concede that urban modernization had given rise to troubling "social problems" (*shakai mondai*) that demanded immediate national attention.

Under the growing influence of progressivist thinkers in Osaka and elsewhere, the Meiji leadership began contemplating a "middle way" to modernization, whereby Japan might experience sustained urban industrial growth while maintaining urban social stability. Although the Meiji leaders were slow to act, they were ultimately pressed forward by two key factors: (1) the verifiable existence of full-blown social conflict in the West; (2) the overwhelming evidence of looming domestic urban social problems. Progressives offered the Meiji leaders the hope that if only they would introduce social policies designed to channel the energy of industrial capitalism, Japan could avoid the fate of the West and secure parallel economic and social progress.

One of the most important figures of the progressive movement in Japan was Seki Hajime. A pioneering political economist, social economist, and labor reformer, Seki went on to become the leading Japanese municipal progressive of the day. When he led the charge toward sweeping urban social reform in the 1920s, in the wake of the Great Kanto Earthquake that devastated Tokyo, he did so as mayor of what had become Japan's largest, most populous, most industrialized, and wealthiest city—Osaka. Elsewhere, I have told the story of Seki's groundbreaking program of urban social reform, conceived to transform Osaka from a problem-ridden industrial metropolis into a "livable city" (*sumigokochiyoki toshi*).[25] Here, I will explore the innovative political framework he promoted for its structural foundation: "metropolitan autonomy." The inspiration for this revolutionary initiative, which went to the core of Japan's ill-conceived system of urban administration, issued from the rich mix of ideas that characterized municipal progressivism as a transnational movement.

Municipal Progressivism in Action

As the turn of the twentieth century neared, and the achievements of the previous century were cast into high relief, an increasingly vocal minority of social critics bemoaned the deleterious effects of economic modernization. These progressives, having removed the rose-colored glasses that had warped the Euro-American vista of the modern world, took a long, hard look at reality.[26] What they saw left them anxious rather than hopeful. The modern world appeared beset by deep-seated social problems that threatened the precious enterprise of progress. The mesmerizing metanarrative of modernization, which had boldly projected the parallel progress of economy and society, had begun to look more like myth than reality.

A new breed of progressivist economists led the way, insisting that the social problems triggered by modernization were pressing but not fatal. As captured by French *économiste social* Charles Gide, social economy was "the science of 'practical realities and possible amelioration,' [and thus] the science of 'social peace.'" It "embraced every effort—within the constraints of the political economy itself—to temper, socialize, and mutualize the pains of the capitalist transformation."[27] Social economy served as what Rodgers calls "the ambulance wagon of industrial capitalism." Scouring modern civilization on both sides of the Atlantic for "social designs to compensate for the privations and pains of the market revolution,"[28] these social economists aimed to cure the modern world's social ills.

What enabled progressives to approach social reform from this transnational perspective was their conviction that the industrialized nations had followed a common developmental trajectory. When they scoured Europe and North America, they saw common "landscapes of fact"—factories, skyscrapers, bridges, cities—that suggested comparable social landscapes and common ground for social policymaking. Equally important, history on both sides of the Atlantic had unfolded in such a way as to permit the sort of transnational mixing and matching of social policies that the diversity and complexity of the industrialized world's social problems demanded. As Rodgers aptly observes, "enough of the real and imagined distance between the nation-states [had shrunk] . . . to make a trade in social policy possible."[29] If progressives still disagreed on critical questions, such as the relative importance of the state, local communities, voluntary associations, and others to successfully implement social policy, they were nonetheless unified in their enthusiasm for proactive intervention in the world of industrial capitalism.

The "intertwined landscapes of mind"[30] of European and American progressives impelled them to unearth solutions to the social problems of the industrialized world wherever they could find them. Those who spearheaded this cosmopolitan initiative focused their attention most significantly on the plight of modern cities, studying the work of urban visionaries and making trans-Atlantic pilgrimages to model communities in search of transferable policies.[31] While the transatlantic "laboratory" was indubitably the central operating theater of progressives, it was by no means the only one. Among others, there was a vibrant trans-Pacific experiment centered on Japan. Like their Western European and North American comrades-in-arms, Japanese progressives were passionate in believing that they could solve the problems of the modern world through the creative transnational transfer of reformist ideas and policies. Indeed, they were convinced that Japan enjoyed a distinct advantage in this challenge. As an industrializing nation, rather than an industrialized one, Japan could invoke "teleological insight" in the process of selection, averting the problems encountered by more "advanced" nations.

From roughly 1900, significant numbers of budding Japanese progressives made the long and arduous "Pacific Crossing" to Europe and North America. Once there, they pored over the same burgeoning literature of social economy and visited the same social meccas as their European and North American compatriots. But, while the Occidental experience was characterized and fertilized by bidirectional exchange, the Oriental one was largely unidirectional. Few progressives from the West ever ventured across the Pacific to the Far East. Fewer still went in search of ideas and policies that might be adopted and adapted at home. Despite this impediment to transnational exchange, Japanese progressives did not resort to the facile Meiji method of cultural borrowing by cherry-picking social policies from the West and transplanting them in Japan. Abandoning the facile notion of unilinear progress, they also abandoned the simplistic version of cultural borrowing that flowed from it. Japanese progressives did not advocate imitation and emulation as a path to progress but instead proposed a complex process of adoption and adaptation that acknowledged the subtle differences between nations and societies.

Following a scholarly and professional path through labor reformism, social reformism, and on to urban reformism, Seki Hajimi was appointed deputy mayor of the city of Osaka in 1914, and in 1923 was promoted to mayor. Later, when the city assembly was awarded the privilege of electing mayors to office, Seki was promptly voted in. The progressive agenda that Seki pursued as mayor of Osaka was predictably dominated by commitments to residential reform and social policy making, which he pursued in a quintessentially progressivist fashion, assiduously adopting and adapting ideas and policies from the West. Like progressives in Europe and North America, Seki was convinced that "great cities" were the primary locus of modern concern. The "contrasts in fortune" and "ceaseless motion of property and populations" found in great cities made them volatile communities in which "the clash between private property rights and public needs" threatened to unleash social conflict.[32] Of all the "great cities" in Japan, as Seki saw it, the industrial metropolis of Osaka came closest to this description and thus stood to benefit most from the transnational exchange of urban ideas and policies.

For all the momentum that Japan's national leaders had gathered in the cause of progress, they remained remarkably ambivalent toward "great cities" as vessels of modernity. If they valued cities as vital repositories of wealth and technology, they also feared the historical processes that fueled their growth. Modern cities had sown the seeds of economic progress but had also become breeding grounds of social dislocation. While the Meiji leaders acknowledged the interconnection between industrialization and urbanization—and treated them as key elements of modernization—they did their utmost to contain the damaging social effects of urban industrialization by maintaining strict control over the nation's largest cities. Most importantly, this meant restricting the autonomy of the nation's foremost industrial metropolis, Osaka, and thereby channeling its modern energy.

As mentioned earlier, from the outset of the Meiji era, Osaka struggled to free itself from central control, finally escaping its "special city" status in 1898. Now able to appoint mayors as chief executives of the city, Osaka was recognized as a local administrative unit in its own right. But this new status arguably created as many problems as it solved. Although Osaka's mayors were municipal appointees, they nonetheless remained under strict prefectural administrative supervision. Moreover, they labored under a national and prefectural tax system that left little room for city levies and thus little room for autonomous action. In short, the mayors of Osaka were condemned to a kind of political purgatory.[33]

From the 1910s, as Osaka grew into an industrial metropolis, its local leadership struggled to secure greater autonomy for the city. Their avowed objective from the late 1910s forward was "metropolitan autonomy." Once the central government had tacitly confirmed the metropolitan identity of greater Osaka, by sanctioning the extension of Osaka's administrative boundary in 1925, local leaders militated for metropolitan administrative autonomy. Calling for the liberation of Osaka from prefectural jurisdiction, in recognition of its regional identity as a metropolis, they urged that it be accorded the legal standing of a prefecture. If Osaka's rapid industrial expansion continued to fuel the "metropolitan autonomy" initiative, earning it parliamentary supporters by the late 1920s, two historical circumstances conspired to give it even greater traction. The devastation of the Great Kanto Earthquake, which struck Tokyo in 1923, transformed Osaka into Japan's first city, and the global economic depression of the 1920s later accentuated the financial injustice that it had long suffered as the urban stepchild of the state. These two events lent special urgency to the "metropolitan autonomy" agenda.[34]

Seki Hajime led the charge toward "metropolitan autonomy," orchestrating the local political movement, and lobbying national politicians and bureaucrats on the issue. Drawing the leaders of the so-called Big Six (Roku

Daitoshi) into the mix—the six largest cities in Japan at the time (Tokyo, Osaka, Kyoto, Yokohama, Kobe, and Nagoya)—Seki transformed the initiative into a national political movement. Taking a distinctly progressivist approach to the issue, he committed himself to proactive urban policy making designed to ameliorate social problems while sustaining economic progress. Toward this end, Seki offered up a searching comparative analysis of the issues—delving into Western scholarship on the subject and exploring Western experience of the issues—which helps explain why he was popularly known as the "scholar mayor" (*gakusha shichô*).

Seki began with an empirical assessment of the problems facing Osaka, including unchecked urban expansion, substandard housing, environmental pollution, and urban poverty. The crux of Seki's argument concerned the character of urbanization in modern cities like Osaka: recent urbanization was not the product of the "natural" growth of urban population but rather a byproduct of urban in-migration. The immigration of rural labor into industrial cities had not merely resulted in inner-city overcrowding, according to Seki, it had touched off the haphazard urbanization of adjacent villages in the urban hinterlands.[35]

If pressing urban problems such as these demanded reforms, however, this could not be accomplished until cities such as Osaka were awarded the authority to act: "While the metropolitan problem has to do with the structure of the metropolis itself, it also has to do increasingly with the place of metropolises in national life and the [administrative] relationship of metropolises to the central government."[36] In Seki's view, then, the metropolitan problem was intertwined with the fate of "contemporary Japan's urban system."[37] Not only did Osaka still come under the direct jurisdiction of Osaka Prefecture, it remained subservient to developmental priorities set by the central government and captive to financial control. Between 1931 and 1935, national and prefectural taxes together accounted for 79.1 percent of tax levies in the city. "By controlling the purse strings [of Osaka]," observes Carl Mosk, "national ministries secured leverage over local government decisions."[38]

Once he had linked the local socioeconomic problems of the metropolis to national systems of urban administration, Seki set out to explain Japan's mistakes. His analysis was at once historical and comparative: the modern metropolitan dilemma had been hopelessly exacerbated by the anachronistic, legalistic, and ultimately irrational provisions of the nation's German-inspired system of local administration. Seki noted that the Meiji leadership had turned a blind eye to the indigenous history of local autonomy exemplified by Tokugawa-era institutions, such as neighborhood associations, choosing instead to impose European juridical standards from the top down: "In my opinion, today's city, town, and village units of local administration do not have Japanese historical roots. The local administrative system is not one that is unique to Japan, but rather one based on German/Prussian law. In short, it is a system imported from Europe."[39]

More specifically, the local administrative hierarchy designed by Albert Mosse for the Meiji home minister, Yamagata Aritomo, simply reproduced the standard Prussian measures of population to distinguish cities from towns and villages.[40] Echoing Charles Beard on the subject, Seki described Japan's system of local autonomy as a "borrowed object" (*karimono*) taken from outside Japan and imposed from above by the national leadership.[41]

It goes without saying that Seki's criticism went to the core of the Meiji predisposition to copy the West—that is, to apply the facile formula of modernization as Westernization. Beyond this, however, Seki's critique reminds us that the Meiji leadership had picked and chosen its models carefully. In the arena of local autonomy, these leaders selected an administrative model that promised to reinforce the central power and stability of the new nation-state. In other words, Japan's German-inspired system of local administration was not designed to stimulate local autonomy but rather to guarantee local discipline. As Stephen Reed points out, prewar "local government in Japan was conceived of primarily as a means of unifying the nation, of undermining localism and penetrating society with public administration."[42]

In an effort to extricate the metropolis of Osaka from the alien framework of local administration imposed by the Meiji leadership, Seki strove to convince the government and the public to rethink Osaka's identity as a community and as an administrative entity. Not surprisingly, he made this argument in a characteristically progressivist way. Placing Osaka's experience in comparative perspective, Seki contended that the city did not just face the same development challenges as Western cities but often the same political ones as well. Like the Japanese, he claimed, Westerners were struggling to retool urban administration to deal effectively with the new socioeconomic entity that urban industrialization had spawned—namely, the metropolis.

In approaching the issue of "metropolitan autonomy," Seki relied heavily on his scholarly background in political economy, social economy, and urban reform. Not only did he endeavor to flesh out the dimensions of Osaka's metropolitan problems, he also cast his net widely in search of ideas and policies that might be adopted and adapted as remedies to them. The Depression added urgency to the issue, impelling Seki as mayor to place "metropolitan autonomy" at the top of his agenda. In a pioneering essay he pointedly attributed Osaka's metropolitan dilemma to the central government's failure to address the revolutionary dynamism of modern urban development.[43]

Seki urged the powers-that-be to begin by reconsidering the "deficiencies of the current structure of [local] administration, which indiscriminately lumps big, medium, and small cities together."[44] Noting that the Japanese were not alone in their myopic adherence to an anachronistic administrative system, he cited William Robson's recent reflections on Britain's outdated system of local government. In *The Development of Local Government* (1931), Robson had called urgently for "an adjustment between structure and function"[45] in British local government, which resonated loudly with the issues that Seki had raised in Japan. Although the obsolescence of the Japanese and British "municipal systems" owed to distinct historical factors—the former, to the imitative imposition of a "borrowed" system of local administration; the latter, to the "fact that burdens [were] being placed on the structure greater than those it was designed to bear"[46]—both faced the same basic problem by the early 1930s. Robson posed the challenge to "conurbations" such as Birmingham, Manchester, and London in a way that hauntingly evoked Osaka's plight: "There is need for a much greater integration of town and country for administrative and financial purposes of common interest. . . . I am convinced that a far more radical solution is now required, particularly in the areas surrounding the great urban complexes."[47]

While acknowledging that Japan and Britain faced the same challenge—to develop new urban administrative frameworks capable of addressing the unprecedented appearance of metropolitan conurbations—Seki did not suggest that Japan should emulate Britain in its response. With a progressive's nose for empirical comparability and analytical applicability, he indulged a new mode of cultural borrowing that transcended the Meiji method of imitation and emulation: adoption and adaptation. From Robson's work, he drew two important elements that were integrated into his own: (1) the notion that (administrative) structure and (urban) function must be aligned for cities to reach their developmental potential; (2) the recognition that Japan and Britain were on the same historical page with respect to their failure to adjust the balance between structure and function in the age of the metropolis.

While progressives touted their rigorous empirical and analytical skills as scientific tools of objective policy making, it is important to recall that they, too, were guided by ideological principles and presuppositions. A key example of this can be found in Seki's critical response to fundamental administrative changes already introduced. Notwithstanding the autocratic obstinacy that he attributed to the early Meiji leaders, for their failure to alter the imitative framework of urban administration put into place in 1889, Seki acknowledged the government's introduction of key structural changes in 1898, 1911, and 1929. The central innovation of 1898—the repeal of the "special city" designation for Tokyo, Kyoto, and Osaka and the accompanying prerogative to appoint mayors—was relatively uncontroversial for Seki. But the administrative changes introduced in 1911 and 1929 carried the sort of heavy ideological overtones that were certain to elicit his progressivist principles and preferences.

While the administrative changes introduced in 1911 strengthened the executive authority of city councils and mayors, and correspondingly diminished the legislative authority of city assemblies, those of 1929 accomplished the reverse. Seki opposed the new principle of "assembly-as-center-ism" (*gikai chûshin shugi*), and it is instructive not merely to examine why he did so but also on what grounds he justified himself. Noting that "assembly-as-center-ism" was symptomatic of a sea change in administrative philosophy—from the German model to an American one—Seki was troubled not so much by the substance of the shift as by the modus operandi of its architects.[48] In search of a new administrative model consistent with the ethos of the new democratic Japan of the interwar era, he contended that the nation's leaders had slipped back into "copy-ism" (*mohô shugi*) by substituting an imitative German system of municipal administration with an equally imitative American one.[49] However neatly and poignantly made, this argument was more than a bit disingenuous: while shielding Seki from the accusation that he had betrayed progressivist principles, it also offered him an excuse to promote his increasingly paternalistic political platform.

Like many other progressives of the day, Seki had long since concluded that democracy was not a panacea. His encounters with the "real world" as a city official of Osaka had convinced him that urban politicians were no less prone to self-interested action than real-estate developers or corporate moguls. Rather than admitting to his reservations about democratic municipal decision-making, Seki suspiciously shifted the grounds of his argument against "assembly-as-center-ism" to lend his perspective the veneer of analytical objectivity, which was designed to mask an unpopular ideological position.

As a frustrated social reformer, Seki was nobody's fool. His opposition to the democratization of municipal administration concealed a hidden purpose born of his experience as a city official: a desire to keep municipal governance above the political fray by treating mayors as city managers and thus maintain a bulwark against the politicization of urban social reform. Fearing a reversal of the 1911 reforms, which had given him the latitude as mayor to exercise broad executive and technocratic authority, Seki conveniently cast city assemblymen as self-interested politicians who would drag city government into ineptitude and corruption. In order to make the accusation stick, he engaged "assembly-as-center-ism" on its home turf: America. Referring first to Austin F. Macdonald, a staunch defender of short terms of office for elective municipal officials, Seki noted Macdonald's odd contention that "public office is a prize not a trust" and attributed this position to the delusional belief that "any man is capable of filling any position in the public service."[50] Seki then spun this neatly into a cautionary tale by reminding his readers that such views were not just "an American thing, but a Japanese one too."[51]

Against Macdonald's blind faith in democracy, Seki held up William B. Munro as a beacon of objective rationalism. In a paean to Munro's cautionary tale about the excesses of democracy, *The Invisible Government*, Seki derided the dogmatism of American democracy and warned the Japanese against a similar fetishization of egalitarianism.[52] As Munro himself made the salient point concerning elective office, "Men may be equal in their capacity to govern, but not for one moment do we hold them equal in their capacity to bear the burdens of government."[53] If Seki obviously meant for his readers to question the wisdom in signing over municipal governance to feckless, unqualified local politicians, he made his point less with substance than suasion. Behind the veneer of scientific objectivity that graced Seki's elegant attack on municipal populism lurked the cynical desire of an embattled municipal progressive to extend the public trust instead to municipal executives and technocrats.

Conclusion

Driven by the conviction that Japan could avoid much of the social conflict and unrest that had littered the road to progress in the West, progressives such as Seki Hajime made the Pacific crossing to Europe and North America with a real sense of national urgency. Fluent in German, French, and English by the time he returned to Japan in 1901—and with a scholar's mastery of social economy and a convert's passion for progressivism—Seki was well equipped for the leadership role he later assumed as mayor of Osaka. Yet, for all the knowledge and passion that he invested in developing a critical comparative perspective on the challenges facing Japan's modern cities, this was no substitute for the critical transnational interchange that animated progressivism in the West. One of the rare occasions when Japanese progressives did have the opportunity to engage in critical dialogue came in 1923, with Charles A. Beard's post-earthquake visit to Japan. Reflecting on the experience later, Seki praised the American municipal progressive for sharing "fundamental inquiries" and "scientific research" from America, and for carefully applying this knowledge to municipal administration in Japan. Then he voiced one telling regret: that precious few of Beard's "invaluable suggestions" had "been translated into actual undertakings."[54]

Seki attributed this failed opportunity to a conspicuous lack of civic concern in Japan. Making much of the fact that few "useful books on municipal administration" were being published and no "civics" courses were being taught in Japan,[55] Seki insisted that the Japanese had only themselves to blame for the nation's failure to tackle its urban problems. Paradoxically, implied Seki, it was not the Japanese who were most poignantly confronting the challenges of urban reform in Japan but rather a foreigner.

For his part, Beard strained to understand this same situation. Praising Japanese municipal policy makers for their technical and linguistic expertise, as well as their "informed and critical minds," he gently took them to task for their naïve adulation of the West and their uncritical adoption of Western urban ideas and policies. Things are not "good merely because they [came] out of the West," Beard cautioned a Tokyo audience. "Do not adopt our institutions and devices without testing them in the fire of your national genius."[56] Like Seki, Beard yearned to make the most of this "transnational municipal moment" by drawing the Japanese into the clutches of a transparently righteous cause. While Japan certainly would have benefited from the presence of more men like Beard—that is, from a truly bidirectional transnational exchange of progressive thinkers and policy makers—this alone would not have triggered civic engagement. As both Seki and Beard clearly understood, meaningful transnational exchange requires mutual understanding but also presupposes a good measure of self-understanding. As long as the Japanese continued to envision their future as some facsimile of the Western present, such self-understanding would remain painfully elusive.

CHAPTER 5

A City in the World of Cities

Lyon, France; Municipal Associations as Political Resources in the Twentieth Century

Renaud Payre and Pierre-Yves Saunier

While contemporary gatherings of city mayors and municipal associations attract media interest, they are usually presented as a "new phenomenon" of the globalization era, even though they are a century old. City networks and associations' past and present activities are, in fact, far from well known. Too often, the existence of these groups is taken as a proxy for their substance, or a token of urban "response" to internationalization, but their operational machineries, functions, and effects have only just begun to be explored.[1] It is true that such an investigation is not easy: historical records are fragmentary and scattered, while contemporary networks' leaders and staff are not inclined to speak freely about their activities and tend to repeat the baseline of their mottoes. This chapter will attempt to observe the constraints and cleavages faced by cities' organizations, through the place and role that a single city has made for itself in their midst. Lyon, France's "second city," offers both archival, direct observation, and oral interview opportunities to bridge a century of intermunicipal activities, because of its presence in several organizations across different generations.[2] Among those we have selected is the oldest transnational association of municipalities, the Union Internationale des Villes, created in 1913, and the more contemporary Eurocities, founded in Barcelona in 1989. We believe the comparison between the role of Lyon within these two groups can help us to understand both the nature of the city's protagonism beyond the national sphere and the basis on which such municipal associations operate, as well as how these change, or exhibit continuities, across time and space.

Sisters in Arms

The Union Internationale des Villes (UIV) was created during the First International Congress of Cities at the Ghent World Fair of 1913.[3] The congress and the union developed out of a dual matrix. Firstly, they were the formalization of hitherto informal networks between European socialist municipal councilors, which the Second Socialist International had been eager to crystalize since its 1900 congress.[4] Secondly, they were shaped by the methods and projects of internationalists Henri Lafontaine and Paul Otlet, who had made it their agenda to organize, support, and coordinate a number of scientifically oriented conferences and associations during the early 1900s.[5] The effects of this mixed origin strongly shaped the form and direction of the UIV up to the late 1940s. A centralized body, according to the organizational framework imagined by Lafontaine and Otlet, the union gravitated around a central headquarters in Brussels, whose mission it was to organize the life and work of the association.

Although it was launched as a voluntary association of individual cities, after World War I the UIV became an international association wherein members were national associations of municipal stakeholders, composed of municipalities, municipal officers, scholars, and national government representatives. Under the leadership of Belgian socialist senator and municipal councilor Emile Vinck, the union lived by the rhythms of its congresses and conferences, which were held in Europe every two to three years, even though the association had expanded toward the Americas and, more marginally, Africa and Asia by the 1930s. Now renamed the International Union of Local Authorities (IULA), the group's rhetoric was very much soaked within a universalist veneer, an aspiration to establish mutual understanding through municipal cooperation. This same rhetoric was also imbued through its routine agendas and through the dissemination of a discourse of scientific knowledge. Documentation was the touchstone of the secretariat's activities, and the circulation of periodicals and bibliographies dedicated to municipal policies and the techniques of municipal action demanded most of the staff's energy. Conference agendas were highly technical, created by lengthy precirculated questionnaires asking for facts and figures from the different member cities. It was often scientists, engineers, political scientists, law scholars, and other specialists who were invited to sketch, administer, and report these questionnaires. The prospect of defining, spreading, expanding, and updating a "municipal science" was, in fact, a central creed of the organization. It was also an effective device to neutralize the tensions that were inherited from the cleavages of World War I, or the mounting ideological frontlines of the 1920s and 1930s.

Eurocities is younger, and its history is still blurred. The organization has generated its own official narrative and often identifies the 1986 Rotterdam meeting of founding cities as its origin. In fact, Eurocities was born in 1989, triggered by the initiative of Barcelona's municipal leaders in their pursuit of visibility and momentum in post-Francoist Spain, while simultaneously preparing for their country's entrance into the European Common Market and the lucrative pay-offs from their victorious bid for the Olympics. A meeting did indeed take place in Rotterdam in 1986—attended by delegations from Barcelona, Birmingham, Milan, Rotterdam, Lyon, and Frankfurt—on the subject of "cities as engines of economic recovery." This was just one among many occasions where the leaders and technicians of these cities met to exchange ideas and foster common interests during the 1980s. However, it was not before the summer of 1988 that Barcelona's mayor, Pasqual Maragall, and the vice president of its metropolitan authority, Jordi Borja, convened a special meeting of "Euro-cities" to discuss "the role of cities in European construction."[6] The invitation was accompanied with a questionnaire that attempted to map "second cities'" relationships with the European Economic Community, as well as their expectations and preparations for the Single Market. On the basis of the answers provided by the Lyonese municipality, it appears that many of these cities shared similar anxieties, not least in finding a collective voice in the new European regime. Others also undoubtedly wished for a permanent structure of "second cities" to liaise with the European Commission.[7] Prompted by Borja and Maragall, those towns in attendance established an organization of large European cities, which they named Eurocities. The conference also marked Barcelona's emergence as a beacon in urban policies, metropolitan management, and municipal leadership—the Latin American extent of which has been explored elsewhere in this volume.[8]

Initially, organizational arrangements were purposively loose and mainly left to thematic working groups led by a single municipality.[9] Meanwhile, *ad hoc* visits by mayoral delegations from various member cities fulfilled the organization's desire for a visible proximity to the main European institutions in Brussels, Luxembourg, and Strasbourg. It was not until the 1991 Birmingham conference, where that city's municipal leaders advocated the establishment of a permanent bureau in Brussels, that the decision was taken to build up as an organization, though. Although Birmingham's proposal was fiercely resisted by cities from southern Europe—who feared higher fees, pared down lobbying activities, and an excessively bureaucratic structure—it was ultimately agreed that a central secretariat was crucial for the organization's visibility and efficiency. The resulting consensus shaped the organizational framework of Eurocities: the member cities would take public center stage, initiate working groups, organize the annual conferences, and hold executive responsibilities, while the Brussels secretariat would pull the administrative ropes and circulate information inside the network.[10]

As the self-acclaimed "network of major European cities," Eurocities is, above all, a pressure group that represents the interests of large cities in and around the European Union's institutions. Its birth was simultaneous with the formation of a European urban agenda, with the European Commission publishing its long-delayed *Green Paper on the Urban Environment* in 1990.[11] Germinated in Jacques Delors' will to connect European institutions with local authorities and other nongovernmental partners, the agenda was devised within the Directorate General for Regional Policy (DG XVI), headed by Commissioner Bruce Millan.[12] As such, Eurocities sought the directorate's ears from the outset, albeit ineffectively since none of its favored projects were adopted in the first urban European program in 1991, Regions and Cities for Europe (RECITE).[13] This desire to more effectively lobby the directorate was cited as another reason to create a secretariat in Brussels, which helped formalize and strengthen Eurocities' relationship with DG XVI. Consequently, between 1994 and 1999 Eurocities was consulted by DG XVI over the design of the Community Initiative URBAN, which was the first European program to subsidize actions to improve the environment and infrastructure of selected urban areas.[14]

From this brief portrait, it should be clear that these two associations shared certain values and experiences despite their obvious temporal and contextual distance. For example, discourses about the need and value of home rule and municipal autonomy are strikingly similar. The two bodies also have a very direct relationship: when Eurocities came into being, it explicitly looked for its place within a landscape where the UIV/IULA and its European branch, the Council of European Municipalities and Regions (CEMR), loomed large.[15] When Eurocities decided to create a secretariat in 1991, it also served as a way to emancipate itself from the tutelage of the CEMR and carve a niche for large cities' collective protagonism.[16] Any new organization thus had to face, and work within, the existing structures and cultures of European associational municipalism.

Opting In, Opting Out: Why Cities Join Municipal Associations

A city historically joins a municipal association, or adjusts its involvement in such organizations, according to a combination of local, national, and international pressures, opportunities, and resource constraints. The political affiliations and worldviews of mayors and councilors, the existence of knowledge-based transnational networks among municipal technicians, and the adaptation or resistance to changes in the urban world order have all been important mitigating factors for municipal authorities in deciding to join or leave a municipal association. We argue here that it was the expectation of political and policy resources from such involvement that triggered Lyon's municipal authorities to join the UIV and Eurocities. During some specific "policy windows," those moments when incentives for the design, proposal, and implementation of new policies were especially high, Lyonese municipal leaders behaved as policy entrepreneurs and embarked on intermunicipal activities to meet specific goals and find new supporters.[17]

Municipal internationalization strategies have taken multifarious forms, from the *ad hoc*, such as dropping a reference to a foreign experiment into discussions about a municipal project or developing a public image strategy, to undertaking systematic documentation and study tours, through the more formalized creation of a network of municipalities. All have provided varying quantities of political, intellectual, and practical resources to enable a given municipality to adjust its presence on the intermunicipal map, develop its agency within national politics, and fulfill its search for local support. According to scholars of political reform, the development of public policy takes its cue from the intertwinement of three streams: first, that of problems (why policy makers pay attention to some problems and not to others), second, policies (ideas generated to answer those problems), and, third, politics (such as elections and the shifting worldviews of political actors).[18] Most of the time, these streams take their own trajectory, and each of them can trigger re-orientations of public policy. But there are some "policy windows" where these three streams merge and provide strong incentives for policy change. These ideas apply as much to historical cases as contemporary ones: at critical points during the twentieth century, Lyon's municipal leaders embarked on transnational journeys into the worlds of municipalities in order to capture new resources, public support, and legitimacy. This detour through the rhetorical and practical realms of municipal international activism provided legitimacy, as well as guidance, for Lyon's leaders, particularly during shortages of political resources or where the governance regime was fragile. Conversely, municipal associations were much less appealing to those municipal leaders with an established status or even to those who reaped similar resources through other, less institutionalized, channels—such as study trips, regular documentary activities, or political and technological networks.[19]

It was a policy window opened out of necessity that sent Edouard Herriot, Lyon's mayor, on a tour of Europe with his municipal team in the early 1900s. Trained as a literary professor, Herriot (1872–1957) arrived in Lyon in 1896, where he soon became the great hope of the local center-left, mostly through his marriage to the daughter of a local political leader. In 1904 he was invited to join the municipal election campaign of the socialist mayor, Victor Augagneur; Herriot accepted. Within eighteen months of becoming a councilor, he had been selected as Augagneur's successor, at the age of thirty-three.

Owing to his rapid rise to power, the new mayor initially lacked the resources to steer or drive the municipal policy machine, not least the political legitimacy, experience, and social capital of his predecessor. As an outsider, Herriot found the intellectual, political and practical resources he needed through his systematic use of expert knowledge as the compass of decision making. Through this he launched a practical program of evidence-based urban modernization. Expanding on his predecessor's sketches, he leaned on specialists of public works, hygiene, and social reform to shape the municipality's decisions and win public approval, hiring many of them to run municipal services. Athough not himself a professional or a technician, as many of those legal or medical specialists who had gradually taken over municipal responsibilities in Third Republic France, Herriot built a team comprised of such individuals who helped him secure political legitimacy and authority.

To inform and legitimize his modernization program, Herriot also launched an unprecedented campaign to learn from the experience of other cities abroad. Between 1906 and 1914, Lyonese delegations of aldermen, councilors, municipal technicians, and experts traveled to many European corners to study the variety of institutions ranging from hospitals to slaughterhouses; to discuss the myriad of questions concerning public health, primary education, and the like; and to inspect a plethora of practical schemes, including housing estates and water abduction schemes.[20] This knowledge of foreign experiences was crucial for Herriot to conceive and gain support for his most ambitious and contested projects. It also posited him as a man of vast knowledge who grounded his policy decisions in empirical, evidence-based findings. All in, this profile—marked by legitimacy through transnational learning—secured Herriot re-election in 1908.

It was upon the occasion of Lyon's Modern City Exhibition, held in 1914, that Herriot won, for himself, personal fame as a "great European mayor" and, for Lyon, the image of a modern metropolis. Modeled on the Dresden Städteaustellung of 1911, which he personally visited, the occasion enshrined Herriot's successful revamping of local politics, as evident in his introduction to the official guide to the Exhibition: "The editors asked what was our leading idea. Here it is: the era of verbose politics, Florentine factions and passionate showdowns is over. Time has come to build our ideas upon the observation of facts; and if this conception cannot yet be applied to the State, let it be that the material, intellectual and moral life of the City be based upon thoughtful and careful study."[21]

It was also during the organization of the 1914 Exhibition that the Lyonese municipal leaders first met with initiatives to formalize these nascent intermunicipal relationships into more structured, associative forms. In 1913, the city was invited to exhibit its accomplishments in municipal child welfare within a special urban exhibition of the "Congrès International et exposition de l'art de construire les villes et de l'organisation de la vie municipale," which was held under the auspices of the Ghent World Fair. Deeming it "very useful" to showcase these achievements to a broad audience, Herriot immediately suggested to his Belgian hosts the idea of holding a second congress, as an additional garnish to Lyon's forthcoming exhibition.[22] To sell the event to potential delegates and exhibitors, the municipal council sent a delegation of six people to Ghent, mostly councilors.

In addition to delegating diplomacy, Herriot was appointed to the UIV's embryonic governing body despite his absence in Ghent. As part payment for this gesture, the UIV's secretary, Emile Vinck, suggested that the Lyon exhibition might well offer his new council an opportunity to meet for a second time. Hoping that Lyon's association with the UIV would help the fledgling association mature and attract a larger membership, Vinck desired to use the Lyon exhibition to mobilize the various national and international municipal associations under the UIV's wings. For Herriot, though, the UIV's expectations were misguided: membership of the UIV served no other purpose than attracting an additional congress to adorn Lyon's exhibition and brighten its visibility around the municipal globe. Forced to organize its Lyon show by itself, the UIV worked out a program that was canceled by the outbreak of the war in August 1914. All that remained visibly intact from this fleeting encounter was Herriot's official reputation as a "founder" and early supporter of the union.

Although a "policy window" had opened through which Lyon's municipal leaders joined the main road of transnational intermunicipal relations, the creation of the UIV came too late for it to provide the resources that Herriot had previously harnessed from *ad hoc* study tours and documentation. The window had (temporarily) closed, and for Herriot, participation within this fledgling intermunicipal associational network was little more than dressing. Lyon's municipal leadership had already found the appropriate resources and, for Herriot, it was of little consequence that the UIV had not.

The decision to join Eurocities, but especially to actively participate in its thematic networks, resulted from another critical historical moment: at the heart of the municipal elections in 1989 was Lyon's international status.[23] In a bitter contest between long-standing center-right Mayor Francisque Collomb (1976–89) and his former deputy mayor, the young Gaullist Michel Noir, the absence of an international strategy was leveled as a symbol of the outgoing mayor's archaism. This attack met with the approval of entrepreneurial groups, which had pushed for a proactive municipal internationalization policy for some years. For example, the Agence pour le Développement de la Région Lyonnaise (ADERLY), a public-private partnership between business groups and local authorities, had published a 1988 report on the city's international assets, which ranked the city as only seventh or eighth among the twelve largest European noncapital cities. ADERLY duly lobbied for a stronger contribution by the municipal government to improve this standing before the arrival of the European Single Market. Sharing ADERLY's concern, the mayoral challenger, Michel Noir, asked ADERLY's treasurer, Christian Boiron, the president of a large pharmaceutical firm, to join his team and coordinate international affairs and development matters.

Noir was elected to the mayoralty in March 1989, a major break in the political history of a city that had resisted Gaullist onslaughts since 1947. Within this new political regime, strong representation for entrepreneurial groups was provided by Boiron, who was appointed deputy mayor, with responsibility for economic and international development affairs. Boiron duly revamped his field, recruiting a host of contractual workers to develop activities. The eagerness of the new team to develop a business-friendly international strategy quickly materialized with the formation of the Lyon International Council, in which local authority executives throughout the region met face to face with entrepreneurs, deputies of formal business groups, and academics. As early as May 1989, the new mayor circulated his guidelines for action: "The development of Lyon's European profile is one of my major priorities. This is why I have suggested the founding of a Conseil International de Lyon, whose mission is to conceive an international strategy and to push for the European dimension to be present in every project of the metropolitan authority."[24] The real challenge lay in putting the new mayor's vision into practice, though. Eurocities provided one way.

Although Francisque Collomb's municipal team had agreed to participate in the Barcelona Eurocities conference scheduled for April 1989, it failed to attend the preparatory meeting in the fall of 1988 and was a late signatory to the resulting manifesto.[25] On taking office, the new mayor transmogrified this lip service participation. Recognizing the potential of the 1989 conference, Noir personally attended, addressing the conference on two occasions and presenting himself as a leader of the emerging network. A member of Noir's cabinet wrote the mayor's speeches after having met with ADERLY executive officers and other local business interests in Barcelona. Echoing Maragall and Borja's call to arms, his script insisted on the central role being played by cities in the exchanges and circulations that would make the new

Europe, and emphasized the European institutions' duty to listen to the collective voice of large cities.

Less than two months after his election, the Barcelona meeting provided Noir with the opportunity to demonstrate to the Lyonese public that his international strategy was moving forward at an unprecedented pace. The icing on the cake was provided by the announcement, shortly before Noir's closing speech, that Lyon would host the second Eurocities conference in 1990. The Lyonese press, whose representatives had traveled as part of Lyon's delegation (at fourteen persons, this was the largest by far of any of the participant cities), celebrated it as Noir's personal success.[26]

After Michel Noir left city hall in 1995, stained by corruption, his successor, former Prime Minister Raymond Barre, campaigned to rescue the right-wing majority. As such, the city's internationalization strategy was adjusted, which included a deliberately lower-key involvement in Eurocities. By 2001, though, a new policy window had re-activated its resource potential for Barre's successor, socialist Gerard Collomb. This was a major victory in a town dominated for decades by right-wing coalitions, but meant that, in its search for support and legitimacy, the new municipal team was forced to re-ignite links with the business community, the majority of which was not among the left's traditional supporters. Collomb's team did so with aplomb, anchoring it to an ambitious internationalization strategy.[27]

While Raymond Barre had relied on his distinguished address book to attract international events or institutions to Lyon (including the G7 summit, which came in 1996), the new team endorsed the substance of a similarly high-profile internationalization policy but dressed it in a very different garb. Mayor Collomb and his deputy mayor for international affairs, the former CEO of an advertising company, Jean Michel Daclin, bet on municipal associations and networks to increase Lyon's visibility and attraction. As they explained it, membership of transnational networks provided the best outlet for the development and dissemination of the Lyon brand. Crafting a policy of active participation in several European and global associations of cities, Collomb and Daclin eyed the chairmanship of Eurocities as their main target. During a period when the cutting edge of municipal government was increasingly simplified into buzzwords—"networks," "governance," "partnership," "benchmarking," and so on—it was not only important to be a member of municipal associations that endorsed this style of slogan politics but also to be at their helm. With leadership would come notoriety; the Lyon brand was being built on visibility.

Networking the Networks:
What Good Are Municipal Associations to Municipal Leaders?

Whatever the initial expectations in joining an association of municipalities, a network's value does not automatically subside. This is because membership does not denote a significant degree of involvement. Some municipalities merely pay their subscription fee, happy to derive benefits by association. Others try to harness the resources provided by the organization, joining a number of thematic working groups, whereas a few municipalities attempt to drive the whole show. Levels of engagement and participation, as we saw in earlier sections, are clearly dependent on individual, as well as municipal, strategies and are fuelled by what the organization has to offer incumbents at any particular time. How the different Lyonese municipalities historically adjusted their participation in these networks—focusing on the IULA/UIV during the interwar years and Eurocities from 1989 to 2007—sheds light on the historic value of intermunicipal associations, and also the continuities and discontinuities in participant engagement.

In the first place, there is the question of the organization's function and resources. The IULA/UIV's life and work took two trajectories during the interwar years. One headed toward the gathering and circulation of specialized knowledge about municipal government and policies. This was written in stone after the Ghent Congress and took shape in 1921, when the Brussels secretariat published the first issue of the *Tablettes Documentaires*, a bibliographic bulletin that collated information from one hundred periodicals in twelve countries—through which union members were provided with the highlights of the most recent research and practice in municipal administration, welfare, electricity, housing, transportation, waste management, and so on. As an intermunicipal clearing house, the IULA/UIV spread its wings further through conferences and congresses, which explored myriad subjects ranging from municipal hygiene to unemployment policies. The Brussels secretariat, beyond coordinating this conference agenda, also answered specific information requests from members, the horizon of which went beyond the mutualization of specialized knowledge. In line with streams of thought that harked back to the late nineteenth century, the IULA/UIV wanted to preside over the establishment of a fully fledged new body of knowledge, a "municipal science," whose content would be the *vade me cum* of municipal employees and leaders all over the world.[28] Such a universal aspiration was coherent with the other side of the IULA/UIV's rationale, which is its loose but constant political discourse for a world in which home-ruled cities would be the basic cells of a democratic order more amenable to peace, mutual understanding, and the resolution of social problems across national borders.[29]

Neither Herriot, who remained mayor of Lyon until 1957, nor his fellow councilors and technicians, made much use of this "municipal science," though. The *Tablettes Documentaires* were never excerpted or systematically used, while the voluminous conference proceedings were never made available in the Municipal Council Library. The Lyonese delegations to the congresses remained erratic and silent, and no attempts were made to tap the knowledge base of the Brussels secretariat. Nor was any sustained attention given to answer the various questionnaires sent by Brussels or its *rapporteurs* for conference preparation or data collection. The interwar municipality's quest for international experiences, which was considerably less important than it had been before World War I, took place through other channels like study tours, correspondence, and the perusal of a limited number of French technical magazines by municipal experts. Though no explicit explanation has ever been given, it seems that the costs in time and energy that derived from active participation in, and maintenance of, the IULA/UIV technological resource base were deemed too important for their possible results. This was especially true because of the weakness of the French national branch of the UIV/IULA, which struggled to aggregate data in the way that the Dutch and German municipal associations did. Furthermore, Lyon's municipal leaders easily retrieved information about nondomestic municipal policies from other sources, all the more since its officials held responsibilities in national political and professional organizations.[30] Not only was there no policy window but routine cross-observation of other municipal policies provided tangible, and economical, results.

The political project of the IULA/UIV does not, on first viewing, seem to have been attractive either. Despite being a long-standing member of its executive committee, and an honorary president, Herriot did not attend a single meeting, conference, congress, or session for about twenty years. Nor were any senior delegates sent in his absence. In all, very little organizational or political support was forthcoming from Lyon. Indeed, when an IULA/UIV conference was held in Lyon in 1934, it took the sanction of special funds by the French prime minister for the event to take place.[31] Having played little role in its organization, the apathetic Herriot briefly attended two sessions, and only then to propagate one of his famous aphorisms about the fact that nation-states have diverging interests, whereas municipalities have converging purposes.[32] The conference nevertheless left a lasting imprint on delegates who attended the banquet, where Herriot flexed his oratory muscles and displayed the spectacular range of the municipal wine cellar.[33]

The weak, but enduring, link between the IULA/UIV and Lyon seems to have been a symbolic transaction only. On the one hand, membership of the union was a sign that Lyon held its rank among the cities of the world.

The IULA/UIV's events and publications provided occasional windows to showcase Herriot's achievements—as at the Lyon conference in 1934, where the city's new hospital was officially opened.[34] On the other hand, the union's leaders were pleased to retain Herriot's patronage. Numerous traces of (unsuccessful) requests for him to chair a session or attend a conference indicate that Herriot's name was, in the words of Senator Vinck himself, held as "a symbol as far as municipal achievements are concerned."[35] Vinck and his associates knew that his prestige and foreign travels as a national leader had won him a visibility that no other mayor in Europe, or in the world, could boast.[36] He was an asset to lure in possible members who were acquainted with those local projects that he had deftly popularized across Europe since the early 1910s.[37] Moreover, he brought credentials to risky endeavors, as in 1936 when he was asked to be a member of the honorary committee for the controversial Berlin Congress.[38] Both parties thus had some interest in this weak but relatively costless and effective link.

Eurocities has also presented itself as a knowledge clearing house, illuminating its rationale to "share knowledge and ideas, exchange experiences, analyze common problems and develop innovative solutions."[39] This added value, the contribution to knowledge production, is justified to members as the payoff for playing an active role within the network, either by leading a working group or forum, or testing innovative experiments. Scientific and intellectual support comes from research groups like the European Institute for Comparative Urban Research (EURICUR), a joint research venture created in 1989 between the Erasmus University of Rotterdam and the mayoralties of Rotterdam and Barcelona. A final clue for this commitment to knowledge production comes through its membership of the European Urban Knowledge Network, a research fund in which member states, the European Union (EU), and its URBACT program[40] are other major stakeholders. By showcasing its expertise from the outset—through its commitment to a scientific approach to urban problems—Eurocities asserted its value to the European Commission, which lacked expertise in urban policy making. This thus transformed Eurocities into a necessary and credible partner for Bruce Millan's DG XVI.

Such bluster masks the meager production of knowledge. Working parties have, according to former participants, operated erratically and ineffectively.[41] The durable mobilization of elected officials and municipal technicians once or twice a year has proved to be a daunting challenge. Although some cities have used such opportunities to evaluate their own policies and winnow foreign experiences, this is far from the sole reason for cities to join, supervise, or create a working group. By and large, most working parties have been thematically focused EU lobby groups (such as the high-speed trains or urban-renewal networks), or have presented windows for members (often working-party leaders) to showcase their domestic achievements and boast about their European recognition at home. This was the case when Lyon headed its first working party, the "child in the city" committee, in 1989. Having campaigned for election on a platform of social inclusion, Noir recognized the benefits back home in chairing this group. Yet the gesture superseded policy substance, since the committee did not even meet before April 1990.[42] Indeed, the working parties quickly became stepping stones for cities vying for visibility and dominance within the organization itself, especially when membership of the executive committee was opened to election in 1992. To muster political support from fellow members, chairing a working party became an exercise in demonstrating administrative and leadership capacity, rather than producing and disseminating useful knowledge.

Moreover, while member cities were asked to contribute to knowledge production, they tended to tweak this activity to their own ends. In so doing, members usually targeted ancillary resources of intangible value for the parent network. Participation in Eurocities and its working groups allowed member cities to play a role within a new configuration of political intermediation, which operated horizontally to facilitate access to a supranational governmental level. For Lyon, the greater a city's visibility in Eurocities, the greater its access to EU resources, more so once Eurocities had cemented its seat around the DG XVI's table. With access came lucrative European funds, from which Lyon benefited.[43]

Although this burrowing undoubtedly fitted the initial lobbying bill of creating an organization to attract resources for its members, it represented a deliberate break from Eurocities' early focus as a modern municipal clearing house. In addition, membership also increased the social capital of municipal leaders, which facilitated relationships with other European cities to generate bids for collaborative European programs. Eurocities thus empowered Lyon to move ahead on EU-connected projects like the European high-speed train network, especially its Lyon-Turin leg,[44] while enhancing the city's profile in other areas. As a Lyonese staff member in charge of Eurocities recently explained: "it helps to sit on the Executive Committee. It also helps to have social intercourse at the European level because you meet commissioners, etc. This network helps to influence European policy, to win visibility and to fill your address book. This is what prompted us to enter the Committee."[45]

There were other derivable political resources from a high profile in Eurocities. Individual leaders have used the intermunicipal stage as a stepping stone for their political careers, as made clear by Michel Noir's annexation of Eurocities. Gerard Collomb's success in this endeavor will be tested in the 2008 election, but it is clear that he has been anxious to build a profile as an intermunicipal leader since 2001. Being a mayor with a voice in the urban affairs of Europe and the world will certainly be presented as one of his main assets during the campaign. Such a quest for status goes beyond the individual: it is clear that the different municipalities of Lyon have always tried to be the leading French city within Eurocities. When, for example, Lyon ceased to be a member of the executive committee in 1997, it created and supervised an informal group of French member cities, in order to retain some driving power while two other French cities (Lille and Bordeaux) sat on the executive.

Mayors Noir and Collomb, their staff, and their deputy mayors were regular participants in delegations to European institutions, conferences, and executive committee meetings. The daily activity that resulted from this involvement was coordinated, between 1990 and 2001, by one staff member, who spent half of her time on Eurocities' work, and since 2001, by a full-time collaborator to coordinate Lyon's incremental campaign to secure Eurocities' presidency. This person made it very clear in an interview that "there are short term and long term strategies. It is true we placed a submission for the Eurocities Awards in 2001.[46] Then we proposed ourselves to preside over a Forum. Saragoza did exactly the same thing. Saragoza ran for Awards, they presented their municipal achievements in thematic sessions and meetings. . . . It is clear that you have to be visible to be elected to the Executive Committee."[47]

Having observed the Lyon general meeting in 2005, we saw the result of these "long-term" and "short-term" strategies. Six cities were candidates for the four available executive committee seats, and they decorated the corridors with printed propaganda material. Most of them had some track record in Eurocities: they had led working groups and forums and had applied for awards long before they ran for the supreme prize. As Lyon had sat on the committee since 2002 and held a vice presidency, this meant that Lyon would automatically be the next president of the organization if re-elected. It was, and it established Gerard Collomb as president of Eurocities until 2008, at which time he will run for mayor again.

Conclusion

Our comparison of Lyon's role within municipal associations during the twentieth century has insisted on its political dimension. During the first half of the century, Lyon's involvement in such networks was not highly visible. It was, above all, a consequence of the symbolic status of Edouard Herriot, the only French mayor with an international profile. Lyon's involvement in the Union Internationale des Villes was born out of an accepted ambiguity and derived mostly from lobbying by the UIV itself. Membership does not automatically translate into involvement. Into the 1990s, membership of municipal associations became a much more serious matter and captured the attention of Lyon's political leaders for several reasons. Firstly, as the city lost its industrial base and moved into tertiary services, visibility across borders was deemed a vital asset by city entrepreneurs. Secondly, Lyon's municipal leaders tried to escape a center-periphery relationship that bound their policy into dependent ties with the national government, while the latter was progressively retrenching its activity and handing over some policy areas to local authorities and to the European level. Thirdly, some policy windows were opened by blunt political changes, which provided incentives for city actors to seek new recipes and resources.

In Lyon, as in several European second cities, cooperation with other municipalities was a strategy that was expected to deliver on these three prongs. In Lyon and elsewhere, it has been used together with other tools for internationalization, which took their cue from the perception that European cities were engaged in a race with many contenders and only a few winners.[48] The consequences were increased competition among cities, which ranged from the development of strategic planning to the race for conference venues, cultural infrastructure, and sporting events or international exhibitions. Municipal associations, despite their front side of cooperation, were also geared toward competition, as shown by the strategies developed by Lyon and other cities to play a leading role in their midst. Many of these tools, as suggested by the genesis of Eurocities, were initially engineered in Barcelona, whose municipal leaders were among the first to develop a systematic political attention to shunt national dependencies, win over national rival cities, and develop a high European visibility that simultaneously embraced municipal associations and other internationalization tools. Lyon, as many European cities, was significantly "Barcelonized" as a consequence of Barcelona's success, not only in placing the city on the map but also in defining the methods and frames of the internationalization game. In the 1990s, membership in a municipal association was one element in the internationalization toolkit that emerged from the Barcelona workshop.

Aside from pointing to clear differences in the structure and operation of municipal associations, our comparison also sheds light on the fact that they have relied on different paradigms of municipal government. The UIV/ IULA was borne out of the Socialist Internationale, and it was mostly supported by a coalition of European socialists who had not embraced the state as the matrix of a socialist society. The model of city government proposed by the UIV/IULA was based on a proactive municipal policy that emphasized the provision of health, welfare, and utilities by the way of municipal trading enterprises. This "welfare municipality" is no longer the paradigm of *fin de siècle* municipal associationalism. Urban services are now mostly provided through public-private partnerships, and municipalities are clients rather than suppliers of these services; enablers rather than doers. Today's municipal associations, like Eurocities, play an important role in the promotion of this enabling style of "governance": their conference programs showcase such achievements, while they provide opportunities for private firms to approach potential customers. As a clue of this propinquity, the municipality of Lyon negotiated for the Global City trade fair, organized by the Reed Midem group, to be held twice in a row in Lyon during 2006 and 2007. This trade fair of urban services, self-branded as "the international forum for urban decision makers," was deemed an invaluable complement to Lyon strategy to win Eurocities' leadership.[49] Being neither completely different nor the same, transnational municipal associations have been both an agent and a product of changes in the realm of municipal government in Europe since the beginning of the twentieth century.

CHAPTER 6

Selling the City-State

Planning and Housing in Singapore, 1945–1990

Nancy H. Kwak

Since at least the 1970s, Singaporean leaders have consistently extolled the virtues of their rapidly modernizing landscape as a symbol of their great success. This success has traditionally been plotted along two lines. First, unlike their Southeast Asian neighbors, Singaporeans swiftly cleared away traditional *kampong*[1] dwellings and shophouses, and ordered the city-state into clean New Towns connected by pristine highways.[2] Second, unlike New Yorkers and Londoners, Singaporeans distributed the fruits of rapid urban development among the populace and consequently better fulfilled the promise of social equality. According to the national government, Singaporeans leveled the field, literally and figuratively. Former Prime Minister Lee Kuan Yew proudly explained at a national rally that the governing People's Action Party's (PAP) vigorous urban planning had resulted in "a deep sense of pride in the progress of Singaporeans as a whole," a collective sense of "security, neighbourliness and well-being of residents in our HDB [public housing] estates and new towns."[3]

In contrast to the nationalist tone of this narrative, however, archival records show the fundamentally international character of urban-planning and housing-policy development in Singapore. Given the emergence of Singapore as a postcolonial city-state and given its role as a major entrepôt in Southeast Asian trade, it is not surprising that the former British colony participated in international exchanges about housing, adopting and sharing nonindigenous ideas about appropriate hygiene, use, and management. What is more interesting, however, is the process of exchange. This raises a number of questions: First, how did ideas circulate between Singapore and other nations? Which local, national, and international organizations (and individuals within those organizations) participated, for what purposes, and to what effect? Second, how did transnational or internationally shared ideas about good housing and best practices in urban planning become incorporated into a national urban identity? How were ideas accepted or rejected?

These international negotiations provide a critical context for histories of national housing development, not only in former British colonies like Singapore but also in other East and Southeast Asian nations after 1945. The late 1940s, 1950s, and 1960s witnessed a convergence of powerful impulses: many of the largest conurbations in the region—Seoul, Hong Kong, Shanghai, Kuala Lumpur—experienced severe central-city overcrowding and the proliferation of informal shelter at the same time that leaders struggled to establish independent, viable, and competitive national economies. Newly formed international organizations, meanwhile, built on the work of predecessor institutions like the League of Nations and the International Labour Organization (ILO) to facilitate development through technical advisory exchanges. Developed nations participated in these organizations for a variety of intertwined motives including anticommunism, business expansion, and benevolent human rights advocacy. An international history of housing policies consequently connects domestic ideas about home, citizens' rights, and urban infrastructure and design with larger questions of security, labor management, and economic competitiveness.

Institutional Legacies of British Rule

Singapore emerged from over one hundred years of colonial governance with self-rule in 1959. Membership in the Federation of Malaysia followed from 1963 to 1965, with independence then secured in 1965. The new city-state unsurprisingly followed many British urban-planning techniques and ideals because of established institutions and practices. In particular, the tradition of British education and the persistence of English as a common language produced more complex historic legacies than the new nationalist rhetoric suggested. As soon as it was established in 1959, the transitional and postcolonial Housing and Development Board (HDB) prided itself on being radically different from the colonial 1927–59 Singapore Improvement Trust (SIT), but in reality, the predilection for English training established important continuities.[4]

Part of this Anglo-centrism resulted from the inculcation of the colonial elite into a British educational system. Lee Kuan Yew, Goh Keng Swee, Lim Kim San, and other key political leaders received most, or all, of their education in British universities. Those civil servants who could not attend Oxford or Cambridge settled for cheaper Australian programs, such as the

University of Western Australia or the Royal Melbourne Technical College. This preference for English education persisted after 1965 partly because of the retention of Commonwealth certification requirements for professionals and partly because of a well-established comfort with the English language and customs.

Professional certification for architects and town planners—begun under SIT auspices—continued relatively unchanged after the HDB took over in 1959. The Singaporean Board of Architects served as a statutory body registering local architects, and it recognized association in the Royal Institute of British Architects (RIBA) as a qualification for membership. The board even mandated stricter adherence to RIBA standards, and Singapore Polytechnic's diploma in architecture was deliberately structured to follow the requirements and examinations of RIBA. Civil and structural engineers, meanwhile, most often obtained qualifications through the Australian Associate Member of the Institute of Engineers' system or as an Associate Member of the Institution of Civil Engineers (UK). Sociologist Lee Sheng Yi noted that over a decade after independence the "great majority of business elites"—particularly the younger generation—spoke English and were educated in English-language universities. This made the Singaporean elite prefer American and British business partners because of the greater ease in communication, and the trend seemed to be mirrored among architects and engineers as well.[5]

The persistence of British institutions after 1945 was deliberately encouraged by SIT officials. Municipal health officer N. A. Canton noted that, given the "large amount of information available in Britain," it would be more efficient to simply apply British data to "suit local conditions" rather than to embark on expensive new research projects.[6] Some of the earliest regional attempts at professional organization, such as the East Asian Regional Organisation for Planning and Housing (EAROPH), emerged in 1954 as part of the South East Asia Conference arm of the British-dominated International Federation of Housing and Town Planning (IFHTP).[7] Unsurprisingly, by the time fully fledged international conferences and training programs like the Colombo Plan (1950–66) had begun, definitions of the engineer, engineering technician, craftsman, and others were generally adopted from those accepted by the professional institutions of engineers in Western Europe and the United States.[8]

The PAP had two interrelated motives for continuing Singapore's dependence on foreign standards. First, the Singaporean leadership understood that current definitions of modernization (and therefore of the more nebulous assessment of national "success") emerged from a framework defined by European and U.S. historical experiences of industrial and postindustrial urban growth. In order to maintain political and economic legitimacy, Singaporeans would need to succeed by these terms. Second, the perpetuation of a British standard facilitated ongoing political interests. English served as a relatively neutral *lingua franca* for the diverse Chinese, Malayan, and Indian residents on the island. In short, Lee Kuan Yew made "industrial modernity the meta-narrative that would frame Singapore's national identity," creating a global city that "could escape the constraints placed upon it by history and geography."[9]

Such historical construction signified the incoming government's attitude toward vernacular architecture and "traditional" housing systems in 1959. The new leaders viewed most working-class houses as liabilities and potential objects of slum clearance or modernization campaigns, regardless of any actual differences in layout and use. Densely packed shophouses with ground-level stores and upper-level residential quarters were unsuited to modern vehicular traffic, offered inadequate living space, and forced business and everyday life onto the streets. In addition, the accompanying congestion and unregulated street life did not fit with the board's ideal of "open development." Terraced houses and tenements presented two equally unsavory variations of the shophouse: the terrace house was all residential, whereas the tenement had a commercial ground level and subdivided cubicles on the second story. Coolie lines were perhaps the worst form of housing available, having been built as communal shelter for laborers. Finally, self-made plank and *attap* (natural fiber) shacks in the municipal area provided another option for those unable or unwilling to pay for shophouse quarters and requiring accommodation close to work in the city. As informal quarters, these dwellings lacked basic amenities such as drainage and sanitation, and constituted a fire hazard as well.

Adapting the British New Town

In place of these dwelling types, the HDB promulgated an ideal begun during the colonial SIT years: it envisioned a "hygienic" Singapore of wide roads, regulated green spaces, and a decanting of the inner city into surrounding environs. IFHTP President (1935–38, 1947–52) George Pepler played a critical role in urging the SIT in this direction in the immediate post-1945 era. Patrick Abercrombie, the British planner and author of the 1943 and 1944 London Plans, likewise met with the governor and sponsored a Town Planning and Housing Exhibition, urging administrators to think of housing as "an integral part in the general planning and development of the Colony" rather than an isolated problem.[10] As Singaporean leaders began to think of housing in connection with the postcolonial urban economy, they looked to New Towns as a useful conceptual tool.

The New Town represented both a crossover and a departure from British planning. In England, Patrick Abercrombie recommended the decentralization of London into satellite cities in the 1940s. George Pepler also built upon wider concern with "the combination of central flat-building" and the "great suburban explosion" when he wrote the "Creation of New Towns" Memorandum (1944), upon which many of Lord Reith's arguments for the New Town Bill (1946) were based. Pepler transferred these ideas to Singapore when he served as Town Planning Adviser from 1950 to 1954, and the British Ministry of Housing and Local Government actively encouraged the travel of "high-powered civil servant[s] with experience of New Town development" from the London office to Singapore.[11] When the SIT prepared for its transition to the HDB in 1959, its chairman J. M. Fraser argued for new legislation along the same lines as the New Towns Act in Britain so that the government and HDB might proceed with similar redevelopment.

British colonial advisors did not transplant the New Town concept without adaptation to the Singaporean context, though. In fact, New Towns were first appealing to the SIT and then the HDB precisely as a tool for managing labor, population, industry, and other resources, and not primarily as a reaction to overcrowding or ribbon development. In short, the New Town idea took hold firstly as part of a larger system of regional planning and tropical housing, and secondly as part of an effort to synthesize housing policy with national aims. These goals made the ultimate scale and scope of New Town construction significantly different from that of Britain or the United States.

SIT workers and visiting experts from around the world laid the foundations for regional-planning and tropical-housing research, which the board developed in the 1960s and thereafter. They argued that tropical regions had much to learn from each other and that Singapore could profit immensely from a regional approach to exchange. Although visiting experts insisted that all shared information ultimately needed to be tailored to local needs, the early decades of regional technical assistance actually brought mostly European and, occasionally, American advisors into the details of Singaporean planning in practice. This "exchange" was not reciprocal; Singaporeans would learn, not teach. The first United Nations (UN) Mission of Experts on Tropical Housing (November 1950 to January 1951) revealed the missionary mindset of these European and American actors. According to chairman Jacob Crane, a civil engineer and planner who, at the time of the Mission, was also serving as Assistant to the Administrator of the U.S. Housing and Home Finance Agency, the UN targeted "more than 100,000,000 Asian families . . . [living] in crowded, unsanitary, sub-standard quarters," since "the magnitude of the

Asian housing problem [was] far greater than that of any other part of the world." In order to eradicate these slums, the mission recommended further technical, financial, and administrative research; the development of a "well-rounded technical team" as "commonly engaged in European and American countries"; an increase in the number of trained professionals devoted to maintaining "the increasingly important international relationships in this field"; the international sharing of construction methods; and the widespread adaptation of New Towns.[12]

Advisory bodies urged the study of New Towns as part of the examination of the "intimate relationship between 'capital planning' and 'environmental planning.'" In a seminar held in Tokyo in 1958, for example, Charles Abrams (an American lawyer who brought about the first federal support for public housing as public use in New York City) and Otto Koenigsberger (a British tropical housing expert active in the IFHTP who would work with Abrams in Ghana, the Philippines, Nigeria, Pakistan, and Singapore) offered the two major presentations on Asian urban development and made suggestions for regional planning legislation focused primarily on the structural organization of the national planning body. These included recommendations to make "the planning agency a board on which the development agencies are represented and in which they have an actual voice in policy," to give "development agencies an advisory or consulting function within the planning agency," to award "the head of the planning agency cabinet rank in the government," and to make "the planning unit an autonomous body with financial and other powers which it can use to induce compliance with its orders." According to Abrams, "if . . . they were specifically instructed to build houses for low-income families, and if loan funds, subsidies or independent revenues were made available to them, the Improvement Trusts might be able to do a better job." In addition, private savings might provide public finance while guaranteeing fair interest rates to the individual. Finally, regional development depended upon careful industrial settlement planning.[13] A decade later, the UN Economic Commission for Asia and the Far East's (ECAFE) Committee on Industry and Natural Resources reiterated some of these concepts, albeit with an emphasis more on Scandinavian models for building and planning than on Anglo-American ones, as in the case of Abrams and Koenigsberger. Nonetheless, the subcommittee rejoiced that their training courses for Asian and African participants provided continuing education on the role of housing in the national economy—pursuing the work of the Colombo Plan and other UN fellowship offerings—and that "regional development planning is now coming to be accepted as an effective tool for integrated development."[14] By the early 1960s, it had become standard for key board members to travel to Britain and study first hand the relationship between central area redevelopment in London and the formation of such New Towns as Stevenage and Harlow in Essex.[15]

Beyond the Empire

Although British connections continued unabated through the 1950s, it is the American as well as the broader international impacts that require more explanation for the transition and independence years. In the last decade of the SIT, various international bodies were active in the region, and of these, the ILO perhaps most. The ILO reported on the development of cooperative movements in Asia in 1949 and formed an Asian Advisory Committee to organize a conference on the relationship between Asian wage policies and workers' housing in 1950.[16] Throughout the 1950s, the ILO organized numerous conferences on the responsibilities of the national government, local authorities, and employers, as well as technical issues like housing finance and standards. One conference resulted in "a widespread agreement concerning the desirability of industrial and urban decentralization" between the governments of South and Southeast Asia.[17] The ILO also sent population control advisors to address issues of urban overcrowding in Asia, Africa, Latin America, and the Middle East; the urban and population crises were closely linked by the ILO and by SIT members who traveled abroad discussing the "Singapore problem."[18]

There was an important difference between the attitude of the SIT and the HDB toward intergovernmental organizations like the ILO: unlike the board, the Trust did not seek validation for a new national identity within the international sphere. Although trust workers certainly wanted to legitimize their colonial presence in addition to learning about specific technical innovations and new practices in such areas as housing construction and finance, SIT participation in intergovernmental organizations lacked the sense of urgency and emergency that so thoroughly imbued their housing policies on the ground in the 1950s. These policies consisted of a "complex and highly spatial political drama" and included "street riots, detentions, the city's merger with Malaya, the city's 'eviction' from Malaysia, and the eventual consolidation of Singapore as a tightly demarcated one-party state."[19] The geography of rehousing campaigns during this decade was symptomatic of an empire in crisis driven to drastic measures by cold war concerns. Although the driving force behind housing policies was certainly international relations, international organizations played a lesser role during these years.

After 1959, the HDB also utilized the language of emergency in order to marginalize "dangerous" elements (such as Chinese communists and other dissenters), but it was much more conscious of its image in the international sphere and participated eagerly in intergovernmental organizations in order to promote a particular image of the new nation-state. From its conception, the board paid attention not only to how its actions appeared vis-à-vis the outgoing colonial SIT but also to how it might appear to the United States, the new player in the region.

During the 1950s, the United States became interested for the first time in technical assistance to Southeast Asia. Although Americans had been consistently involved in shaping the "Urban Internationale" since at least the 1930s, they had been remarkably skittish about being involved in Singapore until that decade.[20] President Harry Truman repeatedly rebuffed British efforts to attract American aid to Southeast Asia, and as late as 1948–49, he insisted that assistance programs be led by the UN and its Specialized Agencies.[21] It was only after Mao Zedong's 1949 triumph over a beleaguered Kuomintang that John Foster Dulles, among others, noticed the potential for the spread of Chinese communism to Singapore. In 1950, the United States became the Colombo Plan's only non-Commonwealth member. Since the HDB was an active member of the plan, it came into direct contact with American advisors in the coordination and exchange of experts and technicians, the establishment of more training facilities, the provision of special equipment to assist with training and research, and the establishment of grants, loans, and private investment for development projects.[22] Truman and Dulles agreed that American financial support for the UN Extended Programme of Technical Assistance (EPTA) and the UN Special Fund needed to increase. Truman's successor, Dwight Eisenhower, encouraged noncommunist American urban planners and architects to travel to the region in order, as the U.S. assistant secretary of state for far eastern affairs put it concisely, "to promote the independence of the free nations in Asia and to help them build strong and free societies."[23] The Ford Foundation, the American Council of Learned Societies, and the Fulbright foreign scholarship program all helped to fund the study of Southeast Asian languages and cultures in order to strengthen the American advisory role.[24] Congress actively recruited the "assistance" of American companies, appointing New York businessman Ralph Straus to head a study on the "role of American business" in "helping other nations expand their economies."[25] By the late 1950s, Americans were involved in Southeast Asia through various venues.

Americans played a critical part in intergovernmental organizations (in particular, advisory committees of the UN) involved in Singapore. U.S. participants simultaneously drew from domestic national experiences while working toward a truly international set of ideals about urban planning in the developing world. Of all visiting planners, the exceptionally capable Charles Abrams played a leading role. Abrams's importance in Singapore stemmed mostly from the board's interest in learning how to proceed with wide-scale slum clearance. In brief, the HDB needed to clear squatters, modernize housing, and provide tangible evidence of its commitment to the people; it had requested assistance from the UN since "urban renewal call[ed] for sound planning and considerable technical know-how."[26] According to UN team members Otto Koenigsberger and Susume Kobe (a Japanese transportation expert), "Singapore is one of the few places in the world which have achieved so large a role of new house construction, that they can afford to think of urban renewal or slum-clearance—or at least, so they think. One of our main jobs is to tell them how to do it—profitably without losing the 1964 elections for which they need the votes of the slum dwellers."[27] Abrams was particularly well suited to help Lim Kim San, chairman of the HDB, because of his experience with eminent domain in the law; "those [questions] connected with urban renewal [were] right in [Abrams's] court." While advising Lim and other HDB members, Abrams referred often to the New York State Urban Renewal Law and the Housing and the Home Finance Agency's hearings on transportation, among other documents.[28]

It was not accidental that the expert on urban renewal came from the United States. Lim used UN Development Programme (UNDP) funds to send architect and town planner Alan Choe to study the U.S. Department of Housing and Urban Development's urban renewal program, and Choe later explained the logic behind this choice: "America at that time was the leading country in the field of urban renewal because they were the ones that saw to it that you had to renew your cities otherwise the decay would just stifle the growth of the city. . . . So they were the first in the world to embark on urban renewal in a systematic matter. Those of us who wanted to study urban renewal, that was the place we would go to because you can see examples of what they did."[29]

This preference for American examples quickly disintegrated in the face of widely publicized urban unrest and racial conflict, though. After returning from his study trip to the United States, Choe spoke dismissively of the ghettoization and segregation that he had witnessed there. Americans had employed a bulldozer approach and used eminent domain against the poor; the lesson for Singapore was to not begin urban renewal until relocation facilities (public housing) were prepared. According to Choe, the United States provided more of a negative than positive example, and Singapore's public housing needed to be designed in a way that would avoid the stigma found abroad.

Beyond Choe's disillusionment with American urban failures was another more important cause for the board's increasing concern with the direct importation of American design ideas: Singaporean architects and planners were increasingly demanding "nationalization" of international design concepts. The national landscape depended upon a careful selection of overall planning and housing decisions, and while low-cost housing could be designed and researched with foreign references, documents, and "the information of the expert consultants," former deputy manager Toh Shung Pie emphasized that "housing in Singapore should reflect the social, economic, climatic, and political conditions of the country and its people."[30] This adaptation could be in motive rather than in actual policy. For example, Abrams recommended Singapore begin careful industrial settlement planning in 1958 as part of a larger vision of well-ordered regional development, but this suggestion appealed to Minister of Finance Goh Keng Swee because he wanted to end the "utter dependence on foreign manufactured products." Goh well understood that modern, high-rise buildings required steel and argued for its production at Jurong, since steel served as "one of the basic industries for sparking off a train of allied industries which will turn Singapore into the New York of Malaysia."[31]

Singapore retained a hyperconsciousness of British and American developments throughout the 1960s, 1970s, and 1980s, but it no longer uncritically admired Anglo-American models. Instead, the city-state's leaders brought a "patchwork" approach to national policy, where international best practices were patched together and assimilated with local needs. Interestingly, this very technique was practiced and promoted by Abrams, Koenigsberger, and Kobe's 1963 UN Mission to the city-state. In their final recommendations, the three men proposed a more flexible Concept Plan, which emphasized industrial development in Jurong and mimicked a Dutch town-planning practice called a "ring city" with "lungs" in the center.[32] In addition, the Expert Mission recommended five-year housing plans; a capital investment program encouraging "capital formation through saving for home ownership"; more reclamation projects, such as those at Bedok, Kallang, and Jurong; self-contained settlements (or New Towns); public transport; systematic urban renewal, without "bulldozer addiction"; and a "programme of publicity and promotion," with a wide range of American and European examples to explain the rationale behind each recommendation.[33] PAP leaders concerned with solving the pressing issues of unemployment and housing shortages listened. The HDB increased its development expenditure from $36 million (1961) to $51 million (1966), and the hike in construction rates, along with industrialization, resulted in a dramatic drop in unemployment rates.[34] As one local newspaper put it, UN experts had given Singapore the "go-ahead" for a "big city face-lift."[35]

UN involvement did not stop there. Shortly after national independence in 1965, Goh Keng Swee and the Ministry of National Development received substantial financial support and a host of UNDP experts for the purposes of "State and City Planning"—that is, for writing a master plan that linked urban with national development.[36] The Master Plan prioritized housing precincts, the British concept of self-contained neighborhoods, and industrial development—all of which depended on the compulsory acquisition of land at affordable prices.[37] The final results of these long efforts were the creation of an Urban Renewal Authority and the passage of the Compulsory Land Acquisition Act of 1966.

The board was not indiscriminate in embracing UN-related assistance. For example, HDB members enthusiastically participated in study-abroad missions of ECAFE but dismissed regional committee meetings as mere "social gatherings for renewal of old acquaintances."[38] The board was quick to realize, however, that Singapore's participation in these meetings could be utilized for diplomatic and public relations purposes. Chief architect Teh Cheang Wan noted that other delegates in ECAFE were coming to the unfavorable conclusion that Singaporeans thought they had nothing to learn from their neighbors, and Teh decided the slight cost in sending a representative was worth the return in goodwill. What was at stake now was clearly the exportation of Singaporean know-how: "Singapore is the only country in this region [which has] successfully solved the housing and building problem and the representatives of other countries are looking forward to [learning from us]."[39] UN and UN-sponsored events were generally deemed important. When HDB Chief Executive Officer (CEO) Tan Kuh Jin explained why he refused to participate in associations such as EAROPH, he simply stated that Singapore should not "throw away the chance of telling our achievement in public housing to the rest of the world" or gaining "international recognition." Such acclaim could only be achieved "through a United Nations sponsored seminar."[40]

By the late 1960s, a new housing ideal had emerged. Unlike the trust, the board did not see the solution to the working-class housing problem in the construction of new tenements, flats, terrace houses, artisans' quarters, and cottages, nor did it welcome wholesale American-style urban renewal. Instead, the HDB and PAP leadership imagined a modern, high-rise Singapore ordered into satellite New Towns with a redeveloped downtown. Unlike the West, redevelopment would not occur until alternate housing had been planned and prepared for the displaced. This new housing would earn international acclaim and mark Singapore as a modern nation uniquely capable of providing decent shelter. Its socialist housing program would simultaneously disenfranchise communists at home and outperform welfare programs in the United States and Great Britain.

Nothing illustrated the new architectural ideal more vividly than a series of stamp contests held by the national government. In the first competition held in honor of National Day in 1963, the winning entry portrayed a Corbusian landscape of widely spaced high-rise slab blocks marching in a line into the horizon, with the word "Perumahan" (housing) emblazoned across the top. The three blocks of twelve-story flats at Queenstown were built of reinforced concrete and were the standard design-type used by the board.[41] The second contest celebrated the Afro-Asian Housing Conference in 1967, while the third boasted the completion of the Board's 100,000th home with an illustration of a multistory block of flats, a shopping center, and a void deck, as drawn by a draughtsman from the Urban Renewal Department.[42] It was not accidental that these images were selected for Singaporean postage, which would travel around the world and showcase the nation's universal high-rise living and planned environments.

Democratic Ownership

While planned, universal occupation of high-rise HDB flats might have fit with the PAP's vision for a modern and economically competitive city-state, the question remains of how the leadership convinced ordinary citizens that such architecture represented a common national identity. The most important tool for achieving popular buy-in was the Central Provident Fund (CPF). Started in 1955 as a compulsory savings-based retirement plan, the fund represented the British effort to avoid replicating their welfare state.[43] Although the use of a fund was widespread throughout the British colonies, the PAP made an important adjustment to this system by liberalizing its terms in 1964 through the Homeownership for the People Scheme—administered by the HDB—which allowed low-income families to use their CPF funds to purchase HDB flats. For the new government, the scheme gave former tenants a newfound respect for their properties, and reduced vandalism and maintenance costs; it accorded historically migrant communities "something to live for, fight for, and defend." Most importantly, it gave the new government a pool of savings from which to build a nation.

The board was undoubtedly influenced by its colonial predecessor in its decision to prioritize homeownership.[44] The British urged owner occupation over other forms of tenure throughout the SIT years, and they strategized legal methods for the encouragement of homeownership. UN advisory bodies echoed this sentiment. As ascertained, the 1963 UN expert mission encouraged savings for homeownership to create capital for national development. By 1970 it had become standard for ECAFE, the Centre for Housing, Building, and Planning, and the Office of Technical Cooperation to recommend "institutional arrangements and measures for mobilizing and channelling savings into housing programmes."[45] In Singapore, the CPF savings system financed HDB construction and played an essential role in capital formation and the government's amassment of foreign reserves. Initially, the PAP only used CPF savings to provide rental units as a direct response to the housing shortage, but with the homeownership scheme, this goal shifted to meet the twin demands "for better housing and [for] a safe form of investment."[46] According to the UNDP, the HDB's rental occupancy dropped from 100 percent (early 1960s) to 38 percent (1981) and then to 16 percent (1989).[47]

Singapore's push to democratize homeownership actually mirrored a larger trend among developing nations worldwide. *The Straits Times* proudly noted that, although the desire for homeownership was "felt by people elsewhere and everywhere," "Singaporeans are definitely better placed than most of their contemporaries to fulfill their aspirations for a home they can call their own."[48] According to the *Times*, the World Bank argued the only way to improve housing distribution was to adopt a strategy similar to Singapore's— namely to sacrifice quality for quantity and only improve quality after everyone had been housed, for "few countries have responded imaginatively to the problem the way Singapore has."[49] The HDB proudly pointed to its skyrocketing homeownership rates, which after a slow start, rose to 76 percent of all board flat-dwellers (1985) and then to 90 percent (1995).[50] Clearly government priorities were shifting as Singaporean society became more affluent: provision of HDB rental provision was not the priority, homeownership was. The PAP also made good use of their successful expansion of homeownership over the course of the 1970s and 1980s as an international public relations tool. Homeownership became a symbol of wealth, not only of individual families but of the nation itself. When the PAP could claim a majority of homeowners either within the HDB public-housing system and affiliates, or the private sector, it was essentially making a claim to national wealth and prosperity as well as to an endowed and content citizenry.[51]

For the "old new bourgeoisie," those "whose privileged class position was secured by professional success before World War II,"[52] the most contentious aspect of HDB design and supervision was the lack of real discussion about meaningful local architectural form. William Lim, Tay Kheng Soon, and other architects and scholars tried to open up the debate, organizing from 1965 to 1973 the Singapore Planning and Urban Research Group (SPUR), "a private citizens' gathering whose aim was to seek involvement in the physical planning process of the newly independent nation state."[53] Most participants had completed their education in the late 1950s or early 1960s in Great Britain, Australia, or the United States, although some rare exceptions, such as Tay, trained domestically. (Even a domestic education still included

British influences, however, since Singapore's system "was and still is, largely modeled on the British educational model."[54]) SPUR members' challenges to the HDB, therefore, emerged in some part from the context of international styles and the "unlearning" of European architectural tropes. Lim recalled that when he first returned to Singapore in 1957 he was "raring to put into practice the International Style of architecture associated with Oud, Wright and Le Corbusier he had been taught to believe in."[55] Although Lim eventually rejected the International Style in favor of postmodernism and a search for region-specific design by the mid-1970s, and although he and other Asian architects began participating in such collaborations as Jacqueline Tyrwhitt's Asian Planning and Architecture Collaboration in the late 1960s and early 1970s, in 1990 he still thought that "At present, even well-meaning policy-makers have to depend on out-dated proposals often recommended by foreign consultants and international agencies. Implementation of these proposals has sometimes led to disastrous consequences adversely affecting the urban poor, for example large-scale clearance of slums and squatter areas, and indiscriminate displacement of hawkers and street vendors, without providing viable alternatives."[56]

The government did not respond kindly to such critiques, nor did it adopt a soft tone with those who questioned what critics called its efforts at social engineering. Chua Beng Huat abruptly left the HDB in 1984 after the publication of an article criticizing the government; in his words, "the political atmosphere in Singapore was still one in which dissenting voices and views circulated in private conversations."[57] After years of outspoken opposition, Tay moved to Kuala Lumpur in the mid-1970s in order to build the "pioneering low-rise, high-density, low-income housing projects" he had been unable to create in Singapore. While Tay, Lim, and others espoused a new regional approach to Singaporean housing and urban development, it is important to note that they were still very much connected to international architectural and planning debates, and that they often drew on an Anglo-American education and vocabulary to articulate their dissent.

Conclusion

It is tempting to revise Singapore's story into one of mutually beneficial international collaboration, but in reality, the process of post-1945 exchange was a deeply contested one both internally and externally. Singaporean planners and government officials fought to increase their city-state's international standing, and they believed that modernization would put them on an equal footing with their European or American counterparts. The circulation of ideas, therefore, represented not only an interest in sharing best practices and in more efficiently managing data but also a tool by which to negotiate Singapore's place in an international hierarchy. The board intended to use international forums not only to glean useful new ideas but, more importantly, to establish Singapore's identity as a new nation, and certain intergovernmental or nongovernmental organizations were prioritized over others in this process. In addition, internationally shared ideas about good housing underwent a domestication of sorts; the PAP deliberately transformed the patchwork quilt of borrowed ideas into a source of national identity and pride. In this carefully constructed narrative, the PAP argued that it provided all citizens equal access to decent shelter in a peaceful, multiracial housing system.

This image was actively propagated around the world. The HDB recruited and ultimately succeeded in bringing hundreds of visitors, with such distinguished guests as Prince Norodom Sihanouk (Cambodia), Dr. Soemarno Sosroatmodjo (governor of Djakarta), the Foreign Minister of Denmark, World Bank officials, Japanese Democratic Socialist Party members, Ernest Weissmann (director of the UN Housing Building Planning Branch), ECAFE representatives, Australian MPs, World Health Organization members, the Israeli Minister of Health, American town planners, U.S. Trade Mission representatives, a professor of sociology from Chicago, teachers from Brunei, India's National Defense Team, and the Duke of Edinburgh. Planners, diplomats, and individuals simply curious to view HDB flats came from Italy, the Philippines, Burma, New Guinea, Fiji Islands, Thailand, Germany, Vietnam, Scotland, the Soviet Union, China, Canada, and Nigeria.[58] The United States encouraged other developing nations to learn from Singapore's successes, and the American Embassy used U.S. Agency for International Development funds to arrange visits to the Ministry of National Development and HDB from neighbors like Taiwan.[59] After the 1973 oil shortage, Minister for Foreign Affairs S. Rajaratnam talked about the potential for advising "West Asia" (the Middle East) on public housing policies.[60] The sharing of housing ideas was fundamentally connected with diplomacy, and much as American and European advisors had their agendas for assisting in Singaporean urban and housing policy development, so also did Singaporeans bring their interests to the international table.

The Singapore "example" was received with varying degrees of warmth and hostility during the 1970s, 1980s, and 1990s. When HDB secretary David Wong showed the film "Happy Homes" in Copenhagen to a group of representatives from the ECAFE, ECE, and UN, among others, the group broke out into spontaneous applause.[61] The board's efforts were not always so enthusiastically received, though, and the prerequisite of a powerful central government in this system of state-managed growth made Singapore less of a model than an anomaly to some. In an interesting response to those who would discard Singapore's system as an exceptional one marked by the peculiar circumstances of size, location, and leadership, World Bank chief economist Lawrence Summers argued that the strong-state model should be exported in order to encourage Singapore-style development. As he plainly put it in a 1992 lecture, "I don't think there is any alternative to increased government action."[62] During the 1980s and 1990s, the PAP continued to build on its fifty-year tradition of international-mindedness and willingness to intervene in private housing—with the government adopting a pioneering role in the diffusion of the Singaporean condominium high-rise, essentially facilitating the export of Singaporean architectural and engineering expertise through such large groups as the Keppel Corporation.[63]

Since the 1990s, Singapore is doubtless becoming an ever-more powerful player in shaping the physical landscape of Southeast and East Asia. The "lessons" for the rest of the world are unclear, though. In being so attuned to international currents, PAP leaders have fashioned a national housing machine less sensitive to domestic cultural currents and local creativity than to the international marketplace. It remains to be seen what the long-term costs—both economic and social—will be for actual residents.

CHAPTER 7

Transnational Municipalism in a Europe of Second Cities

Rebuilding Birmingham with Municipal Networks

Shane Ewen

The relationship between globalization, urban-industrial change, and municipalism is one that has been reconfigured in recent years. The British school of public administration, in particular, has lent credence to the view that local authorities, or municipalities as they are taken here, have been virtually powerless to satisfactorily manage the transition of local economies into a postindustrial global society.[1] The explanations have been clearly formulated: from the late 1970s successive Conservative governments rolled back the frontiers of the state, stripped the powers of a constitutionally weak local state, privatized a multitude of services, and curbed municipal rating powers. Globalization, indeed Europeanization, merely accelerated this pattern, heralding the final demise of the British municipality and introducing a homogeneity that characterized municipal governments from Birmingham to Barcelona. In an urbanized world, the political and economic forces of globalization and Europeanization signaled the Pyrrhic victory of the British central government in its long struggle with municipalities over the governance of modern society. Concurrently, the increasing interest taken by the European Community (EC) in transnational strategies transformed urban governance, leaving national governments to shape policy making by reforming the institutional superstructure, directing the flow of its resources, and shaping the channels through which policies filtered vertically downward to municipalities.[2]

It has also been suggested that "second cities," those Western cities whose growth in the nineteenth century was inextricably linked with industrialization, suffered severe hardship from the political and economic changes wrought by the dismantling of the Fordist industrial society during the 1970s and 1980s. British "second cities" in particular—Birmingham, Glasgow, Liverpool, and Manchester—experienced significant hollowing-out of their economic bases during the 1980s as new tertiary industries bypassed them in favor of growing towns in England's southeast. They were also heavily subjected to the de-empowerment of local government: nation-states increasingly focused resources on their capital cities—trying to turn these into global cities—and "second cities" were left to fight over the scraps.[3]

As a consequence of the centralization and privatization of Western public services and policy making, declining industrial cities adopted economic strategies during the 1980s, which, in recognizing the increasingly competitive global economy, emphasized the importance of diversifying their industrial base into service industries—notably business tourism. This included the creation of neatly packaged images that differentiated them from their decaying industrial heritage, while emphasizing their credentials as cities of European and international prestige. But these were presented as strategies that owed more to the resource inputs and coordination provided by national and supranational governments, a consequence of British inner-city policy during the late 1970s and the EC's social cohesion agenda. Municipalities and their political leaders were given little credit for devising such innovative strategies, for providing the necessary leadership for their implementation, and for coordinating the diffusion of best practice.[4] In this chapter I will challenge this argument and suggest that municipalities, and indeed their political leaders, continued to shape and direct the flow of resources and policy making agendas within late-modern urban governance, but especially during the 1980s and early 1990s.

There was a considerable shift in the cleavages and constraints facing municipalities in governing their urban places during the 1980s. Within the confines of a suffocating regulatory central government, a fragmented public sector, a return to the Victorian heyday of privatized services and heightened social tensions, municipalities sought innovative ways to maintain a voice within the amplified chatter of late-modern urban governance. Changes to local government exerted a significant influence on the changing roles and priorities of the local elite. Traditionally responsible for operational policy, urban governance was redefined during the 1980s and 1990s, with the local elite adopting proactive roles in framing strategic policy agendas to regenerate their cities. Urban governance broadened its membership beyond the conventionally narrow institutional confines of local government to encapsulate the myriad of local, national, and international actors with an interest in running cities.[5] These agendas, patterns, and repertoires for local government were increasingly the object of coordination, cooperation, or benchmarking among European municipalities. It was also multilevel governance that included transnational actors. British municipalities coped with European Union programs and looked overseas for ideas during the 1980s, building on long-established relationships with cities sharing common socioeconomic cultures. Focusing on the case study of Birmingham, one of the largest and most prestigious British municipalities, and a progenitor of late-modern urban governance, I suggest that municipalities continued to play the leading role in forging new policy networks in regenerating cities, through a process of transnational municipalism.

For all the attention the city has received from scholars in recent years, the importance of transnational municipalism—that is the coordination of local services and civic identity, and the sharing of best practices across national boundaries—has been underplayed in examinations of Birmingham's regeneration. Yet in a similar fashion to the complex ways in which transnational cities have been created by migrant networks in places such as Koreatown in Los Angeles,[6] municipalities established and renewed myriad transnational networks of their own. These cut across national boundaries and were contingent on interdependent perceptions of purpose and added value. These networks are not new. Transnational municipalism has a historic continuity, one that extends beyond the late Victorian networks established between Scandinavian and German municipalities, or those forged by social reformers like the American journalist Albert Shaw or Japanese social reformer Seiki Hajime around the *fin de siecle*.[7] What emerges most strongly from this literature is the sense of historic continuity in many of the networks established during the late nineteenth and twentieth centuries. True, the scope and presence of municipal networks accelerated and intensified during the late twentieth century through improvements in communication technologies and the increased availability of global travel, but municipalities have been active in transnational networks for more than a century. Transnational municipalism is a constant and recurring feature of municipalism rather than the product of globalization.

Birmingham: From "Second City" to "City in Decline"

At the center of Birmingham's regeneration was the city council's relationship with the wider world. Indeed how the city council wished to be seen was strongly influenced by its vision to become an "International City," later modified to "Europe's Meeting Place." Such textual images struggled to conjure up reality, yet Birmingham City Council had a clear vision from the early 1980s: to promote the city as a center for business tourism and indelibly mark it on the municipal map. By taking a proactive approach toward regeneration, the city council helped set the agenda for urban policy-making at the national and supranational levels, while becoming a textbook for other large municipalities to learn from studying its working practices. Birmingham's study, along with that of other innovative municipalities like Lyon and Barcelona, sets a deep chronological agenda for those interested in the contemporary history of urban Europe. It also focuses attention on municipalities, recognized here as the motors for urban change, in fostering and engaging in transnational networks and networking activities, which are central ingredients in late-modern urban governance.

Known in Victorian times as "the city of a thousand trades"—producing everything from jewelry to cocoa to electric dynamos—Birmingham was at the heart of the region of the West Midlands known as "The Black Country," so called for its blackened landscape exhibiting the scars of its iron-mining heritage.[8] Birmingham City Council was also known the world over and, along with fellow industrial cities like Glasgow, was a mecca for municipal reformist pilgrims drawn by its tag of "the best governed city in the world."[9] Under the mayoralty of Joseph Chamberlain, the London-born engineer (1873–76), Birmingham epitomized a shared vision of social improvement mixed with prudent and profitable public services. The city's history is thus dominated equally by its accomplishments in the workshop and the council house, a heritage not lost on contemporary policy-makers.[10]

Into the twentieth century, Birmingham successfully diversified its industrial base by moving into skilled engineering, and in particular automobile production, its preponderance of small-scale workshops proving flexible. In soaking up the depression of the 1930s, Birmingham became renowned as "Britain's industrial capital," hosting international trade fairs and acting as Britain's export hub.[11] Under the mantle of a pioneering municipal information bureau, established in 1930, Birmingham was celebrated as a busy imperial city imbued with a historic conception of its contribution to industry.[12]

Postwar Birmingham continued to thrive. Employment remained stable and high into the late 1960s, as "the most go ahead City in the world" cemented its place as the "kingpin of one of Europe's greatest industrial regions." By 1964 the city also hosted Europe's most modern shopping center, the Bull Ring, having imported the design concept of the enclosed shopping mall from North America. Clearly Birmingham was not solely an industrial behemoth but was beginning to tap the region's expanding commercial market.[13] In its physical form, Birmingham too aggressively strove for international notoriety. Driven by the city's chief engineer, Herbert Manzoni, Birmingham embraced the dominant modernist architectural and planning ideals. Manzoni envisioned Birmingham as the archetype of a Le Corbusier modernist masterpiece, which dictated a twenty-five year postwar program of redesign involving the zonal reconstruction of the central core, intersected by two ring roads. The inner ring was initially proposed following a municipal visit to inspect Vienna's progressive road network in 1910, but it was not completed until 1971. In all, this bold program transformed the central residential core of the city from a dense area of narrow, winding streets populated by cramped back-to-back housing into a towering stack of high-rise flats.[14]

Birmingham's increasing specialization within motor-vehicle production ultimately spelled its downfall. In the midst of the 1973–74 oil crisis, the city suffered badly from shrinking market share and spiraling unemployment. Between 1971 and 1981, 191,000 local jobs—around 29 percent of total employment—were lost. With unemployment peaking at 21 percent by 1986, Birmingham and its region faced dire economic circumstances.[15] Meanwhile, the Bull Ring, once the apogee of modernist consumerism, quickly deteriorated amid accelerating de-urbanization and inner-city deprivation. It was no exaggeration when a senior member of the city council noted that "We had a city centre that was dying."[16]

Regeneration as Transnational Municipalism: Tapping the International Convention Market

The narrative of Birmingham's regeneration during the 1980s is one that has been told before.[17] Based on an entrepreneurial progrowth model adapted from the United States, four capital-intensive prestige projects transformed the city center from "cultural wasteland" into "England's most dynamic concentration of [provincial] cultural activity."[18] The flagship project, the £180-million International Convention Centre (ICC), was opened in 1991 to cater to an international convention market, which was further bolstered by the construction of a five-star Hyatt Hotel. A National Indoor Arena (NIA), situated on the banks of the city's rejuvenated canal network, was opened in 1991. Initially part of the city's grandiose—albeit unsucessful— bid to host the 1992 Olympic Games, the NIA enhanced the city's prestige for staging international sporting competitions. Finally, a privately financed mixed-use development, known as Brindleyplace, linked these projects onto Broad Street, which was itself transformed by the attraction of international franchises of hotels, restaurants, and bars.[19]

Despite its shortcomings, not least in failing to tackle Birmingham's underlying social problems, the council's strategy successfully transformed a dilapidated area of the city center, reconnecting it with its Victorian quarter. Similarly, the strategy projected the city's revised image, one that embraced the postindustrial economy marked by conspicuous consumption. It also reinvigorated the council itself, which had seen its powers eroded during the

1970s and early 1980s in the face of central government cutbacks. Birmingham thus re-established itself a reputation as a city for doing, not debating.

But these descriptions fail to account for Birmingham's regeneration in the long run. Moreover, they overlook the city's softening attitude toward free trade and the European Common Market, which captured the essence of Birmingham's outward-looking approach during succeeding decades. Historically protectionist in its approach to business, the chamber of commerce recognized during the 1950s that the region's industrial future was locked into that of the Common Market.[20] Sutcliffe and Smith deem this conversion to be "highly significant of the outward-looking attitude of Birmingham industry," resulting in a flurry of activity during the 1960s—ranging from participation in various international trade fairs to establishing a European Export Section to coordinate business activity within the Common Market—designed to enhance the profile of the West Midlands within European markets and pressurize the government to embrace economic integration.[21]

The groundwork laid by the chamber of commerce during the 1960s in opening up the city to European markets spelled a sea-change in attitudes toward the Common Market and the city's place in the global marketplace. For instance, the decision to build the National Exhibition Centre (NEC), which opened some six miles outside the city center in 1976, owed much to this emerging discourse of transnational municipalism. Originally conceived in the 1950s, but not put into practice until the 1960s, the rationale behind building the largest single-purpose exhibition center in Britain (providing some 90,000 square feet of floor space) recognized that the city benefited from significant locational advantages over London in attracting international exhibitions and trade fairs. By combining resources and expertise within a single company, in 1969 the city council and chamber of commerce and industry purchased land in close proximity to the motorway and railway networks and regional airport, upon which they proposed to build the NEC. Aided by an exchequer grant—despite opposition from the Greater London Council and the Association of Exhibition Organisers, who sought to develop a new exhibition center at Crystal Palace—the NEC was the first truly national meeting place for trade and industry. Despite lacking the "metropolitan glamour" of London, Birmingham usurped the capital as the center of the growing exhibitions market, being ideally placed to take advantage of the move toward European free trade and the need for a purpose-built "shop window."[22]

Opened in 1976, the NEC triggered further investment in the region's transport infrastructure, with a major expansion of the airport to accommodate overseas connections to Paris, Amsterdam, and Dusseldörf, and the building of a new "international" railway station to connect the NEC to the national network. Then Prime Minister Harold Wilson signaled his Labour government's support for the scheme on visiting the site in 1975, noting that the NEC would surpass those continental mainland arenas.[23] Although it would be some years before this aim was realized, the NEC's development signaled Birmingham's intentions to diversify the regional economy, promoting the West Midlands on the national and international stage. An essential precursor for the city's activities in business tourism, this history predates the regeneration schemes of the 1980s.

By the early 1980s the NEC was hosting prestigious national and international fairs, including the British International Motor Show. Its success, coupled with the constraints of its greenbelt development, convinced the council to explore the cost benefits of building an international convention center in the city center. Without the NEC it is difficult to conceive that Birmingham would have embraced the concept of the convention center with such gusto. Even then, the council's experience of the exhibition market aligned its focus onto U.S. cities like Phoenix and Indianapolis, whose earlier successes in building flagship convention centers served as expressions of the value of flagship architecture in driving local regeneration. But this was not mere municipal emulation: the council's ideas were imported in adapted form. In effect this too indicates a sharp eye for ideas since the city's caucus controlled and shaped the diffusion process: first, by selecting which cities to visit; second, by contrasting the constraints and cleavages facing such cities in tackling their "urban development problems"; and third, by carefully selecting a scheme through which it could stimulate growth.

Originally conceived in the city's draft central-area district plan of 1980, the council was alerted to making a decision in 1981 when it learned that similar proposals were being considered in Bristol. Having received a design proposal on land, the freehold of which was municipally owned, its chief executive and lord mayor went on a fact-finding mission to Phoenix. On their return a working group was established within the council's main decision-making caucus, the General Purposes Committee, which further investigated the scheme. After some delays, a consultancy firm was engaged to undertake a feasibility study in 1983.[24] Other firms, notably Hyatt Hotels International and Bovis Construction, were approached as potential investors. The study overwhelmingly favored building an ICC, although it warned that the project would undoubtedly run into financial difficulties unless the council could attract sufficient funds.[25] Thus the decision to build the ICC depended entirely on the accessibility of suitable external funds, particularly in the face of austere exchequer cutbacks and a reticence to place the burden on the local rates. Thus, to secure status as a European City, Birmingham first needed to secure EC funds.

The Europeanization of English Municipal Government: The Case of the Structural Funds

Goldsmith and Garrard note four significant changes to municipal powers during the 1980s: the "rolling back" of the state, privatization of public services, reduced public expenditure, and an attack on vested municipal interests. By introducing market dynamics into the municipal sphere, municipalities now performed enabling roles by entering into partnerships with other agencies.[26] In theory, the pressures placed on municipalities to seek multi-agency partnerships meant that municipal influence would necessarily diminish. In practice, though, innovative municipalities like Birmingham moved beyond their traditional safety barriers and sought new partnerships, which reinforced its traditional role as local power-broker. Municipalities like Birmingham were then both enablers and doers.

More than that, municipalities like Birmingham looked beyond their traditional sources of funds—the exchequer and the property tax—for new revenue streams. This undoubtedly involved astute management of the municipal books, especially in securing low-interest loans during the early stages of regeneration. Most importantly, though, it encouraged a shift in focus from the national to the international stage, mainly to the cash cow that was the EC. Scholars have intimated that urban and regional governments adopted increasingly active roles in relation to economic and political integration after the EC adopted the subsidiarity principle in the Maastricht Treaty of 1992, which statutorily recognized the right of subnational levels of government to be represented in its policy-making process. This injected municipalities with impetus to participate on the European stage by forging transnational partnerships and lobbying in support of a generic urban policy.[27] Municipalities governing "second cities"—and especially those located in stagnant regions like the West Midlands—were encouraged to apply for European structural funds[28] to finance local regeneration and retraining programs. By entering formalized networks of public- and private-sector organizations, employing European liaison officers, and establishing lobbying offices in Brussels, municipalities like Birmingham bypassed the central government in their quest to secure resources and promote a modern, vibrant European identity. The Europeanization of local government further transformed urban governance by introducing transnational spokes to municipal policy-making.[29]

Yet this tradition of municipal engagement on the European stage predated 1992. Indeed the principle of subsidiarity was enshrined by the municipalities themselves in their charter on local self-government, published in 1985 under the auspices of the Council of Europe. Indeed, British membership of the EC in 1973 had an immediate impact on local authorities, especially in implementing and monitoring the plethora of EC regulatory legislation, the great bulk of which stemmed from its harmonization program. To offset the inevitable costs in time and money, membership wielded significant benefits in the field of regional policy.[30] Since the late 1960s the European Social Fund (ESF) (established in 1960 to improve employment prospects for workers affected by structural economic change) and the European Investment Bank (established in 1958 to provide loans or guarantees for EC investment projects) had made funds available for local authorities in the field of housing and labor markets. In addition, following negotiations with the British government to "offset the burden on the balance of payments imposed by the common agricultural policy," a European Regional Development Fund (ERDF) was established in 1975 with the aim to correct "the structural and regional imbalances which might affect the realization of economic and monetary union." This fund coordinated member states' regional policies by providing ring-fenced funds from the EC's own resources to stimulate economic development in stagnant industrial regions.[31]

The absence of any regional tradition within Britain meant that the larger metropolitan authorities took advantage of the resources available. However, strict qualification rules meant that authorities had to be granted Assisted Area (AA) status by the British government before they could apply for assistance. Following years of intensive lobbying, Birmingham secured AA status in November 1984, which automatically "unlocked" EC funds.[32] The ICC project, in particular, was a major beneficiary of ERDF funds since the city council stressed the regional benefits of the development: job creation and the diversification of the regional economy. Following a protracted application period, the ERDF agreed in 1986 to contribute 35 percent of the ICC's cost. The council had initially applied for 20 percent only.[33] By 1987 the city had secured £78 million from the ERDF, which covered important projects like Phase III of the Aston Science Park (1988). Resource transfers across national borders were an important aspect of transnational municipalism in Birmingham, with the council boasting of its "thorough expertise in this area of activity" and insisting that it would continue "to maximise the uptake of available EEC aid."[34]

With the further expansion of the EC into southern Europe during the mid-1980s, the regional discrepancies in economic development were further sharpened. The expansion of the structural funds in 1988 was chiefly targeted toward those Objective I regions whose development lagged behind other member states, most notably in Spain, Italy, Greece, Portugal, and the Republic of Ireland.[35] However, the reorganization and expansion of the structural funds also centralized resources available for economic development into a single scheme—the Integrated Operation (IO)—open to all regions but specifically those with Objective I or II status, the latter embodying those declining industrial regions. In 1989 the West Midlands was designated an Objective II and III region, the EC recognizing that it suffered from high levels of deprivation and structural unemployment.[36] The culmination of years of "intense lobbying," Objective II opened the floodgates for funding assistance during the 1990s. The West Midlands was second only to the North West in the allocation of funds in aid of British economic development.[37] Moreover, with the support of EC Commission President Jacques Delors, Birmingham was the first British municipality to receive an IO, a significant five-year cash injection of £203 million matched funding.[38] And despite the regional tone to the regulations, the city inevitably benefited greatest from the support available. Within the West Midlands as a whole during 1986–89, for example, Birmingham secured 75.9 percent (£72.9 million) of ERDF allocated funding, while between 1984 and 2002 more than £500 million of European matched funding was invested into the city's regeneration.[39]

Birmingham's experience in securing European funds demonstrates the opportunities for regeneration available to municipalities prepared to go beyond national budgetary constraints in seeking alternative funding streams. Under increasingly prohibitive domestic constraints, municipalities tapped into the European scene. In so doing, municipal politicians entered a new political environment through which they developed skills in coalition building and lobbying, shared in a common pan-European regime, and exchanged experiences with municipalities facing similar difficulties in making the transition into the postindustrial society. Of considerable importance to these structural funds has been the fact that "the government does not have total discretion over how these funds are allocated," which protected municipal autonomy in setting selection criteria and evaluating project applications.[40] The important role played by the EC in fostering transnational municipalism since the early 1980s cannot be underestimated.

Thinking and Doing Transnational Municipalism

Birmingham had long recognized the benefits of pursuing an aggressive transnational municipalist approach toward fulfilling its economic development strategy. The council's powerful Economic Development Committee similarly audited the ramifications of membership in the single European market and of the implications of EC legislation for local businesses and regulatory regimes governing social policy, health and safety standards, procurement, and pollution control: "Your [Economic Development] Committee recognises the growing importance of the EC as a catalyst for change in the economic market structure of the member states and as a potential source of funds for economic development in Birmingham." It had even taken the positive message of membership to the city streets, organizing a "Europe 1992 Week" in June 1988 to prepare the community for entry into the Single European Market.[41]

Many of the city's transnational activities involved simple place promotion techniques to sell the city overseas and at home. The city was redesigned and repackaged in order to improve its cultural and physical image, to make it a more liveable city, while simultaneously boosting its economic profile. The creation of new iconic architecture such as the ICC and NIA, the planning of decorative open spaces such as Centenary Square, and the provision of public art such as Anthony Gormley's "Iron Man" (1993) and Raymond Mason's fiberglass sculpture "Forward" (1991) captured the essence of the council's vision of how it wished Birmingham to be portrayed.[42] These were the "municipal cathedrals" of the late-modern age, capturing a vision deliberately designed to put Birmingham back on the municipal map. And it succeeded. The brash, commercial flavor of late-modern urban flagship architecture emphasized the council's ambition to become a European city—a place to meet for work and leisure in a global marketplace. This followed the similar fashion of its late Victorian counterpart, which—through the design of its Renaissance-style Council House (1874–78), the Gothic-spired Chamberlain Memorial (1880), and Victoria Square (1901)—celebrated the city's prominence within municipal circles, and revelled in the spectacle of late Victorian municipalism.[43] Similarly, Centenary Square marked the symbolic connections between the late Victorian municipal golden age and the late-modern municipal revival by linking the redeveloped district with the Victorian heartland, while simultaneously celebrating the city's centenary. Here was a municipality that reveled in asserting its independence from the central state, that did not solely depend on central government handouts to realize its ambitions: "The fact that we are getting so little Government help means that the efforts to help ourselves . . . are doubly justified."[44]

The council's key decision makers were acutely aware of their enterprising heritage and traded on the Chamberlainite memory in their relations with overseas actors. In so doing they were portrayed as "the inheritors of Chamberlain," a small clique of politicians who set the local agenda and represented the city on the international stage.[45] Birmingham's transnational municipalism established and reinforced the connections between the past and present. In effect, by drawing parallels with its Victorian predecessor, this strategy re-established Birmingham as a leading influence in municipalism. Most well known was Richard Knowles, the Labour leader of the council (1984–93), whose pragmatic approach toward regeneration ensured that Birmingham avoided the intense partisan fights that dominated politics in other municipalities. But it was Albert Bore, "a technocrat by profession and . . . a tycoon by temperament," who was responsible for driving Birmingham's rebirth on the international stage.[46] As chairman of the powerful Economic Development Committee (1984–93), Bore authored and championed the city's first economic development strategy in 1985. The central tenets of Bore's strategy were to revitalize manufacturing industries to regain global competitiveness, diversify into tourism and high technology, capitalize on the city's regional dominance by developing its service sector, and mobilize the city's workers through training and community development.[47] As such, the strategy was carefully written to fit with the EC's criteria for awarding grants to stagnant industrial regions: it emphasized the regional economy, and how the city fit into the region's future growth; it recognized the need for change by flagging up the desire to diversify; and it stressed the importance of human resources, striking a chord with the ESF's social policy. The strategy evidently demonstrated Bore's acute knowledge of the opportunities available from Europe and his willingness to redirect the city's radar overseas. By asserting the links between the city's regeneration and its need to attract public investment, Bore thus established the EC's structural funds as a core part of the council's economic strategy.

Although the economic strategy was formative in establishing a purpose to the city's regeneration, it prepared the foundations for additional strategies to coordinate regeneration across the spectrum of local services. In so doing, it established a common location in which to implement this strategy: the city center. Thus, although it was two years before the council published its official city-center strategy, the decision to develop the ICC to the west of the Victorian quarter all but reversed Birmingham's postwar policy of decongesting the center of people and economic activities. The strategy emphasized the twin pillars of environmental quality and accessibility in making the core a welcoming place for residents and visitors alike. Its objective, to recreate the center as an integrated whole, lacked clear long-term policy goals, though.[48] Bore's response, in collaboration with the chairman of the Planning Committee and the leader of the Birmingham City Action Team, a quasi nongovernmental organization, was to hold two symposia to devise a pragmatic strategy. These symposia, held in 1988–89 at Highbury, the former home of Joseph Chamberlain, captured the symbolic link between past and present some "100 years since Birmingham was formally designated a city."[49]

An invited group of distinguished "thinkers and doers"[50] comprised representatives from Birmingham's civic governance, national figures (including urban planners and architects, and financial experts), and a small clique of nine overseas experts, carefully selected for their experience of regeneration.

Four were land developers from the United States (two from Maryland and one each from Chicago and Washington, DC); the others were Professor Peter Jockwsch, an architect based in Kassel, West Germany, which was itself being transformed into a convention city; Rotterdam's head of planning, a city which had similarly embraced modernist planning and was now seeking an alternative strategy; the general manager of Nikken Sekei, a Japanese architectural practice with expertise in flagship developments; and David Mackay, one of the architects behind Barcelona's Olympic Village (1985–91).[51]

The symposia coalesced around the city's ambitious vision to create "a truly international city."[52] The key lesson learned was that community support was critical, since "[f]or Birmingham to succeed as an international city it has first to become a more popular place with its own inhabitants"—that is, a bustling city center offering a range of services to people of all kinds: "The lessons from city centres which have successfully transformed their roles, such as Baltimore and Barcelona, and to some extent Rotterdam and Chicago, are to follow strategies which balance the interests of local people and outsiders."[53] By recognizing that the city needed to plug yawning "market gaps" in the range of retail facilities available, good pubs and restaurants, and public open spaces, the symposia concluded that although Birmingham was no longer "the workshop of the world," it "stands on the brink of establishing a much wider role," in which it would operate "on a European or even global scale."[54] Moreover, by striking a balance between local and international interests, Birmingham exhibited the key characteristics of a *glocalized* city by asserting the local nuances of the global movement of people and capital.[55]

Transnational Municipalism as Logistics

During the 1980s, municipalities gave a higher priority to local regeneration in tune with the process of globalization. More than that, to secure sustained municipal advantages, municipalities prioritized their political representation at the supranational level. By the mid-1980s transnational municipalism in Birmingham had thus taken on a political dimension to complement its economic strategy. With the EC slow to develop an urban policy interest before the mid-1980s, criticisms were leveled at its geographic and psychological distance from the vibrant local motors of economic change. Regional and agricultural interests were high on the political agenda, but municipalities were absent from making the case for a more directed urban policy supported by subsidies to tackle the underlying structural problems they faced.[56]

While the move to create a more cohesive macropolicy foundered, during the mid-1980s a number of "second cities," including Birmingham, began to meet to share their experiences of running cities. At the first such meeting, convened by Rotterdam City Council in 1986, the delegates discussed the theme of the city as "the engine of economic recovery," and considered coordinating resources under an umbrella body, through which they would debate common problems and lobby the EC on urban policies. The title of "Eurocities" was adopted at its 1989 Barcelona congress, at which its innovative POLIS network was also formed to coordinate urban transport policies. By 1991 the now institutionalized club had its own office in Brussels serviced by a small secretariat, with a president and executive committee.[57] In the field of policy learning, the priorities of municipal decision-makers were officially transnationalized: municipalities recognized that they could learn from each other's experiences and, in so doing, coordinate action strategies for securing a more direct influence over European policy. Indeed, by discussing a broad range of topics at their annual conferences—ranging from local democracy and civil society, the quality of the urban environment, to job creation and economic policy-making—Eurocities emphasized the complementarity between economic development, environmental justice, and labor mobility in the transurban knowledge society. Reflecting the emergence of the era of multilevel governance, the vehicle for urban reform was increasingly driven by larger bodies organized on a supranational level rather than traditional bilateral city relationships.

This is not to suggest that the continuity of transnational municipalism had been severed, though. The connections between Eurocities' core group of Birmingham, Rotterdam, Barcelona, Lyon, Frankfurt, and Milan shed light on the embedded nature of transnational municipalism by the mid-1980s. Birmingham, Lyon, Frankfurt, and Milan were all officially twinned with each other and, in some cases, had cooperated in the fields of municipal policy learning, economic promotion, and cultural exchange since the 1950s. Birmingham and Lyon originally signed an "Entente Amicale" in 1951 to mark Western Europe's entry into the new era of peaceful rapprochement by forging "a closer relationship between our two countries and thereby to an ever increasing better understanding," but equally so to cement relations between the two cities.[58] Civic exchanges in ensuing years were generally dominated by technocrats, while local companies exhibited in each city's annual trade fair.[59] The signing of a tripartite twinning between Birmingham, Lyon, and Frankfurt in 1966,[60] which involved reciprocal visits to each city, was heralded with a joint visit to the West Midlands to inspect the near completed inner-ring road. Milan, which was initially expected to join the network in 1971, finally sealed its membership in this elite clique in 1974.[61]

Although the initial flurry of policy learning between the twins dissipated during the 1970s, with the main thrust of the "Entente Amicale" shifting into educational connections,[62] by the early 1980s, relations were re-ignited by the economic transformations faced by each partner: Birmingham's ties with Frankfurt, for example, received special attention in late 1982 when a civic delegation met with German bankers and industrialists to sell the city as "an Industrial and Commercial centre," while promotion weeks were held in local department stores to generate tourism between the two friends. Similar attention was paid to the links with Lyon and Milan.[63] Later twinning agreements, signed with Leipzig (1992) and Chicago (1993), had similar economic motives: a confidential report identified Leipzig as an "enormous" market with advantages for securing jointly funded projects through its status as an Objective I region; while Chicago promised lucrative commercial opportunities in the American Midwest.[64] Into the 1990s, relations with Lyon and Frankfurt remained strong: the former was targeted as the main focus for raising Birmingham's profile as a centre of business services, while the latter remained the city's point of entry into Germany's financial markets and relations with the European Investment Bank. Moreover, Birmingham's fortieth anniversaries with Lyon in 1991 and Frankfurt in 1994 were publicly celebrated as historic examples of Birmingham's transnational municipalism, the latter marking the beginnings of a successful Christmas Market.[65]

Notwithstanding these clear economic motives behind twinning and the fostering of a political voice on the European stage, the creation of a political strategy behind Birmingham's transnationalism during the 1990s merged the policy influences of Eurocities' membership with the promotional aspects of the city's management. With the shift in emphasis toward multi-issue policy groups like Eurocities, Birmingham aligned itself more closely with European municipalities rather than its British counterparts, adapting the models and strategies employed in cities like Lyon and Barcelona to suit local conditions and pooling resources to orient a fledgling European urban policy. Its main organizational resource in this strategy originated in the establishment of a crossdepartmental Joint European and International Policy Sub-Committee (JEIPSC) in 1995. Devising a single European and international strategy for the city in April 1996, the JEIPSC identified one underlying objective to take the city into the new millennium: "To participate in international networks as a means to secure funding from, and to influence policy development in, the European Union."[66] Effective participation in international networks was, therefore, a means to an end in securing economic and political resources.

Seizing the promotional initiative, the city council negotiated with the British government for the ICC to host the G8 Summit in 1998, at which the council, led by Bore, hosted a civic reception for heads of state. Promoted as the "People's Summit," numerous cultural events took place against myriad local architectural backgrounds—Victoria Square, Chamberlain Square, Centenary Square, the City Museum and Art Gallery—which finally heralded Birmingham's worldwide exposure.[67] Moreover, on the eve of the summit, the lord mayor hosted the Summit of the Cities at Highbury to raise the profile of cities and assert their contribution to the development of macropolicy initiatives. All eleven invited cities—Barcelona, Chicago, Congqing, Frankfurt, Johannesburg, Leipzig, Lyon, Milan, St Petersburg, Toronto, and Yokohama—attended and agreed on a common urban-policy agenda that emphasized "shaping, influencing, encouraging and enabling developments" through four overlapping areas: the imaginative use of resources and partnerships, expanded public participation within policy making, greater crossborder coordination of urban affairs, and better support from national governments in nurturing city initiatives. Reporting on the promotional success of the summit, the city's chief executive claimed that Birmingham was now "justifiably recognized as a major city with a significant European and wider international standing,"[68] and so it was.

Conclusion

The idea of municipalism—that is, the ongoing autonomy and integrity of municipal structures, traditions, and powers—and the meanings attached to it link municipalities across the oceans. By establishing formal contacts across national borders, cities like Birmingham have demonstrated the scope of transnational municipalism in shaping the regeneration of late-modern cities. Although many of the place promotional strategies employed by modern municipalities—and especially by resource-hungry ones like Birmingham—have attracted criticism for lacking depth, the empowerment engendered by tapping rich resource bases like the European Commission and the convention market have provided clear tangible benefits to cities undergoing structural transformation.

Birmingham's transnational municipalism challenges the conventional view that local government, and especially British municipal government, has been in perpetual decline since the late 1970s. In identifying a strong sense of continuity in transnational municipalism, and also in the interconnections between the late Victorian and late-modern city council, this chapter supports Trainor's recent contention that "it is time to discard the language of 'decline' in the analysis of British urban governance."[69] Some large municipalities adapted to the constraints imposed upon them during the 1980s by establishing new priorities under visionary leaders. Where once municipalities had not interfered in local economies, those governing older industrial areas turned their functional attention to economic regeneration. In so doing, they switched their allegiance from traditional central-local government funding relationships to new multilevel partnerships involving private enterprise and, at the transnational level, EC initiatives like the European Regional Development Fund.

Birmingham's accomplishments in the workshop and council house continue in modified form. No longer "the workshop of the world," Birmingham is now presented to the world as Europe's Meeting Place. Albeit self-referential, a city's promotional activities are important all the same, especially since its image requires constant re-alignment. Birmingham is more than an international city, in which it participates in the global economy and faces up to the same challenges faced by cities across the planet. It is also a transnational city, one that has actively forged the transnational flows and networks that were created and defined in the fluid economic and political environment of the municipal world. Moreover the continuity of such transnational links challenged the view that the transformative effects of globalization created a new stage in the capitalist process and fractured the history of the urban world into neatly delineated industrial and postindustrial ages. The adaptive capacity of municipalities, in responding to and shaping change, in seeking and establishing new relationships with other municipalities, suggests that transnational municipalism played a more important role in governing late-modern cities than has hitherto been recognized.

CHAPTER 8

Mayor Edward I. Koch and New York's Municipal Foreign Policy, 1977–1990

Jonathan Soffer

Democratic mayoral nominee Ed Koch wanted a public showdown with Jimmy Carter when the president came to New York to endorse him in October 1977.[1] Koch believed that Carter had made "a complete sellout of Israel" by pursuing a joint declaration with the Soviet Union calling for a multilateral Middle East peace conference in Geneva, which aimed at the creation of a Palestinian state. As Carter disembarked at the LaGuardia heliport to meet the press, Ed Koch was there with a surprise: a letter that he had already distributed to the media surrounding the president.[2] Photos of the event show Koch eye-to-eye with the much-shorter Carter, who was standing on a platform. Incumbent Mayor Abraham D. Beame, a former bureaucrat who was famously orthodox when it came to political manners, looked up at them uneasily; his eyes were focused on the letter. The mayoral candidate had been scheduled to drive back into the city with the president. Instead, Carter stranded him on the tarmac.

Koch's display of *chutzpah*[3] helped him keep the loyalty of some conservative outerborough Jews who were slowly moving toward his main opponent, Mario M. Cuomo. Cuomo's campaign had some success at labeling Koch as an elitist Manhattan liberal with TV commercials dissolving his face into that of his congressional predecessor, John V. Lindsay, and by covertly queerbaiting him with the slogan "Vote for Cuomo Not the Homo." Before the incident at the airport, Cuomo vied with Koch to make the strongest criticism of Carter's policy on Israel. Koch's crass but canny confrontation with Carter showed him as tough, countering Cuomo's attempt to effeminize him.

Municipal foreign policy can have a significant effect on presidential elections and on federal-state relations. During the president's reelection campaign, the administration mixed up its political signals and the U.S. delegation voted for a United Nations (UN) resolution that seemed to challenge Israeli "stewardship" over Jerusalem. Carter, who was already under attack by Democratic presidential challenger Senator Edward M. Kennedy for "holding pro-Palestine positions," immediately repudiated the vote, but political damage had already been done.

When Carter, anxious about the outcome of the election, summoned the mayor to the White House, Koch took full advantage of the situation, bargaining with the president for increased federal aid to New York in return for the mayor's political help with Jewish voters. Despite their deal, the meeting increased Koch's contempt for the president, whom he now considered "incompetent."[4] Carter later wrote that the mistaken UN vote "was a direct cause of my primary losses in New York and Connecticut and it proved damaging to me among American Jews for the remainder of the election year."[5] Koch formally endorsed Carter but did everything he could to help challenger Ronald Reagan, partly on foreign-policy grounds, partly because he thought that good relations with Reagan would help the city.

American urban politics has sometimes been wrongly envisioned as the bottom of a hierarchy with the president on top, the state in the middle, and the city on the bottom. Paul Peterson's famous treatise *City Limits* begins with the sentence, "Too often cities are treated as nation-states," and develops the argument that foreign policy is outside the realm of local politics. The U.S. Constitution itself was drafted to make the national government the sole actor in foreign relations.[6] Conversely, Jane Jacobs has gone so far as to claim that all economic relations are interurban, rather than international, and that national economies are just a statistical construct. Saskia Sassen has moreover argued that "sovereignty has been decentred and territory partly denationalized"—that this "reconfiguration is partial, selective, and above all, strategic."[7]

The history of Koch's municipal foreign policy suggests that external relations initiated and administered at the municipal level are central to the politics and economy of New York City, and that they are in greater tension with the U.S. constitution, which seeks to federalize all foreign policy. Koch is best known for the sort of flamboyant statements outlined above, remarks that pleased himself and were sometimes popular among his ethnically diverse constituents. What is less understood are the ways in which he professionalized the city's foreign policy, by appointing deputy mayors for economic development who saw coordinating New York's role in the global economy as fundamental to their jobs, or funding the Commission on the United Nations, with a full-time commissioner who was well connected in Washington and had professional diplomatic skills. These policy professionals worked to re-orient the city's politics and economy to the new realities of global competition that began with the collapse of the Bretton Woods agreements in the early 1970s.

Although the foreign relations of municipalities has generally been a marginal concern of urban historians in the United States, it is time to move the inquiry to the center in order to better understand the role of city governments in the complicated process of reconfiguring sovereignty. New York in the globalizing era of the late 1970s and 1980s is a good place to start, because Mayor Koch was by interests and background self-conscious about having a municipal foreign policy that fit both with the neoliberal vision that gained strong currency among a portion of New York's financial community and with the nationalist aspirations of some of the city's many ethnic groups. Heidi H. Hobbs has argued that the 1980s were a period of "unprecedented growth" for municipal foreign policy, but in the case of New York City, there is a considerably longer history.[8]

The Congressman, the Mayor, and Foreign Policy

Koch's 1977 mayoral victory, following the Carter incident, made him one of the leading Jewish politicians in America. His clash with Carter set the tone for twelve years of municipal foreign policy marked by populist disrespect for the niceties of diplomacy, which his first biographers described in a chapter called "Around the World in 80 Insults."[9] One of his biggest targets was the UN, which had been an object of his suspicion particularly since November 1975 when the General Assembly passed Resolution 3379 declaring that Zionism "is a form of racism." He regularly insulted the institution, at one point declaring that he hoped the UN's headquarters remained in New York, "because every country needs a cesspool."[10]

Despite his own diplomatic amateurishness, designed to appeal to voters' ethnic and nationalist sympathies that paralleled his own, Koch actually professionalized New York's municipal foreign policy.[11] He considered that New York's future lay with its increasing role in the global information economy, as opposed to its shrinking role in the national industrial economy. Koch's formalization of the agencies for conducting the city's foreign policy was new, but the idea that the city could act autonomously from the federal government on foreign relations was not.[12] The first mayor locally to conceive a conscious municipal foreign policy was Ed Koch's greatest hero, Fiorello La Guardia (served 1933–44). The "Little Flower" is generally considered the inventor of the modern mayoralty in the United States; through mastery of media he made the mayoralty a metonymy for the metropolis. Rarely at his desk in city hall, he tirelessly travelled to fires, funerals, events, toured city agencies, and axed gambling machines, all in the name of promoting efficiency and extinguishing corruption.

A former American consul in Budapest, Trieste, and Fiume, Mayor La Guardia delighted in exchanges with the New York consular corps and became so famous for his denunciations of Nazism in the 1930s that he drew torrents of verbal condemnation from Nazi propaganda minister Joseph Goebbels. After the assassination of a German diplomat in Paris provided the pretext for the famous anti-Jewish pogrom of November 9, 1938— Known as Kristallnacht—La Guardia announced that the German consulate and other German property in New York would henceforth be guarded by Jewish policemen.

Ed Koch idolized La Guardia: he even got city hall carpenters to put the 1.57 meter (5' 2") Little Flower's desk on stilts so that the 1.85 meter (6'1") Koch could use it in his office.[13] He also admired and imitated La Guardia's view of the mayoralty as a job that was global in its scope.[14] Koch's background in foreign policy before he came to the mayoralty is significant, though not as extensive as LaGuardia's. Nor did he possess the Little Flower's skills with multiple languages. Koch was never a foreign-policy professional and rarely tried to behave like one. But foreign relations were his passion from a young age. When Mayor La Guardia was denouncing the Nazis, Koch was in high school debating one of his few African American classmates on the question of whether the United States should intervene in World War II. Like La Guardia, Koch favored intervention before Pearl Harbor. Koch became a combat soldier in the European Theater of Operations, and his first experience of municipal government was in postwar Germany, where he presided over de-Nazification in a small Bavarian town for the U.S. Army Civil Affairs Division.[15]

Koch's attitudes toward foreign policy were rooted in his family background. Some of Koch's family had lost their lives in the Holocaust; others had survived and gone to Israel. He kept contact with his Israeli cousins and in 1948 volunteered with his sister in an organization to promote independence for the State of Israel.[16] His father, Louis, was a furrier with a small shop employing his brother Bernie and sometimes one other worker. When thugs from the Communist-oriented Furriers' Union ransacked his shop and roughed him up, "my uncle Max [a bootlegger] had to come and get him out, basically because he had a gun," Koch later recalled.[17] Where La Guardia had accepted Communist support, Koch's foreign policy was dominated by his strong and lifelong anti-Communist beliefs, perhaps influenced by his father's brush with the Furriers' Union, though at the time, New York unions across the political spectrum employed goon squads.

Koch was first elected to Congress in 1968 as a liberal anti-Vietnam War Democrat from the wealthy Upper East Side—a stronghold of moderate Republicans, most notably Koch's predecessor, John Vliet Lindsay. But by his first year in Congress, in part because of the shock of the open anti-Semitism he faced there, Koch became a kind of Jewish exemplar, a reaction to his alienation from, and desire for acceptance in, the white male Christian-dominated House. Koch also found that his own deeply held beliefs dovetailed with his political interests in gaining political support through advocating the national causes of Jews, Greeks, and other diasporic communities in New York. He also learned when to keep quiet, to court the House leadership, and to forge unusual partnerships with conservatives like Barry Goldwater, Jr. By 1975, at the start of his fourth term, he was appointed to the powerful House Appropriations Committee, which approves all federal expenditures, and to its subcommittee on Foreign Operations, which controls most of the money that the United States spends abroad.

Much of Koch's mayoral foreign policy had its roots in his congressional experience. In both jobs, his overriding goal was to ensure American support for Israel. Contrary to popular conceptions of Jewish congressmen, Koch says that he had relatively little contact with the American Israel Political Action Committee (AIPAC), the leading lobbying organization. He maintains that AIPAC never lobbied him (other than sending him their newsletter), "because they didn't have to."[18] Moreover, as the leading pro-Israel congressman of his day, Koch had direct contact with the highest levels of the Israeli government. By the time he was elected mayor, he was personally acquainted with Golda Meir, Abba Eban, Ariel Sharon, Menachem Begin, and many less famous Israeli officials.[19]

Koch perceived his support for Israel as intertwined with ideals of universal human rights. He opposed U.S. aid to Nicaraguan dictator Anastasio Somoza, and because of his powerful position on the Appropriations Committee, one of the bottlenecks through which all U.S. government funds must flow, he was able to block $3 million in military aid to the dictatorship that then ruled Uruguay. He was rather proud when CIA Director George H. W. Bush called to warn him that he might be a target of Operation Condor, the international hit squad of the Chilean, Argentine, and Uruguayan juntas.[20]

Economic Development and Municipal Foreign Policy

When Koch took over as mayor in 1978, the city was suffering a period of austerity since defaulting on its debt three years previously. The 1973 Arab oil boycott, though aimed at the United States, hurt poor countries even more than the rich and caused widespread default on loans to American banks by foreign countries. In the United States, the oil boycott worsened both inflation and unemployment, causing an unprecedented condition of economic distress known as stagflation, which according to most economic theories of the time should have been impossible and for which there was no known remedy. The New York City fiscal crisis can only be understood within the context of these worldwide economic difficulties.[21]

The situation of New York's banks was one important nexus between the world economic crisis and the local one. Major defaults by poorer nations to the same banks that were also the city's creditors led them to tighten the credit reins on the municipal government, making it difficult for the city to keep up its payments. New York State Governor Hugh Carey set up panels of business, government, and labor to prevent the city government from going bankrupt, which would have given a single federal judge the power the run the city. The remedy they proposed was an austerity program that disrupted city services and capital investment, and damaged the city's agency and infrastructure for an entire generation.

When, in the fall of 1975, President Gerald R. Ford initially threatened to veto a bill for federal financial support as a component of the plan to avert the city's bankruptcy, the New York *Daily News* famously headlined: "Ford to City: Drop Dead."[22] The city appealed to Europe for help at the first G5 summit in November 1975. Investment banker Felix Rohatyn, who had been assembling a financial rescue package for the city, persuaded Federal Reserve Chair Arthur F. Burns to ask French President Giscard d'Estaing and German Chancellor Helmut Schmidt, in Ford's presence, what they thought of the possibility of a New York City bond default. As Rohatyn expected, they persuaded Ford that a New York bankruptcy would devastate the already ailing world economic system. The summit caused Ford to reverse course and grant the city a package of seasonal loans and guarantees.[23]

When Koch came into office two-and-a-half years later, the city's physical and social fabric was already falling apart. The crime rate was rising, and during the summer of 1977, a citywide electricity blackout resulted in widespread looting. The budget gap the incoming mayor faced was larger than predicted. Koch successfully appealed for a new round of federal loan guarantees, then made economic development one of his administration's top priorities. The city's economy had previously run on small manufacturing, but by 1978 most manufacturers had left town, causing the loss of thousands of unskilled jobs. At the time, some doubted that the city would ever be able to make itself economically viable again.

Some months into his first year as mayor, Koch persuaded investment banker Peter J. Solomon to serve as deputy mayor for economic development. Solomon had been a major player in the global economy, a partner in the investment banking firm Lehman Brothers, and later, its managing director. Close to President Jimmy Carter, he had been under consideration for chairman of the Securities and Exchange Commission (SEC). Solomon, who had no previous connection to Koch, thus served as an important bridge to Washington, DC.[24]

Along with other members of the Koch administration, Solomon believed that New York's best hope to emerge from the fiscal and economic crisis of the 1970s would be to reinvent the city as a node for mediating transnational relations, at a time when its influence in the national economy had been shrinking for decades. While its manufacturing and port functions had become relatively insignificant, the New York economy could make unrivaled profit by providing a locus for the specialized services necessary to coordinate the global economy. This was expressed in the main development strategy sketched out by Solomon and Deputy Mayor for Policy Robert F. Wagner, Jr., to concentrate the city's resources on promoting the so-called FIRE sector (finance, insurance, and real estate), the most transnationally oriented and information-based portion of the city's economy. Real estate had the additional virtue that, unlike many other businesses, it could not leave the city. The principal means of support for such development was through reductions in real estate taxes for businesses, which were frequently criticized as welfare for the wealthy but were championed by the administration as having little real cost to the city treasury.[25]

By 1983 foreign banks accounted for 20 percent of all loans made in the city and directly employed 140,000 people, according to Herbert Salzman, commissioner of the New York City Office of International Business Development, a subordinate of the deputy mayor for economic development.[26] Two years later, his office estimated Japanese commercial real-estate investment in New York at $500 million—a figure that would be dwarfed in the late 1980s by individual deals, such as the 1989 purchase of a majority share in Rockefeller Center for $846 million by the Mitsubishi Group.[27] These high-profile deals caused some jibes and exaggerated fears that New York was being bought up entirely by foreigners.[28] While the influx of foreign capital certainly helped raise real-estate values, the idea that the Japanese were buying up Manhattan in the 1980s was exaggerated: foreigners owned only an estimated 17 percent of New York office space, and by the end of the Koch administration, the Japanese holdings were less than the huge Canadian corporation Olympia & York and comparable to those of the other largest foreign investors—the British and the Dutch.[29]

However, as early as 1985, the Koch administration's Sister City Program worked to counter anti-Japanese prejudice and encourage investment. The sister-city relationship between New York and Tokyo was the first such formal agreement between New York and another major city, dating from 1960.

Such sister-city agreements were promoted by the State Department as part of its "People to People" program that began during the Truman and Eisenhower administration's efforts to promote America's image abroad.[30]

Although the New York–Tokyo relationship had subsequently become dormant, Peter Solomon discovered that there was still a visiting official from the Tokyo municipal government attached to his economic development office in 1978. Solomon took this opportunity to reinvigorate the relationship, which became a mainstay of the Koch administration's foreign policy. Solomon arranged for the mayor to visit Tokyo in 1980 on one of his first foreign trips as mayor, and Koch returned again in 1985. The Koch administration warmly greeted dignitaries such as Tokyo Governor Shunichi Suzuki with celebrations, business lunches, and New York's first-ever sumo tournament. The committee of citizens that supported the New York–Tokyo sister-city relationship during the 1980s was unusually active and chaired by Maurice R. Greenberg, the influential chair of the insurance group AIG. Extensive advertising on buses and in newspapers, organized by the city, though privately financed, promoted friendly relations with Japan.[31] Koch returned Suzuki's visit after the November 1985 election, his second trip to Tokyo as mayor, and part of a long agenda of foreign travels.

Solomon also liked to look abroad for specific redevelopment models. Although Koch's experiment with bicycle lanes in midtown Manhattan, in imitation of Beijing, was generally thought to be a failure, imitation sometimes paid dividends.[32] In one case, he took a page from the redevelopment of Cardiff, Wales, after a talk with Sir Gordon Booth, a British businessman and diplomat. The result was the Bathgate Industrial Park, originally an area of twenty-one acres of rubble in the South Bronx. Five years after it was built, the press hailed the project because it was soon fully rented and created fifteen hundred jobs.[33]

Manufacturing, however, was not to be New York's economic salvation. Instead, the city has reinvented itself as a node for coordinating the global economy, including the massive flow of foreign capital into the United States in the 1980s, which is why New York's boosters, such as Peter Solomon, increasingly turned outward for capital to spur economic growth. As Sassen puts it, "the nature itself of the leading industries in global cities strengthens the importance of cross-border networks." Moreover, she argues, it is the very dispersal of economic functions that increases the need for central coordination in a few truly global cities.[34] New York, unlikely as it may have seemed from its shabby condition in the 1980s, sought to make its function to be the capital of capitals. The municipality was an active protagonist of this trend.

Recapitalizing New York

New York is by many standards the leading city in the United States. Though it has not been the country's political capital since 1790, it has remained unrivaled as America's financial capital since the mid-nineteenth century. Its bourgeoisie developed much of the rest of the nation.[35] The location of the UN in New York, at the zenith of American political ascendancy in 1945, gave the city the opportunity to recoup as a political capital as well. And this became even more important as the city's near bankruptcy led the city's leaders to try to recapitalize New York both politically and financially. The UN was a significant bolster for this effort.

As headquarters for the UN, New York hosts one of the world's largest diplomatic and consular corps, an estimated 28,000 diplomats at the time Koch took office in 1978, contributing an estimated $450 million to the city economy.[36] The Koch administration set out early to improve their relations with the city. One of Mayor Koch's first appointments in 1978 was Gillian Martin Sorensen as commissioner for the UN.[37] Sorensen provided a discreet diplomatic counterpoint to the brashness of Koch's pronouncements.[38]

Koch gave the formerly all-volunteer UN commission new significance because he recognized the importance of the diplomatic community to trade and commerce, its economic contribution to the city as well as to the figuration of New York as the world "capital of capitals." Sorensen became the first salaried UN commissioner and reported directly to the mayor and his chief of staff, Diane Coffey.[39] Her functions were central to the city's foreign policy; she personally met every ambassador who came to the UN, knew many of them well, and often attended diplomatic functions as the city's representative. She continued programs from previous administrations aimed at helping diplomats find housing and acclimate to New York's culture, and expanded the reach of these programs to junior diplomats, mindful that many third secretaries often returned as ambassadors or foreign ministers. For this reason she saw New York's efforts to aid its diplomatic and consular corps as an important political and economic investment for the city's future. She even organized a conference to train people from other major American cities to support their local consular community.[40] When rumors began to circulate around the UN about moving to Vienna in response to Koch's attacks on the organization, Sorensen wrote an op-ed for the *New York Times* to nip the idea in the bud, arguing that economically and practically the "marriage" was best for both. Privately, she wrote to the consul general of Austria, apologizing for Koch's radio remarks disparaging Vienna, eliciting a friendly letter in return dispelling any rumors of a pending move to the Austrian capital.[41] Two years later, Sorensen was still trying to "damp down" the force of protest in response to Koch's attacks on the UN.[42]

Despite Koch's highly publicized denunciations, he was devoted to keeping the UN in New York and insisted on guaranteeing the city's neutrality as a place for representatives of all nations. Unpopular missions were frequently unable to rent quarters and faced protests from their neighbors when they tried to buy or build. When the Palestine Liberation Organization (PLO) achieved observer status at the UN and sent delegates, the mayor wrote, "I am surprised to learn that the PLO was unable to rent office space notwithstanding the fact that that organization is not held in high repute by the people of the city of New York myself included. Nevertheless, they have to be treated courteously and in accordance with the law, and they will be."[43]

When the Palestinians bought a house on 65th Street, Koch opposed a groundless lawsuit brought by their neighbors.[44] He also supported the right of the Libyan government to build, so long as they obeyed local laws (though he later held up its certificate of occupancy at the request of the U.S. State Department). In the end, despite his often harsh, hard-right anti-UN rhetoric, Koch's real policy seems to have been to mollify himself and his ethnic constituents with philippics, while maintaining the substance of New York as an open multicultural and relatively neutral place for the UN missions of all nations. He did not want the UN to go elsewhere.

Sister Cities and the Domestic Dimension of Municipal Foreign Policy

Sorensen also supervised the difficult logistical and political task of reviving New York's longstanding relationship with Tokyo (signed in 1960) and concluding agreements with four other sister cities: Beijing (1980), Madrid (1982), Cairo (1983), and Santo Domingo (1983).[45] In 1985 she convinced the mayor to fund a separate office under her authority to coordinate the sister-city program. Koch visited and received distinguished visitors from all of these cities, as well as many others in the course of his three terms as mayor.[46] Although the Beijing and Tokyo programs were driven by economics, each also had a specific connection with Koch's own political values and program.

The sister-city relationship with Madrid filled three purposes. It gave New York a relationship with a major European Union (EU) capital in a country whose economy and society were only just emerging from fascist corporatism, with huge prospects for growth. Madrid was also an appealing place to appear in a city like New York with millions of native Spanish speakers and a significant Spanish-language media complex. Perhaps these two aspects were epitomized by the chair of the New York–Madrid sister-city committee, Edgardo Vazquez, head of Banco Popular de Puerto Rico. Finally, Koch hoped to persuade the Spanish government to recognize Israel (which it did in January 1987) and met with Spanish Prime Minister Felipe Gonzalez in an effort to persuade him to do so.[47] The meeting was inconclusive, but it is possible that Koch did help break the logjam; Spain sent an ambassador to Tel Aviv a little over a year later.

The Koch administration also began a sister-city relationship with Santo Domingo, unsurprisingly for a city which at the time had more than half a million Dominican immigrants, the largest group outside the Dominican Republic itself. But under Koch this new tie was very tentative and not pursued as formally and intentionally as the others. The main benefit that came out of it—aside from a visit to the city so that Koch could increase his familiarity with Dominican affairs—was a deal to sell five used city sanitation trucks to Santo Domingo for $25,000. This was not much of a deal for the Dominicans, as the sanitation trucks, veterans of the lack of maintenance and replacement during the fiscal crisis, were due to be sold as junk for $1,500 apiece.[48]

Certainly one of the most interesting sister-city relationships was New York's relationship with Cairo, which began with Koch's 1981 trip there, in the wake of Egyptian President Anwar Sadat's landmark visit to Israel four years previously. Perhaps its most enduring result was the highly ironic postcolonial image of Koch sitting on a camel, "making like Laurence of Arabia" as the caption reads. Its political effects were minimal, though it was popular with part of Koch's Jewish base, as well with as with New York's racial minorities, to encourage the warming relations between Israel and Egypt. But Koch made the trip because Israel's foreign relations were one of his core interests, and it suggested to New York voters that their mayor was facilitating peace between Egypt and Israel. Support for Israel was undoubtedly close to Koch's heart and was not just a tactic.

A foreign policy initiative that was truly sensitive politically for Koch's reelection and driven by the demands of constituents was New York's boycott of South Africa, part of a national movement of localities dissatisfied by the Reagan administration's reluctance to confront apartheid. By 1988, twenty-three states, fourteen counties, and more than seventeen cities had divested more than $19 billion in procurements and investments in companies that did business with the apartheid regime.[49] When Ed Koch wrote to Prime Minister P. W. Botha of South Africa, urging his government "to put an end to the persecution of its black citizens and to provide for the human rights of all its people," a Koch public relations flack insisted that it was not a response to a public meeting held three weeks before in Bedford-Stuyvesant, Brooklyn, where Koch was greeted by chants that he was a "racist." At the time, few political observers accepted his denials that the letter was timed to neutralize that embarrassing incident.[50]

Koch waffled on South Africa issues until 1984, after his increasingly strong denunciations of African American presidential candidate Jesse L. Jackson had significantly sharpened racial tensions in the city. Jackson had not helped matters with his private description of New York as "Hymietown," a term derogatory to Jews. At the time, Koch was facing what was then perceived as a tough battle for a third term.[51] Though Koch is often seen as a candidate with little black support because of his law-and-order rhetoric and high-profile feuds with black leadership, he actually managed to get 41 percent of the African American vote in the 1985 Democratic primary—a substantial number. When he lost the Democratic mayoral primary in 1989, it was in part because his share of the black vote declined to 10.3 percent.[52]

During the 1984 presidential campaign, Koch had denounced Jackson for taking $200,000 from the Arab League for one of his civil-rights projects, saying that it would be equally unacceptable had Jackson's rival for the nomination, Vice President Walter Mondale, taken money from South Africans. Dumisani Kumalo, project director of the American Committee on Africa (ACOA), an organization promoting the economic boycott of South Africa, then disclosed that Koch had taken a $2,000 campaign contribution from Baskin and Sears, a Washington law firm that Kumalo termed the apartheid government's "chief lobbyist." Koch, who is very difficult to embarrass, stoutly refused to return the money, maintaining that it was defensible because he took money from a legitimate law firm, not from the government of South Africa itself. New York Governor Mario Cuomo took a similar position.[53] Around that time, Koch also declared that he would not favor an economic boycott of South Africa unless the Soviet Union, Iran, Libya, and Syria were also boycotted.[54]

Two months later, he radically altered his position and named a panel to study how to sever New York's relations with companies that traded with South Africa. It seems clear that political pressures forced the change. He made the announcement the day mayoral rivals City Council President Carol Bellamy and City Comptroller Harrison J. Goldin, both trustees of the city's employee pension fund, announced a much more sweeping plan.[55] Bellamy and Goldin, along with a controlling faction of the trustees of the multibillion-dollar fund, called for divestiture of all South Africa–related stocks within five years, "except for those firms which meet a strict standard of active opposition to apartheid." Koch probably judged the political fallout from opposing divestment could harm his re-election chances. The *New York*

Times's editorial board commented that "it's hard to avoid a wan smile over New York's City Hall auction of the high ground from which to denounce such racism."[56]

It was politics and persuasion from his friends, perhaps. More than that, though, Koch realized that the Reagan administration's policy of "constructive engagement" with the Afrikaner Nationalist government was on the wrong side of history.[57] The panel, consisting of high-level Koch administration officials, reported in mid-July and called for divestment of pension-fund investments in some companies doing business in South Africa, estimated at $2 billion of the $23 billion of assets held by New York City's five pension funds. The committee also called for modification of city contracting practices to ban purchases from South Africa and from some companies doing business there, and to "look for other ways to express solidarity with black South Africans who were trying to end Pretoria's policy of apartheid."[58] Koch endorsed its recommendations, another example of how he could surpass his reputation for improvised and inconsistent foreign policies. In this case, he allowed a policy process with significant deliberation by a number of people, rather than relying on his own reading and personal reactions. Characteristically, he used his power over public space to help demonstrate the new policy, renaming the corner in front of the South African mission to the UN at 42nd Street and Second Avenue after Nelson and Winnie Mandela.

Koch jumped into the anti-apartheid fight with energy and reaped the benefits of national publicity in photo opportunities with Coretta Scott King, Andrew Young, Jesse Jackson, and other black leaders before his 1985 re-election campaign in which he ran against Bellamy and an African American candidate, Assemblyman Herman D. Farrell. Divestment is one of the clearest interests where Koch used municipal foreign policy to further his own cause with New York voters, in this case African Americans and liberals. In August 1985, the city council passed Local Law 19, which among other provisions, prohibited the city from depositing money with banks if they sold Krugerrands, underwrote South African government securities, or made most types of loans to the South African government. It had a quick effect: companies, including banks, took the boycott legislation "very seriously," wrote city-housing commissioner Paul Crotty in an internal memo to the mayor's office.[59]

Even though economists dispute the effects of South Africa divestment, the city's political action was not inconsequential. After New York announced its divestment policy twenty-eight other municipalities and the state of Maryland followed suit. The boycott had a real effect, forcing numerous companies to reassess their links with South Africa, with AT&T, Bell & Howell, and General Electric withdrawing in early 1986, in response to a new wave of municipal laws, including one in New York City that would have cost them millions in sales by prohibiting purchase of goods from companies doing business in South Africa.[60]

Koch continued these efforts to stop apartheid even after he overwhelmingly defeated his opponents in the September 10, 1985, primary, co-organizing a "national day of mourning" with Dr. Benjamin Hooks, executive director of the NAACP. Then he almost blew it all with a cranky anti-Communist outburst when invited to a UN panel on apartheid. Questioned by Soviet and Bulgarian members of the panel about what the United States and New York were doing to end apartheid, he responded by denouncing the Soviet Union for being "as bad as South Africa" and Bulgaria for mistreatment of ethnic Turks within its borders. Such self-indulgence received unfavorable press as far away as Australia. He seemed to have abandoned the idea of a broad front against the South African regime.[61]

The South Africa boycott of the 1980s may have been one of the most economically and politically effective municipal foreign-policy actions of its time. Perhaps the greatest measure of its effectiveness is that the U.S. Supreme Court found it necessary to declare municipal purchasing restrictions motivated by foreign policy unconstitutional. In *Crosby v. National Foreign Trade Council*, a unanimous court invalidated a Massachusetts law prohibiting the purchase of goods from companies that do business with the authoritarian government of Burma, holding that Congress had preempted the field for the federal government, thereby forbidding states and municipalities from imposing more stringent sanctions. Under the U.S. legal system, this means that any future attempts at municipal boycotts, such as the South Africa disinvestment will be subject to legal challenges that are likely to succeed. While the court's decision limits one of the most effective tools of municipal foreign policy, the federal government is likely to find it impossible to completely eliminate municipalities as factors in external relations, especially large cities that are major centers of international commerce.

Conclusion

Koch used a variety of means to pursue New York's municipal foreign policy. Brash attention-grabbing media statements and the deployment of New York's power to name public space and license in it were among the most important. In the 1980s he renamed streets around the UN after Israeli heroes and Soviet dissidents. In the last days of his mayoralty, after he had been defeated in 1989, Koch renamed the street in front of the Chinese Mission Tiananmen Square, after the massacre, and insulted the Chinese ambassador, urging him "to defect and seek asylum here in the United States and then to tell the truth." Weng asserted that the name change and Koch's statements were "a gross insult to the dignity of the Chinese diplomats and an unreasonable provocation against the Chinese people," yet were gleefully described by Koch as a "demarche . . . one step short of a declaration of war."[62] The State Department disavowed the mayor, and the *New York Times* observed that "Even in the context of Mr. Koch's celebrated astringency in commenting on foreign affairs—the United Nations is a 'cesspool,' the Soviet Government is the 'pits'—the current imbroglio stands out, by virtue of the harsh and personal nature of the communiqués."[63]

The boisterous finale of his administration's foreign policy obscured how Koch generally counterbalanced his verbal excesses with more technocratic ambitions to make New York a smooth-running world city. Beneath his mushroom clouds of rhetoric, Koch fostered a steady, long-term policy that included careful encouragement of foreign business and investment, support for the diplomatic corps, and hospitality for the UN. Ed Koch was no diplomat, but the real measure of his foreign policy was that he appointed people with significant international experience like Deputy Mayors for Economic Development Peter Solomon and Kenneth Lipper, both investment bankers with wide international contacts and experience, and UN Commissioner Gillian Sorensen, a consummate diplomat with important national and international political connections. This was not always an easy job. As Solomon put it, "the job of a deputy mayor was to protect Ed Koch from himself."[64] Such moves ensured that New York's municipal foreign policy would be run with a steady hand, not just a big mouth.

CHAPTER 9

The Municipal Making of Transnational Networks

A Case Study of Montreal's Twinning with Shanghai

Yon Hsu

Crossnational links between cities as the circuits of globalization have been broadly envisaged from the macro scale. For example, John Friedmann's world-city hierarchy and Saskia Sassen's global cities focus on a selection of top-ranking cities, their close connections in facilitating and commanding global flows, and their obtained global/world status.[1] Even though this approach helps us to grapple with the roles played by transnational firms, financial bodies, immigrants, global media, or even cities themselves, it neglects the effervescent looser connections between non-first-tier municipalities.[2] In addition, research on intercity networks often relies on statistical indicators in constructing general frameworks of connections.[3] Nevertheless, the quantitative approach offers few insights into the ways human agency is played out.

This chapter provides a case study of Montreal's twinning with Shanghai in order to penetrate the making of intercity networks through the joint consideration of structure and agency. The focus will chiefly fall on the twinning from Montreal's end. To tease out the actors' own experiences of their participation, fifteen interviews[4] were conducted with senior municipal officers under the Pierre Bourque administration (1994–2001) as well as with leaders

I would like to thank Greg Nielsen and Kathy Allen for reading earlier drafts of this article. This research was funded by the Fonds pour la Formation de Chercheurs et l'Aide à Recherche, the Culture of Cities Project, Major Collaborative Research Initiative, and Social Sciences and Humanities Research Council of Canada.

from business and Chinese communities who participated in the twinning process. The interviews were further verified with archival data and news reports[5] in order to articulate whether interviewees' accounts were rhetorical self-justification without empirical evidence. This is particularly acute when it concerns advantages and disadvantages of the municipal making of inter-city networks.

Transnational Networks, Entrepreneurialism, and Globalizing Cities

Long before being studied under the rubric of globalization, transnational networks were woven at the turn of the twentieth century.[6] Alliances between cities especially mushroomed after World War II for war relief, reconciliation, and peace. Before the 1980s, economic factors had less influence over the nature and direction of transnational intercity networks. Nevertheless, the situation gradually changed during the 1980s when municipalities started to relaunch transnational networks as a means to boost their cities' competitiveness, to find niche markets for local businesses and to generate economic spin-offs. The latter was especially important for Western-Chinese connections because China's economic reform in 1979 required the modernization of know-how and simultaneously dressed the country as a promising land for capitalist development. Thus, when Chinese municipalities embraced intercity networks in the 1980s, their Western counterparts saw the chance to develop projects that promoted local enterprises. This transformation corresponded to the rise of urban entrepreneurialism and gave municipalities an opportunity to develop international strategies.

The transformation of urban governance, as it shifts from urban managerialism to urban entrepreneurialism, has been widely discussed.[7] Simply put, it marks a transformation of cities from a stronghold of the welfare-state system to an outpost of capitalism. This shift subjects urban governance to the logic of competitive economic development and speculative investment in place making. This ongoing transformation first corresponds to the difficulties in maintaining the macro economy of cities, securing the provision of welfare programs, or providing a safety net for those outside mainstream public or private care. It further responds to the global trends of turbulent and flexible economic environments, the excess supply of labor markets, and fluid flows of capital. The general consequence is that urban governance is no longer geared toward taking off the rough edge of capitalism. In contrast, municipalities sharpen up the economic edge in the language of survival, competitiveness, or distinctiveness as ways to globalize cities.[8]

Urban entrepreneurialism in the spirit of neoliberalism has so far been embedded and embodied in downloading (passing tasks without necessarily transferring funds from central to local government), downsizing, privatizing, and innovating flexible ways of governing cities. While conjuring up the desire to integrate cities into global economic flows, neoliberal entrepreneurialism also incarnates through international activities. Using Charles Rutheiser's term, it is also about "imagineering" the global relevance of cities.[9] Central to urban entrepreneurialism is not only the privatization of the public sector but also the promotion of its economic advantages. The encapsulation of neoliberalism in urban governance, often conceived as the facilitation of economic competitiveness, serves as a universal driving force for both Eastern and Western municipalities. This drive is attuned to the strategic interests of global capitalism, intervening in the supply side of the local economy, promoting specific economic sectors, and defining the strengths and qualities of cities. Municipal overseas spending and international projects are often justified through generating economic spin-offs for urban development. Compounded by the hope of creating new global cities, the success of urban entrepreneurialism is also measured by the extent to which cities obtain prestigious global status or fulfill irreplaceable functions in commanding global flows of human and financial capital and knowledge resources.

For municipalities acting as global entrepreneurs, the task of globalizing cities automatically requires them to step out of given local boundaries. The cliché "think globally and act locally" is insufficient, as municipal officials also need to "think locally and act globally." In other words, they not only need to arouse international awareness of their city's distinctiveness but also local awareness of their international reputation, visibility, and significance. They try to cultivate governing capacities beyond the given municipal boundaries as the means to respond to external, or "intermestic," challenges and opportunities. According to Robert Beauregard, local officials "cannot be confined to defined places but must be able to roam across political boundaries, as need dictates, and additionally, through collaborative endeavors that thereby provide another mechanism for responding to the multitude of (particularly external) actors who shape their communities."[10]

Branching cities out, making them known to the world, and bringing the world to cities thus require municipal officials to become entrepreneurs and facilitators. It gradually becomes a municipality's routine and responsibility to lead trade missions, to compete to host international events, to make sister-city arrangements, to develop cooperative schemes with other cities, to promote strategic economic sectors, and to find niche markets by exchanging information with other municipalities.

David Harvey argues that the nature of urban entrepreneurialism lies in the nonzero-sum competition between cities.[11] This argument is valid as we witness competition between cities to host sports events, conventions, and point-of-access or gateway statuses. Nevertheless, creating a "win-win" situation through intercity cooperation is also on the rise. As the main consultant for Montreal's intercity activities during the Jean Doré administration in the second half of the 1980s, Panayotis Soldatos also advocated strategic city alliances by suggesting that not just any city can be included in another city's network. Such alliances, according to Soldatos, should be based upon specific characteristics in order to allow exchanges of urban managerial expertise and the circulation of knowledge.[12]

One Montreal official, who participated in a standing committee on foreign affairs and international trade held by the Canadian Parliament in 1995, bluntly stated that, "I believe most [of our activities] facilitate the marketing efforts of our companies where there are potential markets."[13] As an entrepreneurial measure, creating or maintaining transnational networks tends to downgrade unmarketable cities in the global economy. This in turn explains why Shanghai was chosen over Lyon, Boston, Bucharest, or Hiroshima as Montreal's preferred sister city, since it entailed all the potential and promise to become the next commanding center of the global economy. This was especially the case where Shanghai's own globalizing processes involved large-scale construction projects, which could be translated into business for Montreal-based companies. It further explains why the Montreal government openly endorsed Beijing's winning bid for the 2008 Olympic Games over Toronto. As a government official explained, this was not only because Toronto has been a long-term rival but also because Montreal-based companies in the fields of construction, engineering, urban design, horticulture, and transportation may possibly share a piece of the Beijing Olympic pie.[14] This, as it will become clear, was partially based on the extended political network built up by the Bourque administration between Shanghai and Beijing.

My interviewees certainly echoed this grand narrative about the motives behind the Montreal-Shanghai tie. One of them, working for the city's public-works department, exchanged professional knowledge with his Shanghai counterpart in the construction of the Montreal Garden in Shanghai. When asked about the significance of undertaking tasks in Shanghai, the simple explanation was: "If you are not somewhere, you can't be seen. When ten million visitors from Shanghai go to Century Park in Pudong [the fast-paced developmental area of Shanghai], walk through the Montreal exhibit and visit Montreal virtually, via video camera recordings [about life] on St. Catherine Street, there is visibility."[15] Another Montreal official, responsible for the city's economic development, explained the necessity in leading trade missions to Shanghai and elsewhere: "we have no choice but going out [of the municipal boundary]. If we don't go, we won't survive and stay competitive. Even the World Bank says that."[16] A third high-ranking official, responsible for the city's cultural affairs, argued that "we knew Shanghai is going to pass over Montreal. . . . For urban development, nowhere in China or even in the world is comparable with Shanghai. . . . We started to have a sense of crisis. We must get a firm grip on Shanghai. . . . If we help Shanghai today . . . Shanghai will help us out one day."[17]

Justification for undertaking overseas tasks was expressed in the emotive tones of urgency. Like many municipal institutions turning themselves into international actors, the interviewees resorted to a supranational authority (the World Bank), calculated benefits from the rising status of Shanghai in the global economy, and mobilized the "buzzwords" of international visibility and economic competitiveness. In short, their motives and the ways they situated the role of municipal transnational networks are generated from the discourses of urban entrepreneurialism and measured by the standards of globalizing cities. Municipalities have no choice but to undertake the roles of global entrepreneurs and facilitators in seeking the common good for their cities, which are no longer guaranteed by the Keynesian mechanism of welfare states.

Municipalities are not, however, simply reacting to the international environment nor are they subjected to the entrepreneurial imperative. Reactions differ from city to city as municipal participation in globalization and the creation of transnational networks are ongoing processes where local characteristics and resources are involved. Each network also tends to create economic and political spaces characterized by local conditions and distinctiveness in aspiring for certain controlling functions or access to niche markets. The creation of these spaces is also intertwined with fears of misrecognition or under-representation. The municipal making of transnational networks thus involves complex and tangled motives rather than simple bottom-up or top-down forces. It typically involves an interpenetration of different social spheres rather than the simple "nesting" between the global and the local. Examining those economic and political factors specific to Shanghai and Montreal that shaped the ways both cities developed their networks since the 1980s illustrates this argument.

Montreal's and Shanghai's Economies in the 1980s and 1990s

Chinese municipal governments were keen to undertake diplomatic roles after the Chinese central government announced an open policy toward Western capitalism and modernization in 1979. When Deng Xiao Ping reassured this direction of national development in 1984, more Chinese-Canadian twinning agreements were signed: Edmonton with Harbin, Vancouver with Guangzhou, Calgary with Daqing, Saskatoon with Shijiazhuang, and Montreal with Shanghai.[18] Prior to Montreal, Shanghai had already signed agreements with other port cities like Osaka, Rotterdam, and San Francisco.[19] Shanghai approached these cities with the hope of recouping from the damages and distortion of the Cultural Revolution, which turned China into an economic disaster. As a metaphorical locomotive for China's industrialization, Shanghai particularly hoped that opening up to the capitalist world would ease the heavy burden of revenue sharing with the rest of China. The repercussion of this practice was that it was difficult to invest in the maintenance and improvement of urban infrastructure. When, therefore, the high policy of diplomacy concerning ideological discrepancy was not under the jurisdiction of municipalities, twinning was ideal for Chinese municipalities to open up to the West and to embark on the journey toward modernization and capitalism.

In 1992 the Chinese central government granted Shanghai special status, allowing it to fully embrace the economic reform. Nevertheless, the more autonomous and empowered Shanghai government was under increased pressure to accelerate urban development in order to become the metaphorical dragonhead of China's march into globalization.[20] Shanghai's accelerated development unfolded in the expansion of the city's scale, the transformation of its population structure, in the urban landscape and infrastructure, and through investment growth. Thus, since 1992, there has been a demand for changes in municipal management for the satisfaction of a good business clientele, which also falls under the logic of urban entrepreneurialism.[21] Simultaneously, there is a continued demand for international expertise to redress Shanghai's inexperience in handling rapid urban transformation. If the Chinese city wants to catch up it needs to take advantage of international experience, especially from successful cases. As stated by an interviewee who participated in some large-scale development projects in Shanghai, "it is very good for foreigners in Shanghai. They value our opinions and they want to learn our ways of doing things."[22]

Montreal continued to be preoccupied during the 1980s with its declining position as the foremost trans-Atlantic point-of-access and the shrinking "of its national market. This resulted from, among others, the westward and southward shifts of economic activities within North America, the rising importance of air and road traffic, growing competition from newly developed countries, oil crises, economic recession, and disadvantageous governmental policies. According to the report commissioned by Laurent Picard in 1986, these governmental policies included freer trade and the

Canada–United States Auto Pact of 1965, which benefited southwest Ontarian cities, especially Toronto. The federal policy of the borderline also hit Montreal's petrochemical industry, which lost its Ontario market. The building of the St. Lawrence Seaway also diminished the role of the Port of Montreal, especially as the point of grain transshipment. The provincial policies that disadvantaged Montreal's economy included inimical labor legislation to investment, higher income taxes and wage expenses, and the French language charter. Both federal and provincial governments were also criticized for dragging major issues under their jurisdiction and thus wasted regional energies concerning Montreal's development.[23]

Facing its declining metropolitan status, and as one of the first Canadian metropolises to experience large-scale economic downturn, the Montreal government—under the leadership of Jean Drapeau (1954–57, 1960–86)—was concerned with ways of maintaining and re-enforcing the city's economic vitality and importance. As a result, Montreal pioneered Canada's international exposure. Many urban projects were undertaken, the high cost of which accounts for what Montrealers ironically call the "Drapeau legacy." These projects comprised the hosting of prestigious international events, notably the 1967 Expo, the 1976 Summer Olympic Games, and the 1981 horticultural show, Les Floralies. Meanwhile, they required grandiose construction to support Montreal's aspiration to high status and by demonstrating the city's ability to host international events, including the construction of the Olympic Stadium; the Montreal metro system; the artificial islands on the St. Laurence River; and commercial, cultural, and business complexes, such as Place des Arts, Les Habitats, and Place Ville Marie.

In addition to these structural challenges, Montreal's losing battle with Toronto has long been identified as the ramification of Quebec's pursuit for sovereignty. According to William Coffey and Mario Polèse, the complex interplay among political, social, and economic forces generated from the Quiet Revolution in the 1960s has gradually resulted in a more stringent cultural, linguistic, administrative, and tax environment for business operation.[24] Quebec's uncertain political climate and the tensions with English Canada resulted in Montreal losing its principle economic hinterland to Toronto. The remaining Montreal-based companies exceeded the limited natural hinterland of Quebec and created non-Quebecois economic spaces. Some were, therefore, optimistic about Montreal's twinning with Shanghai because "a huge market could be established through it. It [would] be Shanghai's bridge to North America."[25] Some even wishfully perceived that the twinning was Montreal's triumph over Toronto because this connection would eventually help to "conquer the vast Chinese market."[26]

If Montreal's economic downturn was evident as early as the 1960s, problems became acute during the first half of the 1990s. As admitted in 1995 by Mayor Bourque to Lucien Bouchard, the Premier of Quebec, it was the most distressed city in the country, and the solution was to allow the expansion of large-scale business and to support its search for foreign contracts.[27] Bourque's insistence on the damage created by "political instability" further hints at how national political struggles were central to Montreal's specific local conditions to its international development. However, was Montreal's international development subject to Quebec's sovereignty movement? Judging from the ways that Montreal's twinning with Shanghai were developed, there was insufficient evidence to make such a suggestion. Politically, it reflected Montreal mayoral ambitions, including Drapeau's legacy in internationalizing Montreal and Bourque's leverage of his political influence through his amassing of Chinese networks. The ways in which local economic concerns in Shanghai and Montreal were translated into twinning arrangements and major events reinforce this point.

Twinning Development

The first contact between Montreal and Shanghai was made in 1980, when the latter was invited to participate in Montreal's international horticultural exhibition, Les Floralies, the following year. This was probably one of the first occasions in which Shanghai had direct contact with a Western city since China's Communist Revolution in 1949. In the end, Shanghai won third prize and the delegation donated its entry of *penjing* (bonsai) to Montreal to express its gratitude. Thereafter, horticultural expertise was regularly exchanged as Montreal needed to learn the techniques of tending to *penjing*, while Shanghai was eager to learn about greenhouse construction and maintenance. Les Floralies, and the subsequent horticultural exchanges during the early 1980s, led to Shanghai's proposal for an official twinning relationship with Montreal in 1984, with the agreement signed the following year.

Mayor Drapeau emphasized that twinning was Shanghai's initiative, implying that Montreal was not interested in using Shanghai to advance Quebec's protodiplomacy for sovereignty.[28] It is possible to subject the twinning to the national framework when Shanghai's proposal was made before Premier René Lévesque's trip to Hong Kong and China to promote Quebec's economy, and the positive response of the Montreal government was handed to the Mayor of Shanghai by Premier Lévesque personally. It is, however, difficult to judge if the involvement of the Quebec sovereignty movement's most prominent figure gave the impression that the twinning was part of his plan to promote Quebec's political status overseas, or if the twinning initiative was signed after much controversy over whether the federal government disapproved of his visit to Shanghai in 1984.[29]

Horticulture was undoubtedly the foundation of the Montreal-Shanghai connection, though, and it became the catalyst for consolidating their expanded networks during the late 1980s. As director of the Montreal Botanical Garden from 1980 to 1994, Pierre Bourque invited Shanghai to Les Floralies in 1981. It was not until the Chinese Garden in Montreal was opened in 1991 that he assumed a key role in the twinning, though, through his insistence to carry out the project, which earned the trust of the Chinese. In his autobiography, Bourque stated that he was able to receive the letter from the federal government in order to persuade Mayor Jean Doré, Drapeau's successor, that the continuation of the horticultural project did not undermine Canadian federal sanctions against China's brutal crackdown in 1989. Bourque further discussed how the Chinese treated him like a brother and appreciated his support when the Chinese suffered from world isolation, after he was the only Westerner on the plane to Shanghai in the autumn of 1989.[30]

Although government remained the biggest employer and social actor in China, business opportunities were often intertwined with personal friendships and official patronage. For example, Mayor Bourque introduced a Montreal-based landscape company (William, Asselin, Ackaou [WAA]) to the Shanghai government to win the competition for designing and executing Yanan Zhonglu Park at a strategic point of Shanghai's downtown core in 1999.[31] This firm received further contracts in Shanghai and elsewhere in China. Likewise, S. N. C. Lavalin was involved in a waste-treatment project for consultation, and Dessau Soprin, another engineering firm, introduced a river-treatment project when Shanghai sought urban managerial know-how from Montreal. With the endorsement of the Montreal government, Bombardier bid for Shanghai's mass-transit development and its Chief Executive Officer was later invited to sit on the Shanghai government's foreign-advisory committee. Bombardier also secured a contract to build regional jets for Shanghai's sister province, Yunan.[32] Even the construction of the Montreal Garden in Shanghai in 1999 was not simply about the symbolic friendship between the two cities. This large-scale horticultural cooperation played an economic role in introducing Montreal companies to China. Montreal's twinning activities—from the exchanges of municipal managerial know-how to the construction of a large-scale garden—were explicitly geared toward the pursuit of economic spin-offs back home.

By the time Bourque became mayor (1994–2001), the twinning relationship had intensified in the belief that the networks built up over time would lever Montreal's economy after the 1995 referendum on Québec sovereignty.

That is, Shanghai's booming economy and the constant demands for large-scale public works required Montreal to give Shanghai advice on urban development. In turn, it helped the former to identify opportunities and then create a foothold for local business in establishing a firm grip over Shanghai's risky investment environment. The contents of the twinning programs between Montreal and Shanghai fell into the areas of horticultural exchanges, urban management, trade missions, and some cultural events, which suggests that this agreement served practical purposes to address local concerns in both cities.[33] For example, Shanghai in the 1980s was interested in seeking advice on basic urban infrastructure, such as telephone lines, garbage collection, and sewage treatment. Since the 1990s, twinning also reflected Shanghai's inability to handle more complex urban managerial know-how, such as converting underground spaces from military to commercial use, green-space development, subway construction, river treatment, multimedia and wired cities, the auditing system, and archival management.[34]

The exchanges on civic infrastructural projects shared a fine line with urban entrepreneurialism, especially considering that Montreal's offers of technical know-how to Shanghai addressed its own local economic crisis. The link with Shanghai was regarded as a strategic acquisition of Montreal's internationality at the end of Mayor Drapeau's legacy. It was less the case that Montreal built an international reputation for horticultural or botanical tourism, with the most impressive *penjing* collection outside of China. Yet the significance of forging ties with China's economic powerhouse went beyond horticulture. In Mayor Drapeau's own words, "I'm closer to the end of my career than to the beginning. I'm not interested in just taking trips for the pleasure of it."[35] This was significant because Drapeau held a conviction that echoed urban entrepreneurialism: "[t]he world must not forget Montreal. . . . Even Coca-Cola and cigarette companies, which have been around for decades, spend millions advertising their products. . . . They spent millions so people got into the habit, and keep spending so people don't forget. That's what we must do."[36] This message otherwise conveyed an implied anxiety that "the world is forgetting Montreal" because of its economic decline.

Political Leadership

It is difficult to separate economic and political motives in twinning. Nor is it easy to separate agency and structure in the municipal making of intercity networks. Mayor Bourque's role in the creation and intensification of the Montreal-Shanghai tie is accordingly worth special attention. All the interviewees overtly admitted that the intensified connection with Shanghai emerged from his personal interest in Chinese culture. A government official who accompanied Bourque on several trips to Shanghai emphasized that "Shanghai gave Bourque a lot of inspiration to act [back home]."[37] More precisely, Bourque's development of Chinese networks was an opportunity to cultivate his political leadership in Montreal. Bourque lacked Drapeau's ambitious visions that had shaped Montreal's outlook since the 1960s. Nor did he possess Doré's progressive projection of the city. Since Bourque's leadership lacked Drapeau's charisma or Doré's idealism, he therefore needed to define his own leadership and create his own legacy. In doing so, he singled out his capacity as an ambassador for Montreal, as someone able to save Montreal from economic downturn, and as a globetrotter who would put Montreal back on the world map.

As a result, the Bourque administration actively made transnational networks, including twenty-two twinning arrangements; the promotion of Montreal's film industry in Los Angeles; visits to the World Bank; and trade missions to cities in Asia, Europe, Latin America, and the United States. He was also vice president of the Metropolis organization, a transnational forum for common concerns and challenges to cities with populations of one million and larger. Montreal's twinning with Shanghai was intensified during Mayor Bourque's two mandates through leading trade missions at least once a year.

Montreal's making of transnational networks, in general, and its twinning with Shanghai, in particular, thus required Mayor Bourque to play what Howard Elcock called the ambassadorial and reticulate roles of local leadership.[38] The first role requires the mayor and his administration to represent the city. This role is about promoting the city as a desirable place to live, work and visit. By taking up this role, the mayor and his administration took substantial executive responsibilities in their involvement in negotiations. The importance of playing an ambassadorial role lies in the occasion in which the mayor can extend his networks or improve his relationships with actors in other political agencies. That is, the mayor needs to play the second role of reticulist and develop networking skills to manage increasingly complex intergovernmental relations, as if his position were at the center of a vast system of actors. Consequently, the reticulist role requires the cultivation of networking capacity to offer or share information with others, to remain at a central location in his government where information resources can be accessed easily, to encourage coordination of various demands through established channels, and to develop additional networks. Since multiple networking has become common practice for local political leaders, the mayor is required to be knowledgeable about the structure of intergovernmental relations, formal and informal networks, and political costs and benefits.

Simultaneously, the mayor needs to show interest in other cultures, taste for mobility, and linguistic curiosity as personal attributes.

Bourque played both roles in building up his entrenched networks with Shanghai's government and extending them to Beijing and elsewhere in China. The extended network to Beijing was possible for two reasons. First, the Shanghai administration was a major source of recruiting political leaders into China's central government. Jiang Zemin served as Shanghai's mayor prior to his roles as chairman of the Central Military Commission and president of the People's Republic of China, for example, whereas Zhu Rongji was also mayor before taking up various important positions in the Chinese government.[39] Second, Bourque's attaché, Wen Qi, whose father was Chairman Mao's official photographer, extended his interpersonal networks in Beijing to Bourque, according to a Montreal official who is close enough to reveal Qi's personal background.[40] In his autobiography, Bourque also mentions that "[Qi] opened up many doors for me in the Forbidden city . . . where I met Mr. Li Lanqing, the Vice Prime Minister of China. . . . I was also able to meet many ministers, governors, senior bureaucrats in the areas of justice, science, environment, culture and sports."[41]

Mayor Bourque and his administration also played the reticulist role between other governments in Quebec and China. His role as gatekeeper to China, his privileged knowledge of, and connections with, Chinese economic and political centers could not be matched in Quebec. Bourque mobilized his contacts to help the Quebec government's trade mission to Shanghai and other regions. Albeit expressed in an exaggerated tone, an interviewee who helped out in Team Quebec argued that "[t]he premier asked the mayor to help him to go to Shanghai in 1997. The mayor did. They went there with hundreds of companies. Bouchard could not go to Shanghai without Bourque's support."[42] Premier Bouchard certainly could visit Shanghai, but Bourque and his administration undoubtedly acted as facilitators to ensure a warmer visit.

In Mayor Bourque's estimation, Bouchard's visit to the Chinese Garden in Montreal in 1997—the symbolic hallmark of the Montreal-Shanghai tie—was the point at which the relations between the two political leaders changed for the better. He believed that it was in the Chinese Garden where the premier understood his affinity with Shanghai, which accounted for the financial support granted to some ad hoc twinning projects, including the Montreal Garden in Shanghai. Moreover, government officials from the other Quebec regions urged Bourque to seek Chinese political and economic contacts for their regional development.[43] In turn, making Chinese connections for other governmental agencies in Quebec helped Bourque to create his domestic political reputation as someone capable of opening the door for Quebec to the emerging Chinese market.

Problems and Challenges

The growing municipal interest in transnational networks brought problems and challenges with it, though. Most of all, Montreal's twinning activities with Shanghai were not popular locally, with the link mocked as "flower diplomacy" by vocal sections of the local media and opposition city councilors. Bourque himself was nicknamed "the Chinese mayor" (of which he was proud) to mock his absence during the beginning of the 1998 Ice Storm, while he served on the organizing committee of the International Horticultural Exhibition in Kunming. Nevertheless, such mockery was amplified by other criticisms that clearly entailed a disapproval of Montreal's international activities. An opposition councilor contested that "[r]unning off to China might sound glamorous, but the mayor should never forget how to collect the garbage,"[44] while an angry resident complained that "Mr. Bourque [could] build a garden in Shanghai, but he can't keep our city clean."[45] A Chinese community leader praised him for gaining China's trust and comprehending Chinese business and political cultures but questioned his capacity to bring "something substantial" back to Montreal, especially to the Chinese community.[46]

Montreal officials responded to these complaints by emphasizing the dilemma of balancing external and internal urban affairs. As foreign affairs had been predominately the task of central government, there was limited space and resources for the maneuver of urban diplomacy. One interviewee, whose tasks spanned both cities, argued that "the City of Montreal has a responsibility to its residents, to meet their demands, to supply services, and to offer a secure, clean, wonderful city . . . that's for sure. But the City of Montreal also has a role to represent the city at the international level and to make Montreal interesting for investors from outside . . . as well as to provide an opportunity for Montreal business to have higher visibility. The ultimate good of having a garden in Shanghai is more related to this level."[47]

The dilemma, according to Montreal's government, resided in how limited resources were allocated between internal and external affairs, given that they are two sides of the same coin. The dilemma, nevertheless, lay in the difficulty of shifting from a managerial to an entrepreneurial approach to municipal affairs. The managerial approach emphasized the well-managed redistribution of resources, the maintenance of a better quality of life, and the making of political spaces for equity and justice within cities. This meant that local critics expected the Montreal government to be "an administrative extension of the welfare state and . . . the most proximate infrastructure and social service providers."[48] When international activities did not seem to bring tangible results in a strong and immediate sense, and when they did not match the reminiscence of welfarist managerial ideals, they easily evoked controversies over a municipality's priorities. Local critics thus saw Bourque's transnational networking efforts as his pet projects serving mostly his own interests.[49]

Criticism was amplified in Montreal when the external activities were invisible or inconsequential to the everyday practices of urban life. The Montreal government attempted to make the city visible elsewhere on the globe, but their efforts were simply invisible to the city's inhabitants. This invisibility was also largely due to the lack of an institutionalized channel for constituent participation, such as a twinning committee independent from the municipal government or even from the mayor's office. In other words, there was a lack of public awareness or discursive mechanism in place to ensure the visibility and accountability of the work of cities abroad.

Indeed, institutionalizing citizen participation in transnational networks and networking was a distinctive character of urban diplomacy elsewhere.[50] In addition, the European Commission also advocates the same institutional mechanism to ensure that citizen participation in twinning activities is not diminished along with either the budgetary constraints of local government or any change in political leadership.[51] It is also a means to ensure the balance between non-profit and profitable aspects of transnational networks and networking. In a sense, the institutionalization of a twinning committee is meant to create a discursive and participatory space in which urban residents, rather than local officials, decide the orientation of municipal diplomacy. These committees are also answerable to municipal authorities, whereas local governments oversee grass-root efforts without setting an agenda for the development of internetworks and networking through twinning. In most cases the twinning committees are characterized by volunteerism based on the participation of civic organization, ethnic communities, schools, and professional or business groups.

When asked about the failure to engage citizen participation with transnational networks, a senior Montreal official defended the government's policy to reject financial sponsorship of every twinning committee.[52] This argument is valid considering the limited municipal resources that are allocated to transnational networks. However, one might question whether the funding for travel expenses to Shanghai or other parts of the world, or millions of dollars spent building the Montreal Garden in Shanghai was more meaningful for the Bourque administration than providing financial resources to the encouragement of institutionalizing citizen participation in foreign affairs.

The other explanation for the low level of citizen engagement is that—regardless of how his leadership motivated and united his administration to passionately engage in the intensified relations with Shanghai—Bourque's aspiration to return to Drapeau's ruling style did not welcome the spread of power by institutionalizing a committee of international activities. As Katherine Graham and colleagues explain, the 1994 election not only brought Bourque into power but also returned Montreal to Drapeau's autocratic governing style.[53] For Bourque, citizen engagement through institutionalized channels would simply increase the bureaucratic processes of international affairs, and this was certainly against his regard for a lighter municipal bureaucracy. Downsizing and budget cuts in the spirit of urban entrepreneurialism went hand-in-hand with governmental flexibility and innovation in attracting capital through transnational networking. Bureaucratic processes and institutionalized citizen participation would have crippled their implementation. Furthermore, when there was no possibility to have Chinese citizen participation in twinning, such a committee was accordingly unnecessary. It might even be liable as citizen participation could contest the twinning agreement in the name of human rights.

The accountability of Montreal's twinning was thus questioned. For example, there was no fixed budget allocated to international affairs. Consequently, there was no budget limit when it came to overseas travel expenses, as long as the executive committee granted the approval. In 2000, the travel expenses reached $778,600.[54] When asked about the amount of contracts brought back from Shanghai, only vague answers were given. One interviewee stated that "journalists always liked to ask us 'how many contracts were signed' after our trips [abroad], but we cannot expect the effects right away from a long-term project [like twinning]."[55] Another official bluntly admitted that the exact figures on the economic spin-offs generated from twinning were unknown.[56] The accountability of the Montreal-Shanghai relationship was even more questionable when those Montreal-based companies awarded the project to construct the Montreal Garden in Shanghai were selected without a public tendering process. Even the construction of Chinese arches on Boulevard St. Laurent, which was meant to attract tourists and improve Chinatown's economy, were criticized as beneficial only to the district's merchants at the cost of the prevailing consensus of building a Chinese cultural center, or of social housing for the most marginalized unilingual Chinese elderly. No matter how urban diplomacy is justified as a global trend of urban governance or as a local response to economic crises, the price tag and the ad hoc basis caused the critics to cast doubt on Montreal's twinning.

These problems echo the assumption of Susan Clarke and Gary Gaile that globalizing cities preclude the practice of local citizenship, as in the 1990s local officials tended to select urban policies that did not necessarily encourage citizens to sustain the social and economic resources to participate in an accessible and accountable local governance. Reinventing urban government, while restoring urban citizenship, has been an exigent normative demand for the city's democracy.[57] Disappointingly, what we have observed here is the erosion of citizen participation in decision making and the political marginalization of urban residents. In the case of Montreal's twinning with Shanghai, a parameter of inclusion and exclusion was set to welcome certain types of citizen participation. When the Montreal government was positioned to create political and economic spaces for the local business community, this also implies that economic actors gained more power and access to the municipality's making of transnational political and economic networks.

"The people from Montreal," to be precise, were people of the local business community. Most Montrealers were left behind in the decisions of what types of twinning activities in which they might be interested, let alone Falun followers who wished to share with the mayor their political views on human-rights violation against this spiritual group under Jiang Zemin's leadership.[58] The repercussion of building transnational networks as an entrepreneurial measure is, thus, the rise of economic citizenship. In Sassen's terms, economic citizenship "does not belong to citizens. It belongs to firms and markets, particularly the global financial markets, and it is located not in individuals, not in citizens, but in global economic actors" who seek maximized profits in the shortest term.[59]

Although Montreal's twinning with Shanghai was marked by a lack of institutional accountability, the rise of economic citizenship, a low level of constituent participation, and a high suspicion of the return of the autocratic governing style, it further faced the problem of sustainability. In fact, it went dormant right after Bourque's electoral defeat in 2002. The newly elected mayor, Gerald Tremblay, showed no strong interest in maintaining the Chinese networks.[60] Montreal's twinning with Shanghai suddenly became insignificant to politics in Montreal. The lack of institutionalization or citizen participation eventually made the transnational political and economic spaces between Montreal and Shanghai ephemeral.

Conclusion

Illuminated by the case of Montreal's twinning with Shanghai, this chapter has singled out the importance of understanding the motives of city halls going abroad to build new networks with foreign municipalities. Montreal's twinning with Shanghai was propelled by local, economic/political, and structural/agency forces, and there is no evidence that it was subject to Quebec's sovereignty movement. Nevertheless, it could not be decontextualized from Mayor Drapeau's promotion of internationalism since the 1960s, as a result of the transformation of the international political economy and the changing political dynamics between Canada and Quebec. In addition, the intensification of the Montreal-Shanghai tie (and Montreal's engagement in other transnational networks) during the 1990s cannot be understood without considering Mayor Bourque's personal interests in China and his aspiration to build a political legacy as the mayor who repositioned Montreal toward China, the new center of the global economy. This attempt to define political leadership should also be understood within the intergovernmental context in which Bourque mediated between China and Quebec.

The final part of this chapter turned to the problems and challenges of building transnational networks through urban diplomacy. Repositioning the city in relation to the emerging Chinese global city was pitched as increasing Montreal's visibility and carving out transnational economic spaces for its local business community. The entrepreneurial approach underlined by the neoliberal logic was mingled with local aspirations to escape the economic slump and walk free of the political shadow of the 1995 referendum. However, as expressed in local criticism, Montreal's transnational networks, while opening the door to the global economy, wrestled with local aspirations for better and more tangible municipal services and fairer social justice.

When this dilemma could not be worked out satisfactorily, the discontent of urban diplomacy and transnational networks was amplified. Repercussions included the absence of bottom-up constituent diplomacy, the lack of accountable and institutional mechanisms to ensure the sustainability of transnational spaces created by urban diplomacy, and the rise of economic citizenship, which benefits those who are already advantaged the most. Compounded by the neoliberal demands for flexible, innovative measures for creating or accumulating urban competitiveness, and by returning to an autocratic ruling-style, those transnational political and economic spaces created by the Bourque administration were uneven, unstable, and transient. These factors further contributed to the sustainability of the municipality's transnational networks.

This case study demonstrates that intercity networks are not simply woven by transnational firms, financial institutions, immigrants, or global media. Municipalities have also eagerly transformed themselves into active players in the global economy. This eagerness to seek international exposure, status, and importance in the process of globalization is commonly achieved through fierce intercity competition to host international events or organizational headquarters, as well as attracting capital investment and human resources. This chapter nevertheless provides an understanding of how cities are globalized through cooperative mutual support and exchanges between non–first-tier cites. Montreal's twinning with Shanghai further shows that twinning has been transformed from its traditional symbolic significance of friendship to mutual economic advantages between cities since the 1980s. Finally, this chapter has helped to identify the macro and micro factors in twinning and to understand how global trends and local conditions interpenetrate each other in the making of intercity networks. Through a microscopic view of actors' motives and their engagement in urban international affairs, this approach not only infuses our understanding of global networks with a sense of lived experiences but also teases out how agency, especially political leadership, cannot be ignored as it contributes to the specific characters of intercity networks.

CHAPTER 10

Latin American Municipalities in Transnational Networks

Reforming Municipal Government in Rosario, Argentina, and Montevideo, Uruguay, in the 1990s

Silvia Robin and Sébastien Velut

L ong distance connections are not new for Latin American municipalities: in fact, many cities were founded as nodes for the global networks of the Spanish and Portuguese empires in the sixteenth and seventeenth centuries. European influence also materialized toward the end of the nineteenth century, when several city planners traveled to Latin American cities to inculcate them with urban modernity. At the same time, poor rural migrants, moving from southern Europe to Argentina, Brazil, and Uruguay, created their own original urban life through the interbreeding of imported and native urban practices. These exchanges contributed to keeping overseas connections alive, particularly with Europe.

Transnational networks enjoyed a renewed importance from the late 1980s. Under predominantly democratic regimes, Latin American countries shifted from state- and nation-centered models of development and political relations to more open ones, in which international influences were allowed to filter. Simultaneously, decentralization increased the autonomy of municipalities in various aspects of urban policy, which subsequently became involved in international relations, or what has been termed "paradiplomacy"—that is, the diplomacy of subnational governments.[1]

This chapter is the result of research carried out in the network "Cuenca del Plata." It elaborates on an earlier and shorter version published in Géocarrefour 80, no. 3 (2005): 207–14.

These efforts were supported by national governments and international bodies, particularly the European Union (EU) and the United Nations (UN). The former issued a document on "decentralized cooperation" in 1992, while the latter stressed the importance of local places within the logic of Agenda 21—the plan of action that emerged from the 1992 Earth Summit. New frameworks for international cooperation and development were cast, a common language was invented, and a group of influential individuals devoted their energies to subnational governments networking. This new transnational political framework saw the definition of a series of terms that permeated the activities of urban management, including "strategic planning," "urban marketing," "governance," "competitiveness," "sustainable development," and "popular participation." All of these concepts belonged to the general category of "best practices," a similarly new denomination, defined and disseminated by international bodies like the EU and UN agencies, that relied on the assumption that experiments conducted in some cities should became sources of inspiration or models for others.[2]

The Spanish city of Barcelona gained a special place in Latin America as a central reference for its effective combination of city planning and urban management. After the 1992 Olympic Games, Barcelona was presented worldwide as a success story of late-modern urban transformation, encapsulating private investment, a greater international profile, and widespread popular consensus.[3] Circulating through various channels, the strategic planning of Barcelona was replicated in more than eighty Argentinean towns and regions between 1993 and 2000.[4] But the reference was not unique, and flows did not merely run from north to south. Indeed, Latin American cities also became places of reference, particularly Curitiba and Porto Alegre in Brazil, the former for its environmental policy and the latter for its participative budget. Many of them actively engaged in transnational networks of local governments devoted to the exchange of urban-management tools and experiments.

For municipalities that sought, received, and adopted these models as solutions for their own problems, networks made the picture more complex but also more interesting. They could select different experiences from participating cities and build their own devices according to local conditions. They also participated in transnational networks on an equal footing, as peers who could contribute their own innovations and experiments, not only as recipients of information. Consequently, the benefits for municipal teams to participate in transnational networks were manifold: they discovered new ideas, adorned with an international label and some flavor of universal validity; they chose from various possibilities the option that best suited their own agenda; and they engaged fully in one of the "best practices" of the decade—that is, international networking itself. On the other hand, the great circulation of city-management models was also a source of confusion: a given model had to be adapted to suit specific needs and local conditions, but in doing so, the political meaning attached to it evolved considerably.

The Left coalitions that won the elections in Rosario, Argentina, in 1989 and Montevideo, Uruguay, the following year, exemplify this evolution. Both coalitions were responsible for running large cities (with more than one million inhabitants each in the late 1980s) and sought to demonstrate that left-wing parties were fit for purpose and more reliable than traditional political forces. Their involvement in transnational municipal networks was a major resource exploited on the path toward legitimacy. The two cities eventually became important references for the whole continent and beyond, with international awards and a recognized status of leadership. Rosario and Montevideo, whose local governments shared similar political profiles, originate from countries with polar administrative traditions. Yet both municipalities constructed and implemented innovative administrative policies, which relied on strategic planning and decentralization in order to foster political participation, gain legitimacy, strengthen urban governance, and address the challenges of a new economic order. In this process, they actively participated in transnational networks by building explicitly on methods of urban management borrowed from Barcelona and also from Porto Alegre's participative budget. It is our concern in this chapter, after a brief overview of the municipal systems in Brazil, Argentina, and Uruguay during the 1990s, to examine how municipalities in Rosario and Montevideo sifted and winnowed foreign experiments and know-how. We then turn our attention to examine some of the personal and political actors involved in this transnational networking relationship, particularly the urban planner Jordi Borja and the academic sociologist Manuel Castells, as well as the role of institutional networks. In our final section, we assess the way in which imported models were incorporated into the local agendas.

The Municipal Turn in the Southern Cone

The state-centered social structures, which characterized many Latin American countries, lost momentum during the second half of the twentieth century. Politically, this reflected the end of military dictatorships; administratively, it indicated the different states' failure to solve social problems; and, economically, it was the product of increasing public deficits, foreign debt, and inflation. A longlasting discussion about local autonomy was revived with the end of these authoritarian regimes. In Argentina, Brazil, and Uruguay, local governments were given broader responsibilities, not only as supposedly more-efficient administrative units but also as genuine cells that could breathe democracy after years of dictatorship.

As a result of institutional reforms, greater autonomy was granted to regional and local units. The Brazilian Constitution of 1988, for example, accorded a similar political status to the three tiers of government (the Federal State, Federated States, and municipalities). In Argentina, the nation-state promoted municipal responsibilities within the general legal framework of federalism.[5] In the case of Uruguay, a traditionally centralized state, its Constitution of 1997 presented a series of norms to initiate decentralization. The election of the head of local government (the *Intendente de departamento*) was separated from the national election, which introduced local issues when voting for the *Intendente*, and imbued local councils with greater autonomy.

Decentralization was justified by theorists of local development, who stated that local administration centered on locally accessible resources was more likely to induce development.[6] Several scholars have stressed the new role of cities and regions in the global economy as places where major social changes occur, but simultaneously, where wealth production takes place.[7] This assumption, grounded in the empirical evidence of developed countries, needs qualification for Argentina and Uruguay, where a substantial share of the gross national product is derived from agriculture and the cities are essentially centers of redistribution and consumption. Still, with rates of urbanization over 80 percent in both countries, cities are major political and social stages and actors.

During the 1990s, structural reforms were implemented in several Latin American countries. Privatization and lower tax barriers were the most visible part of the agenda, but it also included the devolution of policies and legal responsibilities from the national and provincial governments to municipalities, which redesigned government and governance in the process. Packaged with this ideal of the small and efficient state was the transfer of tasks and powers to local authorities. Being closer to the population and everyday social problems, municipalities were deemed the most appropriate unit to deal with pressing issues like education, health, unemployment, and also, critically, economic development. The creation of the Common Market of the South (MERCOSUR) by Argentina, Brazil, Uruguay, and Paraguay in 1991 provided the backdrop for the protagonism of local authorities.[8] This meant an enlargement of the spatial scope of cooperation and competition for both firms and local governments. MERCOSUR was conceived on the model of the EU and municipalities were logically expected to promote initiatives involving civil society in the process of regional integration. On the other hand, low taxation and trade facilities presented firms with a wide spectrum of location choices, fuelling competition between cities to attract investment.

From this starting point, ambitious designs were drawn up to make cities more attractive places for investors, wherein crucial inputs (including advanced services, technological resources, skilled labor, and highly effective infrastructure) were made available to firms. In the context of shrinking employment and fiscal resources, this had to been implemented through a re-engineering of urban governance—that is, the way in which municipal authorities interacted with private and public actors. Municipalities became places of experimentation, where practical techniques and governing procedures could be devised in order to improve the performance of the public apparatus.

To fulfill the new tasks that decentralization, privatization, democratization, and liberalization placed on their shoulders, municipalities had to rely on constrained resources. Their limited economic revenues, which relied on a meager fiscal base, particularly when urban economies underwent major crises, were a limiting factor. Other elements such as geographical location; the relationship between municipal, regional, and national governments; local educational standards; and wealth accumulation also differed from cities in Europe or North America. Political and social leaders, as well as economic actors, had to be highly creative to elaborate policies and agreements that would enable them to take advantage of scarce and quite volatile opportunities.

Rosario and Montevideo:
The Challenges of Decentralized Administration

The urban structure of the MERCOSUR countries exhibits a major imbalance between the huge metropolitan areas of São Paulo, Rio de Janeiro, and Buenos Aires—each with more than 10 million dwellers—and the other metropolises, the majority of which have populations under 2 million (with the exception of Santiago de Chile, with 5 million, and some of Brazil's regional capitals). As a consequence, Rosario (with 1.16 million inhabitants in its metropolitan area and 0.9 million in its municipal district in 2001) and Montevideo (with 1.34 million inhabitants in 2004 within its *departamento*) are important towns from a continental perspective. The social democratic coalitions that led the reforms of municipal governments were eager to prove their ability to administer large cities, showing greater efficiency than traditional political parties and coalitions. Nevertheless, they had to deal with the specificities of the national conditions, particularly the legal and fiscal limits to municipal autonomy.

In Argentina, the reform of the National Constitution (1994) stressed the importance and autonomy of municipalities. However, within the framework of Argentinean federalism, the municipal regime remained regulated by the provinces. These provinces had responsibility for setting municipal boundaries and local tax bases, as well as for defining municipal powers and competences. Consequently, each province established a municipal system regarding each municipality's functions, rights, and powers. Most of the provinces subsequently reformed their own constitutions to include articles regarding municipal autonomy, which granted municipalities the right to enact their own laws and define their own responsibilities. Yet, the five most heavily populated provinces and particularly the province of Santa Fe, in which Rosario is located, have still to enter the process. Although the provincial constitution does not expressly recognize municipal autonomy—making it impossible for local governments to define their own statutes—the definition of municipal powers is so vague that it accords municipalities the leeway to take charge of any matter deemed appropriate, such as economic and social development. Moreover, the provincial constitution makes no mention of cooperation among municipalities, therefore preventing the creation of metropolitan authorities.

Such a situation presents a problem for Rosario. This city, the largest in the province, is the functional center of an area that includes a dozen municipalities. A focus for Italian immigration at the beginning of the twentieth century and an important industrial center, Rosario has a strong radical identity and a left-wing political tradition supported by the National University. However, this central municipality has no means to coordinate resources and powers among provincial municipalities, still less an official metropolitan authority. The historical rivalry between the municipalities of Rosario and Santa Fe (the provincial capital) partly explains this impotence, alongside a clear political dispute between Rosario's local government and the provincial authority. The latter is in the hands of the Justicialista (Peronist) Party, whereas the former belonged to the opposition Radical Party (Unión Cívica Radical) until 1989, and then the Popular Socialist Party (PSP), a local movement that originated in Rosario University and is affiliated to the Argentinean Socialist Party. Most of the smaller towns within Rosario's metropolitan area are under Peronist rule. The provincial government thus perceives it a threat to either grant autonomy to Rosario or install a metropolitan government to administer the main economic and demographic center of the province.[9]

Uruguay, on the other hand, is a Unitarian state with a strong tradition of centralization. The country is divided into nineteen districts (*departamentos*), each under the authority of an *intendente* (executive) with an elected legislative assembly (*Junta Departamental*). There is no municipal political-administrative level. The 1997 Constitution introduced a series of reforms that followed a logic of "centralized decentralization," but the political elite exhibited a lack of will to press this issue forward.[10] This is unquestionably the consequence of a strong centralized political culture and a historic two-party system that has maintained itself by either crushing or absorbing local political forces.

The internal decentralization initiated by the capital city during the 1990s should be analyzed in this context. Montevideo is not only important as the capital but also because it is home to more than half the national population and 85 percent of its industrial and commercial activities. Moreover, the organizational capacity and political mobilization of its urban society differentiates Montevideo from the rest of the country. Under the responsibility of the *Frente Amplio*, a left-wing coalition elected in 1990, and the leadership of Tabaré Vázquez, the *Intendency* set up mechanisms and structures for social participation that were a true innovation for Uruguay. Its political program sought to transform Uruguay's political life by improving the standard of urban administration and sustaining a deeper level of political participation. This was deemed to be the only way to overcome the two-party system that dominated Uruguayan political culture for over a century and successfully sidelined the Uruguayan Left from power until 1990. As a first stage, the national administration emphasized civic participation and municipal decentralization, a successful strategy that led Tabaré Vázquez to the presidency of the Republic in 2004.[11] Like Rosario's Mayor Hermes Binner, Tabaré Vázquez felt that he had to devise bold solutions to urban problems in order to fulfill his political aims. This was the beginning of a series of reforms relying largely on local elements mixed with an array of imported ideas and know-how, particularly from Barcelona during the first half of the 1990s and later from Porto Alegre.

The Barcelona Model: The Making of a Brand

After General Franco's death, a new Spanish Constitution (1978) recognized the right to autonomy for "nations and regions" (Article 2), with democratic local elections held the following year. This was particularly meaningful for Barcelona and Catalonia, since it reinvigorated autonomy on the basis of a regional cultural identity, a left-leaning political culture, and a history of resistance to Franco's dictatorship since the civil war of 1936–39. These political transformations, and in particular those carried out in the region of Catalonia, coincided with the exhaustion of industrial capitalism.

During the 1980s, Barcelona, once Spain's industrial heartland, showed signs of a deep structural crisis. Pascal Maragall, an economist, member of the

Socialist Party, and the city's mayor from 1982 to 1997, launched a decisive program to transform Barcelona from the beginning of his second mandate (1987–91). The purpose was to transform the city from a place of industrial decay into a postindustrial city, a showcase for democratic Spain, which had gained full membership of the European Economic Community as recently as 1986. That same year, Barcelona was designated as host of the Olympic Games for 1992. This triggered a series of urban transformations related to the development of the "strategic planning" management device; the first documents of which were published in 1988. The Catalans then received intellectual and practical support from leading figures, such as the sociologist Manuel Castells, who became an adviser to the regional government and, subsequently, played an important part in the dissemination of Barcelona's model throughout Latin America.

The purpose and challenge was to make Barcelona an attractive metropolis, combining Spanish and European cultural identity. This was a modernity that would cater to a wide gamut of economic uses, from industrial production to service consumption. This was to be secured by applying methods borrowed from contemporary business strategy, namely goal-based strategic planning and marketing, with the use of tools such as SWOT (strength, weakness, opportunity, threats) analysis. The first social and economic strategic plan (1990) defined three main objectives that were developed in the ensuing plans.[12] Adapting its methodology from business to city planning made it possible to retain planning as a core activity for the municipality, whereas central planning had lost any credibility. It also facilitated greater dialogue with firms, since a common vocabulary was used, and underscored the usefulness of advertising aspirations and projects on city dwellers, in order to make them feel that they were part of this great transformation.[13]

Logically, the relationship between public and private actors was central to urban interventions: private firms gained a leading role in municipal administration, taking advantage of the business opportunities offered by the urban renewal process and steering the political transformation jointly with the mayor and city council. That conjunction facilitated Barcelona's integration into international capitalist circuits. Its authorities claimed that they succeeded in combining free-market economics with social welfare and political legitimacy, through a three-tier system of governance that made it possible for politicians, business, and the local community to map out the city's future.

Since then, the "Barcelona brand" has become a model, which epitomizes late-modern urban governance and planning, a model that was widely disseminated throughout Latin America and Europe. After the Olympic Games, major events with a global reach, such as the Universal Forum of Cultures (2004) and the UN urban forum of the same year, continued this strategy. In so doing, they gave Barcelona a significant place on the map. Indeed, recognition was actively sought, with the mayor, Pasqual Maragall, himself occupying several leading positions on the bodies where municipal policies were discussed, evaluated, and exchanged. For example, he became president of the Council of Municipalities and Regions of Europe (1994–96) and of the Committee of Regions of the EU (1996–98). With the city councilor, Jordi Borja, Maragall made Barcelona the prime driving force behind the creation of the Eurocities network (1986) and was elected Europe's vice president of the International Union of Local Authorities (IULA), a position he coterminously held in the World Federation of United Cities during the mid-1990s. Barcelona not only participated in municipal networks but created them as well. This was a central component of its strategy to make the "Barcelona brand" a global one, opening up lucrative markets for architects, city planners, engineers, and other local firms.

Through this active participation in international forums, and with the help of the intellectuals employed in the transformation, such as sociologist and urban planner Jordi Borja, Barcelona sold itself as an example of urban renewal in Europe and beyond. The city sought acknowledgment of its achievements by submitting applications for international awards, such as the Prince of Wales prize for architecture and design awarded by Harvard University in 1990. The effort was completed by installing ad hoc structures for the conquest of Latin America, such as the *Centro Iberoamericano de Desarrollo Estratégico Urbano* (the Iberian-American Center for Strategic Urban Development [CIDEU], 1993), a network devoted to strategic planning and to the diffusion of the Barcelona model.[14] The network gathers cities from Spain and Latin America exclusively and is supported by the Spanish Agency for International Cooperation (AECI).

Scholars argue about the existence of a "Barcelona model," stressing the absence of a complete coherence between the various approaches used to transform the city.[15] Jordi Borja, himself a key figure in this narrative, stated that the model could not be replicated everywhere.[16] Nevertheless, from the viewpoint of transnational relations between local authorities, the Barcelona experience serves as the closest approximation to an exportable model for urban governance, involving a series of procedures and methods; a team of planners, politicians, and intellectuals discussing, promoting, and applying the methods; and a global strategy of diffusion.

Porto Alegre: From Liberation Theology to World Bank

On the other side of the ocean, the new Brazilian Constitution promulgated at the end of 1988 also modified the balance of power within that country, transferring responsibilities and attributions previously centralized in the federal government toward the regions and the municipalities. It also stressed the importance of direct and indirect participation, underwriting various procedures such as the referendum, the plebiscite, and laws of popular initiative. The municipality of Porto Alegre (the regional capital of the Rio Grande do Sul state) built on these possibilities to launch its participative budget, a method involving a wide level of popular participation to define the priorities and spending strategies of the local government in order to achieve a better distribution of public expenditures within the city of 1.4 million inhabitants in 2005.

The participative budget was devised when the Workers Party (PT) won the local election under Olívio Dutra (1989–92) for the first time and was subsequently developed by Tarso Genro (1993–96, 2001–2).[17] The PT was eager to demonstrate its capacity for governing an important town in order to prepare for the election of Lula da Silva as president. The PT and its members had a deep culture of political participation, grounded in trade-union activity, as well as in grassroots assemblies inspired by religious movements but especially the Liberation Theology.[18] They were willing to transform society from the bottom up, through direct democracy. This strategy was also useful for tactical reasons: Olívio Dutra did not have a majority in the city council, thus the appeal to direct popular decision making was a way to bypass his opponents.

This conjunction gave way to the participative budget (*Orçamento participativo*), as a process whereby the financial decision would be made locally by the inhabitants themselves. The first stage involved the city being divided into sixteen districts, where general assemblies were held with the technical assistance of the municipal staff, in order to decide upon spending priorities for the following fiscal year. Each assembly provided the participative budget's technical secretariat with a ranked list of projects for the districts, including sanitation, local school or health centers, and street lighting, among others. They also selected their designated representatives, who attended the council of the participative budget, which met weekly to prepare the annual budgetary estimates and monitor the execution of the present budget. From 1994, thematic assemblies were organized to discuss transversal matters such as culture, education, transportation, urbanism, education, and health. Meetings were held with the local community in order to prepare a full budget proposal, which was presented to the city council and was usually rubber-stamped with minor amendments, since councilors recognized that the proposal had strong popular support.[19]

The participative budget proved to be an effective device in decentralizing and sharing public spending between the districts, in giving an institutional framework to popular participation, and in fostering a participative culture and social accountability. This was an important result that allowed the PT municipal government to sever links with the clientalist political culture. The participative budget also exhibited good results by improving living conditions in the rapidly growing neighborhoods.

The participative budget was gradually systematized, making it an important reference for local governments, international bodies, and political parties seeking innovative ways to rejuvenate governing practices. Although it was not conceived as an exportable device, it proved to be so from the mid-1990s. In 1996, the participative budget was distinguished by the Dubai International Award for Best Practices, a joint program launched by UNESCO and the Dubai municipality, to implement the decisions of the 1996 UN Habitat conference of Istanbul. The Dubai program was intended to create a database of local governments' "proven solutions" in order to give them a world audience. This was also a step for the PT to gain international respectability.[20]

In 2001, with the help of several nongovernmental organizations (NGOs), the municipality of Porto Alegre and the PT organized the first World Social Forum (WSF), an antiliberal forum where new forms of governance and resistance to multinational capitalism were discussed and popularized under the slogan, "Another world is possible."[21] The WSF proved to be a great success, with more than six hundred participants, and was subsequently held in Porto Alegre in 2002 and 2003, and moved to Mumbai, India, in 2004. In 2005, Barcelona hosted the Mediterranean Social Forum.

Under the umbrella organization of the WSF, a special place was given to local authorities, through the Forum of Local Authorities, which comprised 180 mayors from America, Europe, and Africa in the first event, their number growing in the following years. This forum agreed that "Local authorities should commit with the direct, democratic participation of their citizens. . . . Such efforts will entail a better and fairer redistribution of public resources." In so doing, its participants committed themselves to promoting their "recognition of the right of cities and their democratic governments to act in the political, economic and cultural life of the world. It is therefore important to maximize local alliances, as well as direct joint and collaborative efforts between cities."[22]

A clear link was made here between globalization, its drawbacks, and the need for cities to experiment and share new "best practices" of government, with a greater involvement of civil society and the support of transnational networks. As activists and municipal officers from around the world discovered first hand, Porto Alegre and its budget became famous as a central resource for the global Left and alternative political movements. This also supported the principle that global political actions had to be undertaken in local stages, particularly from the larger cities.

Barcelona and Porto Alegre gained international notoriety through different channels and circulations that were supported by local and national governments. Personal and formal contacts were facilitated through linguistic and cultural proximity. The historic relationship with Spain was explicitly kept alive, particularly by the Spanish government's cooperation policy that made the best of decentralized cooperation between local governments and took advantage of a common political trajectory. The Spanish democratic transition, which included a strong dose of decentralization, easily matched the needs and expectations derived from Latin American municipalities, which were caught in a similar turmoil of new responsibilities a few years later. Between 1996 and 2002, Spanish cooperation funded more than twenty courses and internships on different topics for the Rosario municipality. This contrasted to a single program financed by the French government. The agency of some key characters was part of the process of establishing or maintaining informal and formal networks, and feeding them with experiments and know-how in municipal governance. Their role in the success of the Barcelona brand is especially interesting as it showcases the interaction of migration, political and intellectual networks in the operation of municipal circulations, and it is on this case that we will now focus.

Characters in the Networks

Some key figures have thus played leading roles in the exchanges between Spain and Latin America, particularly the urban planner Jordi Borja and the sociologist Manuel Castells. Borja designed and implemented strategic planning in Barcelona and then became the guru for strategic planning in Latin America.[23] He advised, lectured, and consulted on the creation of many strategic plans. In Latin America, this was the case of Río de Janeiro, Bogotá, Medellín, and Puerto Madero in Buenos Aires—cities where Borja also sat as a steering committee member for their own plans. From 1989 to 1995, Borja was also president of the *Tecnologías urbanas de Barcelona sociedad anónima* (TUBSA), a joint venture between public and private partners from Barcelona and its region that offered services in urban engineering, including water facilities and networks, energy provision, and garbage collection and processing.

Close to Catalan Socialists and the Spanish Left, Manuel Castells became an adviser to the government of the Catalonian region from the beginnings of national democracy. He also held a significant intellectual magisterium for many Latin American planners, urbanists, and politicians. Born in

Barcelona in 1942, Castells had to leave Spain due to his political opposition to Franco's dictatorship. He completed his degree in France and was appointed in Nanterre, where he taught alongside important figures like Henri Lefebvre, Jean Baudrillard, and Alain Touraine. After his involvement with the May movement in 1968, Castells had to temporarily leave France, traveling to South America. *La Question Urbaine* (1973) was quickly translated into Spanish, establishing his work as fundamental reading for students in social sciences throughout Latin America. Castells was subsequently hired by the University of Berkeley, where he taught sociology from 1979 until 2003. The strong relationship between Berkeley and Latin America contributed to install Castells as a prominent figure for the continent's urban development, one who was sought out by national governments and international bodies for his expertise.[24]

Castells's focus on cities evolved from an orthodox Marxist perspective combined with a strong empirical approach in the 1970s to an overarching view of the globalization process, resulting in his series on the "Information Age" in the 1990s. In the meantime, he concentrated on new forms of urban and regional planning, grassroots movements, and the role of technology in local development, shifting from a radical to a more pragmatic perspective. He also toured and lectured extensively in Latin America to present theories on the information society, and especially the importance of technology, networks, and identities. He was not directly associated with the practical implementation of urban planning techniques, but certainly provided a strong theoretical background.

Borja and Castells joined forces in the mid-1990s to write a handbook for city management that was presented at the UN conference on human settlements in Istanbul and quickly became a reference source for city planners all over the world.[25] The work demonstrates a great ability to mix theoretical and practical approaches with an impressive empirical material, a combination that gave great strength to their views on city management. It stressed the role of cities in globalization and promoted strategic planning as a central philosophy of it, in order to create "cities with a project." The authors admitted that "the final objective [of the strategic planning] is the diffusion of the strategic thought," and the latter was clearly a success.

On a more personal level, many Latin American politicians were familiar with the Spanish situation or had contacts with Spanish, particularly Catalan, individuals as a result of their own history during the years of exile. Mexico was a meeting place, and this is where Alvaro Portillo found a haven. A member of Tabaré Vázquez's team, Portillo was born in 1948 and fled to Mexico in the 1970s, where he became acquainted with Catalan refugees. There, he added a doctorate in sociology to his initial training as a lawyer and worked in several public agencies in the fields of planning and regional and urban administration. Portillo returned to Uruguay in 1986, where he was appointed Professor of Urban Sociology at the University of the Republic. He entered the *intendency* of Montevideo in 1990, as part of Tabaré Vázquez's team, where he was in charge of decentralization and social programs.[26] Another two of Vazquez's ministers had similar histories, living for many years in Catalonia where they militated in the Catalan Socialist Party.[27]

Indeed, political parties provided venues for exchange. Rosario's Popular Socialist Party and the Socialist Party of Uruguay belong to the Socialist International, and their members participate in meetings where they have the opportunity to exchange views. The Socialist International works upon the basis of thematic committees with regular meetings, one of which is dedicated to local authorities. The mayors of Rosario, Hermes Binner and Miguel Lifshitz respectively, were very active—particularly in 2000 when Rosario hosted the meeting, but also in 2001 in Athens where Binner chaired the Conference of Local Authorities, and in Mons (Belgium) in 2004 where Lifschitz was appointed vice president of the committee. The meeting was held in Porto Alegre in 2005 as part of the World Social Forum. The Charter for Cities, governed by the Socialists, and initially framed at Athens in 2001, offered new forms of urban management as a guideline for socialist municipalities.[28]

In Rosario, the architect Mario Corea, who was born in Rosario before moving to Barcelona, was the nexus between the municipality and the Spanish urbanists. As a young architect, Corea fled Argentina, before settling in Barcelona where he was responsible for various important projects and taught at the Universitat Politécnica de Catalunya. As a personal friend of Hermes Binner, he connected Catalonian architects and planners with Rosario's municipal team. During Binner's mayoralty, Correa was a close adviser, becoming project manager for implementing Rosario's master plan in 1997 and also for two important urban renewal projects. He also played a key role in making Rosario a node of the formal URB-AL networks supported by the EU, which made the circulation of foreign experiments a keyword among Latin American municipalities. Like other characters, Correa also contributed to the expansion and functioning of the more institutional networks, especially those that are the more visible part of local authorities' transnational relations, to which we now turn.

Institutional Networks

Institutional networks are the most visible part of the interactions between local authorities and have gained a remarkable momentum during the last decade in Europe and Latin America, as well as globally. They proved to be valuable instruments for the dissemination of new forms of governance, as suggested by the case of the Eurocities network.[29] An interesting case in point is the URB-AL Program (the title being a contraction of "urban" and "Latin America"), created in 1995 under the aegis of the European commission. URB-AL's purpose was to foster "decentralized cooperation" between Europe and Latin America and to promote the exchange of "best practices" between local authorities. This was the consequence of the importance given by the European Union to decentralized cooperation—that is, international cooperation between local governments or NGOs. Networks were constituted to seize resources offered by the European Commission to fund international cooperation. In the first stage (1996–2000), funds were made available to finance thematic networks and organize meetings. In the second stage (2001–6), funds were also made available to undertake demonstration projects that built on those intermunicipal exchanges fostered during the first stage.

Local authorities thus organized themselves into thematic networks. For example, Montevideo coordinated a network on urban social policies, while Rosario established the network: "management and control of urbanization." From 2002, during the second stage of the program, Barcelona's municipal government took a more active role and coordinated the network for "promoting the role of women in decision-making bodies," while Porto Alegre became responsible for a network on "local finance and the participative budget." Each network held regular meetings dedicated to exchanges between members, under the supervision of experts. In the case of Rosario's network, the experts were Jordi Borja, the French economist and consultant Hervé Huntzinger, and the architect Mario Corea: formal networking and circulation slipped between the channels of previous connections.

The URB-AL program proved to be a great success in terms of the involvement of local authorities. From 1996 to 2000, the program involved more than one thousand entities, city councils, and other local authorities. In Latin America, local governments from all countries were eager to participate, whereas in Europe, one-third of the five hundred participants were from Spain (124), Italy (88), France (50), and Portugal (43).

In the MERCOSUR itself, the *Mercociudades Association* was conceived as a municipal version of the commercial integration carried out by national authorities. This network, like Eurocities, intended to give a local dimension to regional integration. It was fostered in 1991 by members of the *Unión de ciudades capitales iberoamericanas* (UCCI), an association of Spanish and Latin American capital cities, which had itself been created in 1982. *Mercociudades* was launched in 1995 in Asunción, reaching a membership of 180 local authorities a decade later. Rosario, Porto Alegre, and Montevideo were among the first members of the network and became responsible for working groups on social development, strategic planning, municipal management, and urban planning. Their leadership is also acknowledged by the fact that they each held the rotating executive secretariat: Porto Alegre in 1996–97, Montevideo in 1998–99, and Rosario in 2000–1. Although *Mercociudades* was distinct from URB-AL, it worked on a similar basis in being composed of a large network with thematic working groups. An agreement was signed between *Mercociudades* and Eurocities in 1999. The main documents issued by *Mercociudades* are fully consistent with the widespread discourse on local spaces and large towns in globalization. As a practical tool, *Mercociudades* organized working groups and collected "best practices" to be shared among its membership. However, for all their success, it was up to the cities themselves as to how, if at all, they adopted and adapted the models of urban management agreed on by these pioneering new thematic networks.

Adapting the Models

In Montevideo, as in Rosario, the adoption of new models of urban management was intended to signify a break from the previous municipal regimes. Both relied on a corpus of knowledge and practices, which included decentralization, important physical transformations of the built environment, and the implementation of participatory mechanisms. Decentralization primarily meant the reinforcement of municipal autonomy, but it also included internal decentralization as a step toward making the city a focus of democracy. This covered a range of measures to make the municipality more visible, accessible, and accountable in the neighborhoods. The building of administrative centers in the districts was, in the case of Rosario, part and parcel of this dual goal to change the material and political landscape of the city. Other operations included the renewal of harbor brown fields and the construction of buildings concentrated on the banks of the Paraná, for Rosario, and the Rio de la Plata, for Montevideo, respectively. This geographical focus was certainly a consequence of the availability of cheap vacant land, due to changes in port activity, but it also derived from the fact that the revamping of limited sections of the cities' former industrial areas was also part of Barcelona's toolkit, which privileged the visible transformation of that city.

The absorption of the Barcelona model was not a mere transfer, though. This was evident in the ways that Rosario and Montevideo adopted and, indeed, rejected aspects of Barcelona's decentralization experience. For Barcelona, local participation was necessary to foster social consensus. However, this has not been a priority in Rosario where, as in Montevido, the coalition of the *Frente Amplio* envisioned it as a crucial tool to reinforce political consciousness. From Barcelona, Uruguyan leaders learned the way in which public debate was organized in neighborhoods to build consensus on local projects, but also as a way to create local political spaces that would ultimately reinforce the coalition. Different aspects of Barcelona's "best practices" had a better fit in Latin American cities than others, and cities like Rosario and Montevideo adapted, shaped, and molded the constituent parts of Barcelona's model to fit local conditions. The strategies, policies, and language of "best practices" do not always translate neatly across national spaces.

Yet the Barcelona brand is more evident in Rosario than in Montevideo. Rosario's municipal authority explicitly mentioned the experience of Barcelona when they started to elaborate their strategic plan in 1994. They appointed Catalan experts to advise on the process. More symbolically, Rosario was increasingly labeled "the Barcelona of Argentina." To transform its image, Rosario used benchmark events like the international congress of the Spanish language (*Congreso internacional de la lengua española*, 2002) and launched major interventions into the built environment. Avenues were opened, while the harbor was transformed into an urban park called *Parque España*, along which expensive housing was built. Old buildings, such as the customs offices, were renovated, making it possible to trade on Rosario's historical identity and its relationship with the River Paraná.

Popular participation was not part of the program until the great Argentinian crisis of 2001, when popular discontent, directed especially against politicians, spurned municipalities into action. Local assemblies were spontaneously held, which represented a threat to political parties. In the ensuing weeks, Rosario's municipalities launched programs to foster local participation and started to study Porto Alegre's participative budget in an attempt to regain political legitimacy.

In the case of Montevideo, Barcelona's influence was also present, but Porto Alegre was a closer reference, and the political programs of the *Frente Amplio* and the PT shared many features. As a result, Montevideo's local government mainly stressed political participation and decentralization: it built institutions, such as local councils, to foster and organize popular participation, rather than premises and equipments. These institutions aimed at giving citizens greater influence over decision-making processes and providing the *Frente Amplio*'s militants with political legitimacy. The process of participatory budgeting started as early as 1990, before Porto Alegre became famous, and was consolidated by the election of local councils within Montevideo in 1993. The entire reform of urban management stressed the way in which citizens participated in the decision-making process. Thus, although Montevideo's policy-learning horizon was more localized than

Rosario's, its newfound commitment to transnational networking should not be undervalued as a major contributing factor toward its embrace of "decentralized cooperation." Sometimes municipalities do not have to travel too far to adopt and implement models and "best practices" from neighboring countries: overland networking is just as valid as its overseas counterpart.

Conclusion

During the 1990s, the protagonism of the Latin American municipalities was manifest through the circulation of references, tools, and experts. It combined the strategy of commercial continental integration, the explicit will of the local authorities to secure a place for their cities on the globalization map, and the will of national governments to strengthen the relations between MERCOSUR and the EU. Exchanges among key actors took place in horizontal and nonhierarchical networks where relations did not coincide with the rank/size or status/power order of traditional urban hierarchies. Individual lifetime trajectories, the political trajectories of countries and communities, linguistic and cultural bonds, and communities of learning played considerable roles in shaping these networks. The channels of such circulations were multiple, shifting from bonds of kinship to friendship, from business to governmental relationships, from associative networks to national and regional foreign aid policies, or multilateral institutions. The result was a certain homogenization of the language of municipal government in Latin America and beyond. This took place notwithstanding the fact that strategic planning and its toolbox were not deprived of their contradictions, and the whole set-up was not initially intended to serve the specific needs of Latin American cities, or more generally, cities of developing countries.

Nevertheless, strategic planning was adopted as the idiom for municipalities to find their way in this transitional economic and political process between a Fordist and post-Fordist economy, and between an authoritarian and a democratic political regime. The fact that strategic planning was a problem-setting, rather than a problem-solving, machine and could easily work as a self-fulfilling prophecy, certainly contributed to its success. However, national and local conditions always appear to be decisive in defining the local agenda and in choosing the specific model and its modification.

Local and national government worked better when they shared common guidelines. Municipal networks were supported by the building of the MERCOSUR, or the relationship between MERCOSUR and the European Union. The circulation of experiments was also enhanced by the involvement of the Spanish government and its foreign-aid policy toward "Iberoamerica." The transfer of "best practices" from Spanish cities to the cities of its former empire was also a conduit for the sale of private services in consultation, urban engineering, and architectural design.

On the local scene, political leaders demonstrated a great ability to select and use imported ideas and methods according to their own needs. This was a powerful source of legitimacy, when "experts" could certify that the methods applied locally were internationally proven. Yet the whole philosophy of "best practices" was misleading, since it relied on the assumption that a series of methods could be used in different contexts. This was not only because methods had to be adapted to specific contexts but also because the general meaning of those practices was transformed during the transfer: Barcelona's business-inspired methods became a standard tool for left-wing local authorities, whereas the participative budget, which was intended to make local administration accountable to local electors, became a legitimating tool for discredited politicians in the aftermath of Argentina's economic collapse.

Independent of methods and impacts, one result has thus far been an intensive search for municipal success stories and "best practices." This search has created and strengthened transnational networks funded by the municipalities, national governments, and international bodies alike. These networks allowed professionals to receive specific training and familiarize themselves with foreign management methods, contributing to a homogenization, or convergence, of municipal governance methods and vocabulary. In this networking process, the political elite and municipal civil servants harvested resources and legitimacy that proved useful for their voters and peers, making them eager to pursue that kind of exchange. As a result, municipal transnational networks acquired a self-sustained momentum, yet they simultaneously became a common stage for a homogeneous practice of urban management, losing their potential for innovation in the process.

Lost in Translation?

Mapping, Molding, and Managing the Transnational Municipal Moment

Shane Ewen

Globalization has been conventionally identified by scholars as heralding a historic rupture in city-state relations, shifting from a state-centric to a city-centered configuration of socioeconomic, political, and geographical power. Leading protagonists argue that, in the wake of unprecedented transnational and global flows of capital, trade, people, and ideas since the 1970s, "global cities" like London, New York, and Tokyo have emerged as the engines of economic and social transformation. These flows have, in turn, reshaped patterns of urban development and wealth accumulation. Globalization, then, has compressed the space-time continuum, removing cities from their territorial straightjackets and allowing them to effectively inhabit the spaces "in between" conventional national borders, through which they steer the flows of capital and information that together constitute the neoliberal capitalist economy.[1]

For those suspicious of the analytical category of globalization, or for those who question its historical specificity, the scale and pace of integration within the world economy between the 1890s and 1914 was more marked than during the past three decades.[2] Others still have identified qualified differences between early modern and modern globalization, the latter gathering pace after 1820 with the quantifiable flows of people, goods, and capital around the Western world. For Adam McKeown, if we want to better comprehend the interaction between these flows and the mutability of national borders, "only a broad periodisation reaching at least back to 1820 can account for all of these entwined processes."[3]

The historical specificity of globalization was not the core motivating drive behind this volume. Our concern with the alleged "interregional" or "intercontinental" interconnectedness of the neoliberal global economy is one of scale and unit of analysis. If historians are beginning to historicize the uneven pulses that linked regions and nations across the modern world, they have thus far neglected the role of the local state—represented here by urban municipal governments—in forging and crystallizing this interconnectivity: the political map remains defined by nation-states and empires.[4] In seeking to reterritorialize historical studies of globalization, we enroll support from Jeffrey Sellers, one of the few scholars to examine the historical continuity of this interconnected world through an urban and municipal lens: "However globalized the world is, the local generally remains the level of analysis that is the closest to individuals. The effective character of policy, the dynamics of markets and class formation, the opportunities for political and civic participation, and the everyday constitution of identities all need to be analyzed at this micro level to be fully understood."[5]

The local remains an important variable for understanding the origins and function of this interconnected world, not least because the global cities literature has shown that cities have not been rendered insignificant outposts of multinational corporations or supranational bodies. Cities continue to matter and not solely on the "global" stage. The rescaling, or "reterritorialization," of "urban governance"—taken here to broadly describe "the set of institutions, rules, and procedures" by which urban municipal governments are managed—in recent years has shifted the structure and practice of power but also its study, vertically from the national to the local state and, additionally, horizontally from the global to the transnational arena.[6]

In this volume, urban municipal governments provided rich conceptual and empirical pickings for a historical examination of the construction and diffusion of policies, knowledge, regulations, and technical know-how through and across the limits of nations and empires. Taking our lead from the growing interdisciplinary focus within transnational studies, we advocated adding an additional spoke to the wheel of existing research on transmigration, transnational social movements, the locational interface between global and "glocal" capital investment, infrastructural communications, and the transnational interconnectivity between religion and culture.[7] Located in the spaces "in between" municipalities, the transnational journeys of municipal protagonists has been the underlying focus of this volume.

Historicizing the "Transnational Municipal Moment"

In his study of "transnational urbanism" among transmigrant communities, Michael P. Smith cites two important reasons for historicizing transnational practices. First, historical context accords transnational movements with historical specificity, challenging the romantic misconception that they are "timeless cultural wholes." Transnationalism is a hybrid movement, combining elements of the past and present, and blending a plethora of actors whose own identities (class, race, gender, etc.) are themselves historically constructed. Second, historical examination "helps us to differentiate between what is new about contemporary transnationalism and earlier instances of transnational migration, cross-border political or religious movements, trade diasporas, and the like."[8] By removing the historical blinkers on the different waves of transnational activity, the case studies in this volume corroborate the historical immaturity in regarding transnationalism "as a recent offspring" of neoliberal globalization, rather than as "a constant [and recurring] feature of modern life."[9] Thus, Rosario's and Montevideo's interest in Catalan urban planning have their origins in the political, cultural, and linguistic legacy of the Spanish Empire and not just the global brand that is "Barcelona."

In the introduction, we mapped out the three schematic waves of municipalization, with their respective "regimes" of circulation. The first was constituted from the informal transfers of the later nineteenth and early twentieth centuries, shaped and conducted by individual transnational entrepreneurs such as Seki Hajime, Osaka's cosmopolitan "scholar-mayor." In Jeffrey Hanes' chapter, Seki's exhaustive studies of European and U.S. municipalism were mined to establish and inform "metropolitan autonomy" as an adjunct of Meiji Japan's modernization. From Seki's "Pacific Crossings," to the myriad "Atlantic Crossings" identified by Daniel T. Rodgers, to the manifold intra-imperial crossings examined in this volume by Nora Lafi and Andrew Brown-May, the selective borrowing, adaptation, and adoption of ideas and regulations lent themselves to the uneven diffusion of urban modernity.[10] This exposes the temporal and ideational variations inbuilt into municipal engagement in international and transnational activities.

Succeeding these peripatetic practices from 1913 was a more structured transnational organizational impulse, one that attracted some of the early individual entrepreneurs into formalized and long-lasting institutions like the Union Internationale des Villes, the progenitor of transnational clearing houses of municipal knowledge, "the basic condition of progress" for its leader, Emile Vinck.[11] But still, key protagonists—represented in this volume by Edouard Herriot, the noted Lyonese municipalist—flitted between the formalized organizational structures and their own individualized networks, seeing the transnational arena as transient and mutable, shaped by a municipality's own logic and its window onto the wider world. By the 1950s, though, in a world worn out by war and facing geopolitical instability from decolonization and the cold war, municipalities had embraced transnational relations—epitomized by the wave of town twinning and sister city agreements signed between municipal leaders and local communities between the 1950s and 1970s—as a means for sharing the values of international solidarity, peace, and cooperation. Coordinated by various supranational bodies and twinning committees, the age of formalized, institutionalized, and specialized bilateral and multilateral partnerships had been established.[12]

This recharged wave of municipal interchange was marked by the growth of professional institutions, through which urban questions were problematized according to a technocratic logic. The pursuit of technical solutions for universal urban social problems such as sanitation and housing demanded increasingly technical knowledge shaped as much by professional, than municipal, associations. These professional connections transcended conventional local and national boundaries, and brought about a transnational discourse that hinged on worldwide understandings of technocratic expertise and professionalism. This is most evident in Nancy Kwak's chapter on housing in Singapore, in which she traces the growing involvement of internationally trained architects, the U.S. government, as well as the technical advisors to IGOs like the United Nations (UN) and the International Labour Organization, in funding and planning Singaporean urban development during the 1960s. Recognizing the importance of "sound planning and considerable technical know-how," the Singaporean planning authorities themselves recognized the embedded professional discourse that now shaped the "Urban Internationale."

The third wave created the global and regional maze of the 1980s, marked by the creation of an array of thematic multilevel networks. The key protagonists themselves sensed a change in the balance of power away from the redistributive welfare state of the post-1945 generation to the post-Fordist competitive mania signaled by the new global vocabulary of "public-private partnerships" and "urban regeneration." Symbolically represented in Europe by Eurocities and in South America by Mercociudades, two organizations that appear in chapters by Robin/Velut and Payre/Saunier, networking gathered a collective momentum in the competition over ever-scarce political and financial resources. Even then, the virility of bilateral networks continued apace, particularly with the opening of diplomatic and trade relations between China and the advanced Western economies, as explored by Yon Hsu. Represented here by the twinning agreement signed between Shanghai and Montreal in 1985, the exchange of municipal technical expertise for market opportunities, initially sown by expert horticultural diffusion, has given the transnational spaces "in between" urban municipal governments renewed breadth and depth. Even for those like Smith who are sensitive toward the continuities in transnationalism, greater access to the spaces "in between" (through personal mobility and more integrated

technologies) has rendered "the scope and complexity of transnational relations . . . more extensive now than in past historical periods."[13]

For our own part, we contend that these regimes intertwined, rather
than neatly succeeded each other chronologically, and that there is no
neat break in scope and complexity. As such, we identify a "transnational
municipal moment" taking place between the mid-nineteenth and late
twentieth centuries. This "transnational municipal moment" was characterized by the common rules and conventions shared by urban municipal
governments across the globe and the multifarious connections that these
governments created across time and space to make sense of the "municipal-
ized world." Chapters by Nora Lafi and Jeffrey Hanes, for example, express
how the architecture of the Ottoman and Japanese municipal systems were
the product of such crisscrossed circulations: municipal leaders in Tripoli
winnowed rules and conventions from within and beyond its imperial
borders to match its own municipal traditions, while the vast journeys
undertaken by Japanese social reformers across Europe, the United States,
and the Ottoman Empire saw its cities transfer or adapt foreign innovations
suited to local systems. Transnational networks have thus remained locally
focused throughout, within which municipal actors played the most active
roles as both donors and recipients, leaving traces of their own systems and
conventions in their wake. The contributors followed this cue: their case
studies examined how their respective municipalities sought a set of ideas,
policies, and methods—Robin and Velut call this "a huge empirical
toolbox"—to more fully comprehend the role of cities in these historically
rich transnational flows.

To capture this set of shared rules and circulatory connections, Ewen
identifies transnational municipalism as a discursive concept and lived practice, which he posits as the coordination of local services and civic identity,
and the sharing of best practices across national boundaries. As we see in
the chapters on Birmingham and Lyon—two "second" cities with a strong
heritage of transnational activity, but lacking sufficient weight to unilaterally
tap the growing riches of the European Union—transnational municipalism opened various "policy windows" through which second cities developed
coherent strategies in "uploading" and "downloading" policies and practices.[14] For us, the transnational municipal moment that took place between
the mid-nineteenth century and late twentieth acts as a window onto the
complex social organization (the municipality and its institutionalized rules
and procedures), process (i.e., the activities of networking between municipal
protagonists, expressed through transnational municipalism), and outcomes
(the formation and implementation of municipal policies) that comprised
transborder networks. The municipal category of analysis, in its institutional

and cultural form, offers a route into examining the interconnectivity of these planes.

Beyond this shared commitment to rescaling historical studies of globalization and transnationalism onto the level of translocal activism, the contributors to this volume have examined a number of interdependent characteristics in their case studies, which intertwine notwithstanding conventional national, continental, and imperial boundaries. The remainder of this conclusion focuses on such features: (1) the diffusion and translation of key concepts and indicators across cultural and linguistic borders; (2) the role of policy entrepreneurs in steering and mapping transnational municipal networking; and (3) the constraints and cleavages between the center and the locality in forming and managing municipal "best practices."

1. The Transnational Municipal Dictionary

In their case study of Rosario and Montevideo, Silvia Robin and Sébastien Velut demonstrate that during the 1990s the two South American cities were governed by municipalities keen to learn the rules of the game of the transnational political framework. In a renewed logic of "decentralized cooperation," the two municipalities were flooded with a plethora of concepts and indicators designed to assist them in their pursuit of administrative efficiency. Through the circulation of policy manuals, circulars, and advisors, both municipalities learned about "strategic urban planning," "governance," "sustainable development," "competitiveness," and the like. Only by being armed with this set of "best practices," as much discursive and linguistic constructs as policy initiatives, could municipalities in all corners of the globe hope to learn from, adopt, and adapt innovations that had been tested in city laboratories elsewhere.

We might be diagnosed as suffering from déjà vu. In Lafi's re-assessment of the complex circulation of modernizing laws around the Ottoman Empire during its *Tanzimat* reforms between the 1830s and 1880s, we also learn how the discursive and linguistic impulses of nineteenth-century political transfers were equally pivotal within an empire's vast administrative boundaries. Istanbul's circulation of facts and figures to inspire urban modernization was not the product of a simple center-periphery, or "donor-recipient," relationship. Provincial technicians and governors could not learn from best practices deployed elsewhere—whether in Istanbul's Galata district, where European-style municipal reforms were tested in the late 1850s, or in studying the Meiji reforms in Japan—if they were unable to decipher and fit them into local traditions and power structures. Thus, the empire's official gazette, which was distributed to all provinces, was translated into local languages, while local almanacs did their best to keep up to date with the myriad constitutional reforms. Provincial cities like Tripoli then digested this information, which were then married with existing rules and conventions to create their own dynamic municipal regimes, while others, like Tunis, under pressure from European consuls, resisted modernization. Intra-imperial circulations were as important as the transnational diffusion of ideas: here was a process involving the sharing of knowledge about policies, institutions, and ideas across an imperial landscape replete with a number of localized political regimes and traditions.

In a similar vein to the connotation and translation of the word "local" in different countries, the transnational dictionary of municipal leaders has had to be sensitive to national, local, and even temporal nuances in language and cultural identities. Concepts and indicators are subject to the traditions of localism and municipalism; they are rarely ready-made transfers. This means that ideas are invariably made to fit, however imperfectly, with the adoptive regime. Hence, Tripoli's notables accepted administrative modernization from Istanbul on the condition that they selected their preferred chief officer, who would respect local traditions, whereas both Rosario and Montevideo rejected aspects of "the Barcelona model" of urban management, especially alien practices designed to increase public participation in urban governance.

2. Transnational Entrepreneurs

Recent studies of late-modern urban politics emphasize that changes to the configuration of conventional central-local relations has necessitated a more expansive leadership style among local actors. Local authority chief executives, mayors, and their staffs are obliged to feel at home on the supranational and transnational stage as they are at home. In the context of the European Union, this "new political class" builds coalitions and networks in order to agitate for resources and even, in some instances, to further a political career on an international stage. Chapters by Payre/Saunier and Ewen stress that municipal politicians like Pasqual Maragall of Barcelona, Albert Bore of Birmingham, and Michel Noir of Lyon have had "to be at home welcoming Japanese would-be investors, or dealing with European Commission bureaucrats on the streets and in the corridors of Brussels."[15] The same ideas ring true beyond the confines of Europe, as shown by Robin and Velut: Hermes Binner and Miguel Lifshitz, as mayors of Rosario, have, through their transnational journeys around South America and Europe, played active roles since 2000 in placing their city on the international map. Others still, like New York's mayor, Ed Koch, had to welcome foreign diplomats, UN's officials and chief executives representing the largest multinational corporations.

Local leaders are both intensely local, in fostering partnerships with other local stakeholders to shore up their domestic power base, and intensely global, in going abroad to build partnerships and seek resources: Martins and álvarez describe this "renewed personalization" of local power as "glocal leadership." Thus, although these entrepreneurs work within the structural constraints of urban governance, they are able to assert their agency in moulding and managing their transnational municipal moment according to their own personal and political logics.[16]

Yon Hsu, for example, while noting the difficulty in separating agency and structure in studying transnational municipal networks, emphasizes the pivotal role played by Mayor Pierre Bourque (1994–2001), Montreal's local leader, in remapping the city's visibility on the world stage. The extensive and intensive networking activities undertaken by Bourque, chiefly as part of the Montreal-Shanghai twinning partnership, were clearly conducted within the ordinary constraints and cleavages of late-modern Canadian urban governance. Yet Bourque's globetrotting went above and beyond the call of municipal duty, extending his own personal networks in addition to those of his administrative apparatus. In seeking his own political legacy, Bourque sold Montreal to the Shanghai municipal authorities: here was a city that, despite suffering from a postindustrial economic malaise, posed strong financial and political investment opportunities for an up-and-coming Chinese metropolis.

A more direct example of agency overriding structural constraints is found in New York between 1978 and 1989, where Mayor Ed Koch's outspoken political style fed into an aggressively bold municipal foreign policy that, at times, emphasized style over substance. For all his "mushroom clouds of rhetoric," though, Jonathan Soffer notes how Koch's main legacy to his city was by fostering "a steady, long-term policy" built around foreign investment and pragmatic paradiplomacy with supranational behemoths like the UN. Koch was obviously supported by a strong managerial and administrative team, headed by major players recruited from the existing transnational arena. To identify New York's success at reinventing itself solely with its experts in investment banking and international diplomacy would be to underplay Koch's value, though, not only in recruiting them, but in having the "technocratic ambitions" to carve out a fresh path in the pursuit of urban growth. Indeed, Koch himself had studied his municipal forefathers, basing his administration on that of Fiorello LaGuardia (1933–44), who kept his eye trained firmly on the international, as well as the domestic, scene. Here, we see how enmeshed and intertwined our "regimes" of transnational municipalism can be: politicians can govern by looking backward and learning from the past, while particular styles of governance can be translated temporally and made to fit in different geopolitical contexts. Clearly the interrelationship between personality and paradiplomacy circumnavigates the constraints of institutional structures, rules, and formal procedures.

3. A Transnational Crossroads

As much as "there is no such thing as a single global city," there is no such thing as a single transnational municipality.[17] By their very nature, networks have rarely been singular unidirectional exercises, but have usually involved at least two municipal actors. These might take the form of a relatively straightforward donor-recipient relationship, but in most cases transnational municipalism is multidirectional and all participants give and take in unequal measure. We see this in the cases of Melbourne, Osaka, New York, Singapore, Birmingham, and Lyon. Hence, the majority of transnational networks are reciprocal: twinning involves cultural, political, and educational exchanges as much as economic opportunities, as exemplified in Hsu's study of the Montreal-Shanghai agreement. Urban municipal governments act as policy makers as much as policy takers, as is evident in the case of Rosario and Montevideo, whose municipal elite carefully cultivated the transnational arena, selecting programs before adapting them into concrete practices. They can also be policy givers, as with Montreal's offer of technical knowledge to help Shanghai cope with rapid urban growth.

The multidirectional nature of transnationalism is as much the case in imperial networks. Lafi's chapter, in particular, challenges the existing Ottoman historiography, which has been conventionally shaped by the binary oppositions of East/West. In so doing, she calls for a more complex schema for interpreting Ottoman reforms, one that involves the circulation of ideas both within and without the empire's borders. Hanes's chapter on Osaka's "Pacific Crossings" further questions the conventional dichotomy between the East (as backward) and West (as progressive) binaries: Japan's modernization was not a simple importation of Westernization but involved selective borrowing of Western practices, which were then subjected to intensive research, analysis, and comparison. Indeed, Japan's own technical and linguistic expertise meant that such practices could never be neatly translated. Transnational dialogues, such as those in 1923 between Viscount Gotô Shimpei, the mayor of earthquake-ravaged Tokyo, and Charles Beard, the famed American municipal progressive, have important implications for "*histoire croisée*" more generally, since they dispel the myth that the circulation and adoption of innovations was invariably the product of the East's subordination to the West. They call for a more nuanced treatment of relationships, one that could beneficially begin with Stephen Ward's useful typologies of diffusion for urban planning.[18]

Nancy Kwak's examination of Singapore's Housing and Development Board since 1959 further shows how transnational networks fulfilled a dual political and cultural purpose for the governing People's Action Party (PAP): the city-state's participation in international forums was not only useful to gain practical information about urban planning and housing but also to establish a Singaporean national identity. By resisting British efforts to appoint Anglicized Singaporeans to senior municipal positions, the PAP signaled its intention to pursue urban modernization according to its own logics, drawing on broader ideas and audiences beyond its imperial heritage. Transnational circulations, therefore, served as a tool by which Sinaporean planners and government officials increased their city-state's international standing as an exemplar of postcolonial urban modernity. Similar spin-offs are evident in Hanes's chapter, where Seki's pursuit of "metropolitan autonomy" saw the Japanese nation benefit from the construction of its cities as vessels of urban modernity. With industrialization came administrative and political modernization, which in turn ensconced Japan and Osaka equally on the world map.

Transnational municipalism is multidirectional precisely because it is also multidimensional. Christian Lefèvre and Ernesto d'Albergo identify myriad generic motives behind a municipality's overseas activities: these range from improving a city's competitiveness, entering formal bilateral relationships, and establishing multilateral partnerships to tap the growing supranational resource-base (as with Eurocities and Mercociudades), to the more altruistic or paradiplomatic strategies designed to show solidarity with the developing south, or express a city's authority through "diplomacy from below," expressed most acutely by Ed Koch.[19]

To these we would add routinized policy-learning initiatives such as the circulation of municipal bylaws, regulations, and yearbooks concerning specific urban policies. The shelves of Melbourne's town clerk's office, as detailed by Andrew Brown-May, were replete with the manuals, yearbooks, proceedings, and accounts of British municipalities. But this too was more complex than a simple center-periphery relationship involving the importation of practices from the metropole, since volumes from Bombay, Dunedin, Toronto, and numerous U.S. cities were just as visible. As demonstrated, Melbourne's municipal leaders closely studied trends that transcended continents, hemispheres, and most significantly, empires. At the same time, Melbourne's own bylaws were sent to any interested parties, establishing the Australian metropolis as a precinct of the global city. Other precincts were less prominent: the "missed connection" between Ottoman and Japanese urban reformers—symbolically marked by the wreckage of the Turkish frigate *Ertugrul* on the shores of Wakayama in 1890—indicates that policy learners were prepared to move off the well-trodden path in their exchange of ideas. Standing at the crossroads of the modern world, urban municipal governments together crafted an intricate web of circulations and relations.

The proliferation of research on municipal networking in recent years has been a direct response to the increasing transnational circulation of social, economic, and political capital within a global urban system. As part of the modernity project, these "municipal connections" have taken a variety of forms—"formal and informal, permanent or ephemeral"—during the long century and a half since 1850.[20] They have thus bound municipalities across time and space: crossing continents as much as national borders, and linking past and present practices and protagonists. To borrow a well-used phrase, municipalities are not "bowling alone" but co-exist in a networked and iterative world that transcends national and temporal borders, as well as legal and cultural boundaries.[21] Throughout the modern age, municipalities, far from being turned into passive actors by the rise of the nation-states, have been interested in each other's existence, their concomitant problems, and the policies they have framed and implemented as solutions.

The late nineteenth and twentieth centuries are epitomized by the emergence of the transnational municipality in all its guises, which faced universal urban problems associated with health, crime, fire, planning, and so on. How city actors sought practical solutions to these problems has received increasing historical attention since the publication of Marjatta Hietala's seminal *Services and Urbanization at the Turn of the Century*.[22] Contemporaneously, social scientists have scrutinized the internationalization of cities and the changes to urban governance since the 1970s. However, for most of these, including Hank Savitch and Paul Kantor, and even Patrick Le Galès, the global networked city is, really, a product of post-Fordist decline and the rise of a global entrepreneurial spirit. For these scholars, it was only from the 1980s and mostly in Europe, with the strengthening of the European Union and the retrenchment of the nation-state, that municipalities found a window of opportunity to renew their urban economies. Even then, many remain the dependent agents of an entrenched corporate economy.[23] This volume is our modest attempt to reconcile these two streams of research, providing a long-term perspective on these more recent transnational and global flows of capital, trade, people, and ideas that seem to herald a "return of cities," though we suspect they never had left.

Taking its cue from this growing scholarly interest in the urbanized world, this conclusion reflects the notion that the recent past of the world, as well as its present and future, is an urban one. As such, the municipality is the basic cell—as well as one of the key actors—within this urbanized world. In identifying and examining the myriad networks and municipal connections from the mid-nineteenth century onward, the contributors to this volume have repositioned the municipality closer to the center of studies of modern cities. Through their extensive and intensive journeys, urban municipal governments had a direct impact on the modern world's capacity to identify its social problems, and devise and disseminate common solutions. During an age when the nation-state was crystallized in its modern form, this transnational municipal moment emerged as a new embodiment of urban agency, in its most institutionalized form.

EPILOGUE

Cities, Competition, and Cooperation
Prospect Meets Retrospect

Marjatta Hietala

In today's "global world," competitiveness is one of the key aims for cities. Municipal authorities across the world strive to enhance the economic capacity of their cities by attracting businesses and workers. This, in turn, has shaped local and regional policy in many Organisation for Economic Co-operation and Development (OECD) countries. For these countries, major determinants of a city's competitiveness include such policy keywords as "accessibility," "infrastructure," and "human capital." In addition, "entrepreneurship," "innovation," and "investment" are identified as facilitating new business growth and product development, while fostering the growth of a new urban economy centered on knowledge creation and innovation. Cities thus compete to attract and retain mobile factors like labor and capital, which they do through their provision of tangible local amenities, such as green spaces, affordable housing, business support, and multinational corporate headquarters.[1]

When exploring a city's competitiveness, new trends are evident, at least in the OECD's 2006 report, *Competitive Cities in the Global Economy*. Chief among these are economic opportunities, which are sought through a sustainable growth vision of "competitiveness" and "livability." However, the OECD also recognizes three dilemmas in this strategic vision. The first

Marjatta Hietala was the first historian to systematically examine the circulation of know-how between municipalities. Her memorable study, *Services and Urbanization at the Turn of the Century: The Diffusion of Innovations*, published in 1987, aroused our own interest in the similarities and contrasts between our own municipalities. When we embarked on this venture, we were keen to invite Marjatta to contribute an epilogue to this collection, twenty years after *Services and Urbanization* was published. To this she kindly accepted.

concerns the spillover of metroregions, those sprawling conglomerations of urban people. The report questions whether metroregions have become major centers of growth in contemporary economies. It cites greater accessibility, lower transaction costs, social capital, and urban agglomeration as positive externalities not just for businesses but also for public authorities, educational institutes, and local civic associations that are keen to benefit from increased competition and livability. For all their benefits, though, there remain various negative externalities associated with large conglomerations of population. These include congestion costs, dilapidated or obsolescent infrastructure, and also weak social, political, and fiscal cohesion, which together dilute the impact of spatial planning on a city's growth prospects.[2]

The second dilemma deals with the public strategic vision. The authors describe the risks in developing policies based on a focused strategic vision, citing the example of the Montreal metropolitan region as evidence of the diversity of specialized targeted clusters in a multiplicity of different metroregions.[3] The third dilemma concerns the relationship between economic dynamism and the livable city. The authors emphasize that there exists considerable evidence that an attractive and functional metropolitan environment is not contrary to economic growth, noting several examples of how public authorities regulate air pollution, energy utilization and conservation, renewable energy sources, and water conservation.[4] Seoul, for example, has developed a restoration project that has replaced an elevated expressway and supplied its disadvantaged neighborhoods with fresh stream water and green spaces.[5] Of course, this resonates with the destruction of city walls that encircled historic European cities during the nineteenth century, in place of which were built green belts or ring roads. This point explicitly connects "competition" with "innovation," or "competitiveness" with "innovativeness," as the mindset oriented toward innovation.

Every city now wants to promote creativity and innovativeness, which necessarily involves encouraging greater mobility and networking, in and around various formal and informal clubs, and common interest networks. A city's innovativeness is connected to the mentality of its people, but equally so to its prominent institutions, public buildings, and support services, such as transport links and telecommunications. All of this belongs to what Charles Landry calls "hard infrastructure."[6] For Paul Edwards, infrastructure is an invisible background, the substrate or support, of the modern environment, the system without which contemporary societies cannot function.[7] In its widest definition, infrastructure includes several features: the material capital (e.g., land and buildings), the immaterial capital (e.g., educational attainment, health and research potential), and the institutional infrastructure (e.g., the city council and other service providers).

Various infrastructural indicators are identified when ranking the most livable cities. Mercer's schema, for example, is based on thirty-nine indicators, which include the political and social environment, schools, recreational facilities, and health and sanitation. According to this, the top three ranking cities worldwide are Zürich, Geneva, and Vancouver, and, if health and sanitation are exemplified, Helsinki is high on the list.[8] Mercer's rankings can be contrasted with others, such as Saskia Sassen's, which are based on explicit economic factors. In these, when the location of headquarters of private companies is quantified, many metropolitan cities rank higher than nonmetropolitan ones.[9] But much of this is not new, since history tells us that a city's urban infrastructure has always been built in reference to that of other towns, even if this has been done through different processes and channels until now. It is to this historical analogy that this epilogue briefly turns.

Competitiveness through Cooperation

The need for cooperation and networking among cities historically grew out of acute problems caused by industrialization and rapid urbanization, including unsanitary living conditions, air pollution, and city disasters such as fires and earthquakes. In my opinion, crises and catastrophes have sped up the construction of infrastructural services in many cities. During the mid- to late nineteenth century, for example, poor health conditions, epidemics, and high death rates "gave birth" to public health officers and school health services, while the laying of water pipes also reflected heightened anxieties about fire. In time, the common problems and demands for solutions engendered by rapidly growing cities meant that cooperation and networking could take place nationally as well as across national borders. In the search for solutions, cities turned to their hired experts for help. In turn, these experts tested and compared the suitability of solutions innovated by cities in other countries.[10]

Toward the end of the nineteenth century, reforms to state administration and industrial organization created the conditions for various new professional categories to emerge, among which were geologists, chemists, and railway engineers. The traditional political and economic elite needed efficient experts in specialized fields, who in turn secured the status as highly trained, well-paid, and mobilized professionals. With the modernization of urban society came new regulations to deal with the myriad urban social problems, all of which required supervision by this new professional elite. A great variety of inspectorates were formed, all demanding specialized knowledge. However, although efficiency and rationalization in urban services demanded a specialized degree of skill similar to certain medical fields, teaching, and urban planning, countries differed in the status that they accorded this academically trained class. Thus, in Germany and Scandinavia, the state's active contribution to economic progress was enhanced through professional further education. Cities and towns invested in human capital by distributing money among city officials and professional groups to assist their pursuit of foreign know-how. Through their accumulation of knowledge, these technicians weighed the constraints and cleavages of municipal ownership of core infrastructural services (notably water supply, sewerage, transport services, energy, and health care). As such, the municipality has historically provided the institutional infrastructure to the urban substrate and has coordinated the investment of the material and immaterial capital. That the municipality remains the infrastructural backbone in the Nordic countries, among others, indicates the durability of municipalization as a disseminating practice.

These technical and administrative infrastructural innovations were passed along via conferences and congresses, which have historically functioned as markets for the exchange of municipal knowledge. Most cities developed a process to systematically follow-up the achievements of other cities from the late nineteenth century to World War I. For example, municipal policies were keenly observed and exchanged across national borders, while the open exchange of knowledge facilitated the widespread adoption of urban infrastructures across Europe. It was during this intensive period of "creative internationalism" that international conferences, congresses, and exhibitions were in full swing.[11] At these world exhibitions European and American cities alike competed to demonstrate how progressive they were in adopting modern infrastructure and new technologies. English and German cities provided the markers for other towns to follow, having become wells of inspiration through their early management of urban problems. Taking one example, the municipal exhibition organized in Dresden in 1903 illustrated the tremendous progress that had taken place in municipal development within Imperial Germany. Invited experts flocked from across Europe and North America to observe the many infrastructural innovations on display: these ranged from physical infrastructures—such as building regulations, tramways, and street lighting—to economic ones—such as savings banks—to less visible, social infrastructures—such as schooling, poor relief, health, and the public's well-being.[12]

It was at this time that cities and towns also started to form their own ever-expanding networks, which functioned on both the national and international arenas. Through these they initiated city meetings, enforced municipal cooperation, and most significantly, asserted their own nexus of decision making. In so doing, they followed a process of cooperation that transcended national frontiers. Transnational mutual cooperation was established—first, on a regional basis and, second, on a national basis; soon it blossomed into an international phenomenon. A first wave of the national municipal associations were founded between 1890 and 1925, only six of which were located outside Europe, and in 1913 the first international congress of towns was convened at the occasion of Ghent's World Fair. Interested in common questions concerning the building of city infrastructure, this congress gave birth to the Union Internationale des Villes (International Union of Local Authorities [UIV/IULA]). From inauspicious origins, the UIV/IULA quickly grew after the resumption of its activities from 1925. By 1935, thirty-two national unions from twenty-two countries were affiliated members. Membership included sixty-three national unions in 1953 and was steadily rising until, a decade later, it included fifty-five different countries spread across the world: twenty-one from Europe, fourteen from Asia, eight from America, ten from Africa and two from Oceania.[13] By 2003 the UIV/IULA had over one hundred members representing regions across the world. United Cities and Local Governments (UCLG), which was born out of the merger of the UIV/IULA with other intermunicipal groups in 2004, now has members in over 127 countries.[14]

Intercity networks can take diverse forms, including those between citizens and professional groups of city authorities, networks comprising trusted persons and authorities, and others between cities and city-owned facilities. The networks forged between municipal officials and policy makers, as well as the transnational transfer of municipal knowledge between different European and North American municipalities, have recently attracted much research, evidence of which is replete in the endnotes to the chapters in this book. One such urban actor in this process was Helsinki, to which the remainder of this epilogue focuses. As an early municipal innovator in the diffusion of infrastructural know-how, Helsinki's municipal council played a formative role in the systematic organization of cross-municipal observation for several decades around the turn of the twentieth century.

Networks and Individual Observers: Examples from Helsinki

During the late nineteenth century, fact-finding tours undertaken by individual experts and municipal authorities were of considerable importance to Helsinki. Analyzing the destinations and determinations of those tours ascertains the reference groups with which experts, institutions, and cities have identified. In Finland, the "frame of reference" was provided by the municipal authorities and city officials of Helsinki, the country's administrative center. These actors sought to develop Helsinki in the same direction as other "model" capitals—notably London, Paris, Berlin, Vienna, and Stockholm, of all which were larger centers of population. During the early twentieth century, Finnish officials were driven by the need to keep pace with other civilized states. To such ends, Helsinki's municipal authorities, as well as the leaders of the Association of Finnish Cities (founded in 1912 as the Municipal Central Office), developed a follow-up system to their transnational activities.[15] This system consisted of five stages: first, they read studies and printed articles, including international statistical compendiums; second, they tapped the experience of decision makers in other cities by obtaining the written proceedings issued by city councils and municipal boards; third, they considered the statements of various experts from professional associations; fourth, they deliberated on their own personal observations and travel reports; and fifth, they invited foreign experts to Helsinki for closer scrutiny and discussion. The follow-up system and diffusion of innovations can thus be seen as a policy-learning process whereby Helsinki targeted specific cities from which to winnow and adapt ideas for their local adoption.

Helsinki's city council valued information from multiple sources. It was not enough to collect a single model or one person's observations: the greater the venture, the more comprehensive was its approach and the more thorough its preparation. Such examples were found when new hospitals were planned, or when water purification and electrification schemes were debated. For twenty years, Helsinki's city engineers searched far and wide for the best methods to purify water from the mid-1880s: they visited several English, Dutch, and German water plants, comparing different purifying methods and tapping the expertise of foreign engineers. Indicating the multilayered nature of transnational networking, the city council's final decision, taken in 1907, was to adopt American quick filters, an innovation adopted from their engineers' European travels.[16]

The result of tapping these channels of information was that the innovation or idea was often adapted to prevailing domestic conditions. Indeed, direct copying was rare. According to data sampled from 390 tours undertaken by Helsinki's city officials and elected representatives from 1875 to 1917, almost one-half (187) of tours involved ascertaining other cities' experiences in connection with elementary schools. Next came health care, with 115 tours, while adult education and training accounted for 31. For city planning and social services, 41 journeys were made, with another 16 to study lighting techniques. These tours usually visited several cities, often in several countries, the major targets being Scandinavian neighbors and Germany. Sweden's popularity, but especially its capital of Stockholm, obviously reflected historic cultural and linguistic links. Moreover, Stockholm was en route to the continent and was a major venue for elementary school conferences, which drew interested observers from across the region. Danish cities, particularly Copenhagen, were also frequently found in Helsinki's itineraries. In Germany, Finnish municipal authorities visited sixty-three towns, of which Berlin was the most popular.[17] However, although capital cities provided the main reference source for Helsinki, Finnish municipal experts also journeyed to cities in smaller European countries, but with reputations for "good practice" or "innovation." Thus, in Helsinki's itineraries, Dutch, Belgian, and Swiss cities appeared alongside the other Nordic countries, Germany, Great Britain, France, and Austro-Hungary.

Helsinki's core infrastructure had already been completed before 1914, but transnational journeys continued unabated afterward. From 1919, the city council included a general grant for city officials' foreign-study trips in its annual budget—the condition of its award being that the recipient would later write a report and remain in the city's service for a minimum of two years. In the years that followed, the grant system became an entrenched practice: the aggregate sums increased throughout the 1920s and 1930s, while representatives from each of the different divisions were awarded grants in almost equal proportions, justifying their receipt in language that was couched in terms of the economic and business benefits to the city. Between 1936 and 1940, the city granted 201 travel grants; while in the four years after 1946, a total of 402 were awarded.[18] The inclusion of travel grants in Helsinki's annual budget illustrates the importance of foreign know-how in the eyes of its municipal authorities and taxpayers. Through travel reports and municipal proceedings the latest information on innovations was collated and widely disseminated. More significantly, the diffusion of infrastructural innovations was a temporal process, the ideas and journeys themselves taking time to germinate and the infrastructure designed to last for decades. Municipal leaders and their officials thus participated in transnational journeys in order to build projects that would last.

Challenges for the Future

Many of the problems that have been tackled through institutionalized and personalized networks throughout nineteenth- and twentieth-century Europe are today topical across the developing world. Historically, the need to keep up with the latest developments has been of vital importance for small countries and cities such as Helsinki, Oslo, and Stockholm, located far away from Western European metropolises. The pattern remains, yet it has shifted its geographical focus toward the global south. The main problems and challenges faced now, and in the future, are the growth of megacities, their offshoots of slums, and their manifold environmental problems: carbon dioxide, dust and noise pollution, as well as climate change and their resultant catastrophes, which have thus far included floods and hurricanes. The issue of effectively preparing for natural disasters, including adopting regional warning devices, is top of the agenda for supranational institutions like the United Nations at the moment, especially in the wake of the South Asian tsunami of December 2005.

Even today, among the challenges faced by cities and towns, are the common problems concerning the (re-)building of infrastructure and the growing demand for a multitude of different services. Service demand has become particularly acute in the megacities of the developing, as much as the developed, world: Mexico City and Delhi, as well as Tokyo and New York, are common examples of megacities with populations exceeding twenty million. These exploding cities are weaving extraordinary new urban networks, corridors, and hierarchies, which as yet show no end to their growth. The problems of such global metropolises include intense traffic congestion, a severe lack of clean water in the urban periphery, incapacitated sewerage systems, and social and ethnic residential segregation. Within these megacities are megaslums inhabited by millions of impoverished city dwellers: the eight biggest in 2005 were in Mexico City, Caracas, Bogota, Lima, Lagos, Baghdad, and Gauteng (Soweto).[19]

The challenges are multitudinous. While we talk about creating sustainable cities, we also now discuss "resilient cities"—that is, those which persevere regardless of major natural and manmade disasters.[20] Moreover, at a time when digital communication networks play an increasingly vital role in fostering urban growth, global terrorism threatens the very vulnerability of this urban infrastructure. The twenty-first century's cities are susceptible not only to overt attacks on buildings but also to the covert disruption of cyber attacks on the nodes and links of critical networks.[21]

In their book, *Crucibles of Hazard: Megacities and Disasters in Transition*, the authors from the International Geographical Union's Study Group conclude that the natural disaster potential for the world's megacities is expanding at a pace far in excess of the rate of urbanization. Moreover, new amalgams of hazard are being created in metropolitan areas with overlapping natural, technological, biological, and social risks, exposing more people and places to environmental hazards. Safety and security have, in the long term, become the common interest for cities. The vulnerability of megacities is obvious.[22]

Transnational organizations like the United Cities and Local Government (UCLG) face a plethora of unparalleled and, for some, insolvable problems to rectify. However, UCLG is not alone, since there are many other global organizations that help local authorities plan and prepare for possible future scenarios. Cities Alliance, for one, is a coalition of local authorities' associations, national governments' developmental assistance departments, and intergovernmental organizations that claims a commitment to poverty reduction and slum upgrading. The UN-HABITAT is a subsidiary organ of its General Assembly and emphasizes the implementation of its Habitat Agenda, in particular achieving the goals of adequate shelter for all and sustainable human settlements.[23] The Mega-Cities Project (founded in 1987) is another example of a new kind of agency: a transnational, nonprofit network of leaders from government, business, grassroots organizations, academia, and the media, which is dedicated to sharing innovative solutions to common problems faced by megacities.[24] Recognizing existing failures in global urban governance, bodies such as these are building new coalitions and starting to work toward solutions for these ever acute urban problems. The achievement of competitiveness is a challenge that faces all cities, including megacities, but first they have to become livable: cooperation is thus the flip side of the search for competitiveness.

Throughout history municipal authorities have faced difficulties in prioritizing and municipalizing services when planning infrastructure. In this, political and economical factors have played a decisive role. Now when infrastructure is being built in developing countries the future prospects are often presented in an overly positive tone. It is assumed, for example, that information technology will solve all of a megacity's problems regardless of whether the basic infrastructure has been installed or not. These same authorities forget that European and North American city infrastructures took many decades to build.

In one respect, though, cities today face different responsibilities to their predecessors: during the later nineteenth century, cities had to shoulder the financial burden for their core infrastructure, whereas today there is financial support available from several private and public sector sources. European cities and regions, for example, can secure money from the European Union. Meanwhile, other foundations like the World Bank, the Asian Development Bank, Cities Alliance, and the UN-HABITAT allocate funds to cities outside Europe and North America. For all this financial muscle on show, though, this new global governance regime cannot solve all the world's problems on its own. Once again it falls to the army of municipal technicians and elected officials to identify, winnow, and adapt workable technical and organizational innovations to fit local conditions. For the new megacities of the world, it is this that will make the critical difference.

Notes

Preface

1. Arjun Appadurai, "Disjunction and Difference in the Global Cultural Economy," *Public Culture* 2, no. 2 (1990): 1–24.
2. Carl Nightingale, "The Transnational Contexts of Early Twentieth-Century American Urban Segregation," *Journal of Social History* 39, no. 3 (2006): 667–702.

Chapter 1

1. Shavings and sparks of this debate can be caught through the pages of the dedicated journals *Urban History* and *Journal of Urban History*, as well as from a series of articles and chapters, among which is Eric Lampard, "Urbanization and Social Change: On Broadening the Scope and Relevance of Urban History," in *The Historian and the City*, by Oscar Handlin and John Burchard (Cambridge, MA: MIT Press, 1963), 225–47; Richard Rodger, "Theory, Practice and Urban History," in Richard Rodger, ed., *European Urban History* (Leicester: Leicester University Press, 1993), 1–18; Harry S. J. Jansen, "Wrestling with the Angel: On Problems of Definition in Urban Historiography," *Urban History* 23, no. 3 (1996): 277–99.
2. Charles Tilly, "What Good Is Urban History?" *Journal of Urban History* 22, no. 6 (1996): 710.
3. Tilly, "What Good," 702.
4. Cf. Stephan Thernstrom, "Reflections on the New Urban History," *Daedalus* 100 (1971): 359–75; David Cannadine, "Urban History in the United Kingdom: The 'Dyos Phenomenon' and After," in *Exploring the Urban Past: Essays in Urban History by H. J. Dyos*, ed. David Cannadine and David Reeder (Cambridge: Cambridge University Press, 1982), 203–21.
5. There is no major contrast, from this point of view, between Kenichi Ohmae (*The Borderless World: Power and Strategy in the Interlinked World Economy*

[Cambridge, MA: MIT Press, 1990]) and Richard Falk (*Predatory Globalization: A Critique* [Cambridge: Polity, 1999]), though they disagreed on the consequences of globalization.

6. The sense of a "rupture" and the presentation of the last few decades as a break is most evident in Ulf Hannerz, *Transnational Connections: Culture, People, Places* (London: Routledge, 1996).

7. Arjun Appadurai, *Modernity at Large: Cultural Dimensions of Globalization* (Minneapolis: University of Minnesota Press, 1996), 64.

8. For economic aspects, see Kevin O'Rourke and Jeffrey G. Williamson, *Globalization and History: The Evolution of a Nineteenth-Century Atlantic Economy* (Cambridge, MA: MIT Press, 1999). For international relations, Barry Buzan and Richard Little, *International Systems in World History: Remaking the Study of International Relations* (Oxford: Oxford University Press, 2000).

9. Significant examples are Giovanni Arrighi, *The Long Twentieth Century: A Preliminary Sketch* (London: Verso, 1994), and Andre Gunder Frank and Barry Gills, eds., *The World System: Five Hundred Years or Five Thousand?* (London: Routledge, 1994).

10. For example, Margaret E. Keck and Kathryn Sikkink, *Activists beyond Borders: Advocacy Networks in International Politics* (Ithaca, NY: Cornell University Press, 1998), chap. 1.

11. Landmark exceptions were Charles Bright and Michael Geyer, "World History in a Global Age," *American Historical Review* 100, no. 4 (1995): 1034–60; and Prasenjit Duara, "Transnationalism and the Predicament of Sovereignty: China 1900–1945," *American Historical Review* 102, no. 4 (1997): 1030–51.

12. See Ian Tyrrell, "American Exceptionalism in an Age of International History," *American Historical Review* 96, no. 4 (1991): 1031–72; and Daniel T. Rodgers, *Atlantic Crossings: Social Politics in a Progressive Age* (Cambridge, MA: Belknap Press, Harvard University Press, 1998).

13. Leila Rupp, *Worlds of Women: The Making of an International Women's Movement* (Princeton, NJ: Princeton University Press, 1997); Ian Tyrell, *Woman's World/Woman's Empire: The Women's Christian Temperance Union in International Perspective 1880–1930* (Chapell Hill: North Carolina University Press, 1991); Bonnie S. Anderson, *Joyous Greetings: The First International Women's Movement, 1830–1860* (New York: Oxford University Press, 2000).

14. Robin Kelley, "'But a Local Phase of a World Problem': Black History's Global Vision," *Journal of American History* 86, no. 3 (1999): 1015–72.

15. Ewa Morawska, "The Sociology and History of Immigration: Reflections of a Practitioner," in *International Migration Research: Constructions, Omissions, and the Promises of Interdisciplinarity*, ed. Michael Bommes and Ewa Morawska (Aldershot, England: Ashgate, 2005), 203–41.

16. Alejandro Portes, "Immigration Theory for a New Century: Some Problems and Opportunities," *International Migration Review* 31, no. 4 (1997): 799–825.

17. Benefits of this mutual attention are clear in Andreas Wimmer and Nina Glick Schiller, "Methodological Nationalism and Beyond: Nation-State Building, Migration, and the Social Sciences," *Global Networks* 2, no. 4 (2002): 301–34.

18. One outstanding example is Frederick Cooper, "What Is the Concept of Globalization Good For? An African Historian's Perspective," *African Affairs* 100 (2001): 189–213.

19. World history, a subspeciality that came of age after World War II, is being reinvigorated by the desire of several world historians (among others Patrick Manning and Jerry Bentley) to steer the field toward the study of connections and circulations. Bruce Mazlish and Akira Iriye, in the early 2000s, came forward with the project of a "new global history" that seeks to chart globalization, which was seen as a distinctly twentieth-century phenomenon, with its roots in the age of expansion of the early modern world, http://www.newglobalhistory.org.

20. See Thomas Bender, ed., *Rethinking American History in a Global Age* (Berkeley: University of California Press, 2002), in which the internationalization of U.S. history is established as an attempt to capture "the historical spaces opened by globalization."

21. Sanjay Subrahmanyam, "Connected Histories: Notes toward a Reconfiguration of Early Modern Eurasia," in *Beyond Binary Histories: Re-imagining Eurasia to c. 1830*, ed., Victor Lieberman (Ann Arbor: University of Michigan Press, 1997), 289–315.

22. Serge Gruzinski, *Les quatre parties du monde: Histoire d'une mondialisation* (Paris: La Martinière, 2004).

23. Anthony G. Hopkins, ed., *Globalization in World History* (New York: W. W. Norton, 2002); idem, ed., *Global History: Interactions between the Universal and the Local* (New York: Palgrave, 2006). See also Carlo Fumian, *Verso una società planetaria. Alle origini della globalizzazione contemporanea(1870–1914)* (Rome: Donzelli, 2003).

24. Christopher A. Bayly, *The Birth of the Modern World 1780–1914: Global Connections and Comparisons* (London: Blackwell, 2004).

25. One of them, the Geschichte.Transnational gateway, set up by a team of German and French scholars, offers a good overview of resources in the field, http:// geschichte-transnational.clio-online.net/transnat.asp?lang=en.

26. "Globalization is a long-term historical process that, over many years, has crossed distinct qualitative periods," writes Manfred Steger, identifying this point as one of the few points of convergence of scholarly views (Manfred B. Steger, ed., *Rethinking Globalism* [London: Rowman & Littlefield, 2004], 1).

27. Jean François Bayart, *Le gouvernement du monde: Une critique politique de la globalisation* (Paris: Fayard, 2004).

28. An interesting up-to-date survey of this theme is in Gunilla Budde, Sebastian Conrad, and Oliver Janz, eds., *Transnationale geschichte: Themen, tendenzen, und theorien* (Göttingen: Vandenhoeck & Ruprecht, 2006). A review in English by Michael Geyer is available at http://hsozkult.geschichte.hu-berlin.de/ rezensionen/2006-4-032.

29. For our initial forays into the field, Shane Ewen, "The Internationalization of Fire Protection: In Pursuit of Municipal Networks in Edwardian Birmingham,"

Urban History 32, no. 2 (2005): 288–307; Pierre-Yves Saunier, "Changing the City: Urban International Information and the Lyon municipality, 1900–1940," *Planning Perspectives* 14, no. 1 (1999): 19–48.

30. One such project in which we had direct experience in collaborating with political scientists, sociologists, and economic geographers was the Cities as International Actors (CITTA) network, funded by the European Science Foundation, between 2002 and 2005. Its results are published in a special issue of *Environment & Planning C: Government and Policy* 3, no. 25 (2007).

31. Jeffrey Sellers, "Transnational Urban Associations and the State: Contemporary Europe Compared with the Hanseatic League," in "Formation and Transfer of Municipal Administrative Knowledge," ed. Nico Randeraad, *Yearbook of European Administrative History* 15 (2003); Jeffrey Sellers, "Re-Placing the Nation: An Agenda for Comparative Urban Politics," *Urban Affairs Review* 40, no. 4 (2005): 419–45.

32. Neil Brenner, "World City Theory, Globalization and the Comparative-Historical Method: Reflections on Janet Abu-Lughod's Interpretation of Contemporary Urban Restructuring," *Urban Affairs Review* 36, no. 6 (2001): 124–47.

33. Janet Abu-Lughod, *Before European Hegemony: The World System A.D. 1250–1350* (New York: Oxford University Press, 1989), 161.

34. John Rennie Short, *Global Metropolitan: Globalizing Cities in a Capitalist World* (London: Routledge, 2004).

35. http://www.lboro.ac.uk/gawc/projects/projec55.html (accessed February 1, 2007).

36. A. D. King, *Global Cities: Post-Imperialism and the Internationalization of London* (London: Routledge, 1990). On the disconnection of the 1980s "global/world cities" scholarship from previous scholarship on cities and globalization in the developing world, see Diane Davis, "Cities in Global Context: A Brief Intellectual History," *International Journal of Urban and Regional Research* 29, no. 1 (2005): 92–109.

37. A significant exception is Bob Jessop and Ngai-Ling Sum, "An Entrepreneurial City in Action: Hong Kong's Emerging Strategies in and for Inter-Urban Competition," http://www2.cddc.vt.edu/digitalfordism/fordism_materials/jessop.htm (accessed February 1, 2007). However, the role that municipalities claim to play on the international relations scene was a tangential feature in landmark collections, see Andrew Kirby, Sallie Marston, and Kenneth Seasholes, "World Cities and Global Communities: The Municipal Foreign Policy Movement and New Roles for Cities," in *World Cities in a World-System*, ed. Richard Knox and Peter J. Taylor (Cambridge: Cambridge University Press, 2001), 267–79.

38. M. Mark Amen, Kevin Archer, and M. Martin Bosman, eds., *Relocating Global Cities: From the Center to the Margins* (London: Rowman and Littlefield Publishers, 2006).

39. Saskia Sassen, "Searching for the Global in the Urban," in ibid., x–xiii.

40. Peter J. Taylor, World City Network: *A Global Urban Analysis* (London: Routledge, 2004), 15.

41. Recent examples are Peter Kresl and Earl Fry, *Urban Response to Internationalization* (London: Edwar Elgar Publishing, 2005); and Hank Savitch and Paul Kantor, *Cities in the International Marketplace* (Princeton, NJ: Princeton University Press, 2002).

42. Patrick Le Galès, *European Cities: Social Conflict and Governance* (Oxford: Oxford University Press, 2002).

43. It is interesting to note that the French version of the book is titled *Le retour des villes européennes* (The Return of European Cities).

44. John Bennington and Janet Harvey, "Transnational Local Authority Networking within the E-U: Passing Fashion or New Paradigm," in *Comparing Policy Networks*, ed. David Marsh (Buckingham: Open University Press, 2003), 149–66.

45. A good introduction to this field is Sidney Tarrow, *The New Transnational Activism* (Cambridge: Cambridge University Press, 2005).

46. Harriet Bulkeley and Michele Betsill, *Cities and Climate Change: Urban Sustainability and Global Environmental Governance* (London: Routledge, 2003).

47. Harriet Bulkeley, "Transnational Municipal Networks and Urban Governance," paper presented at the Joint Sessions of Workshops—Uppsala 2004 Policy Networks in Subnational Governance: Understanding Power Relations.

48. For example, Harold L. Platt, *Shock Cities: The Environmental Transformation and Reform of Manchester and Chicago* (Chicago: Chicago University Press, 2005); Dieter Schott, Bill Luckin, and Genevieve Massard-Guilbard, eds., *Resources of the City: Contributions to an Environmental History of Modern Europe* (Aldershot, England: Ashgate, 2005).

49. Michael P. Smith, "The Global City: Whose Social Construct is it Anyway?" *Urban Affairs Review* 33, no. 4 (1998): 482–88.

50. Michael P. Smith, *Transnational Urbanism: Locating Globalization* (London: Blackwell, 2001).

51. See, for example, chapters in R. J. Morris and R. H. Trainor, eds., *Urban Governance: Britain and Beyond since 1750* (Aldershot, England: Ashgate, 2000).

52. Rodgers, *Atlantic Crossings*, 33–34.

53. In this sense, the "great transformation" was preceded by a "little transformation," which took place in municipalities. This is the point made by Renaud Payre, who identifies Karl Polanyi's observation of the municipal achievements in Red Vienna as the beginning of his reflection about the relation between economic, social, and political change. See Renaud Payre, *Une science communale? Réseaux réformateurs et municipalité providence (CNRS Editions, 2007), 9–15.*

54. For two overviews of literature in the field, see Pierre-Yves Saunier, "Taking Up the Bet on Connections: A Municipal Contribution," in *Municipal Connections: Cooperation, Links, and Transfers among European Cities in the 20th Century*, ed. Pierre-Yves Saunier, Special Issue of *Contemporary European History* 11, no. 4 (2002): 507–27; Pierre-Yves Saunier, "La toile municipale aux XIXème et XXème siècles: Un panorama transnational vu d'Europe," *Revue d'Histoire Urbaine* 34, no. 2 (2006): 163–76.

55. Charles Tilly, *Coercion, Capital, and European States AD 990–1990* (Oxford: Blackwell, 1990).

56. See Fabio Rugge, "L'auto governo comunale tra Germania ed Italia (1880–1914). Note per uno studio sulla circolazione di dottrine, Modelli istituzionali e pratiche amministrative," *Jahrbuch für Europäisches Verwaltungsgeschichte* 2 (1990): 103–21; and Federico Lucarini, *Scienze comunale e pratiche di governo in Italia 1890–1915* (Milan: Giuffré, 2003).

57. Patrizia Dogliani, *Un laboratorio di socialismo municipale: La Francia, 1870–1920* (Milan: Franco Angeli, 1992), 163–82; Marjatta Hietala, *Services and Urbanization at the Turn of the Century: The Diffusion of Innovations* (Helsinki: Suomen Historiallinen Seura, 1987); Rodgers, *Atlantic Crossings*, chaps. 4 and 5.

58. For a contemporary account and a few clues, Roger Wells, "Foreign Government and Politics: The Revival of German Unions of Local Authorities after World War II," *American Political Science Review* 41, no. 6 (1947): 1182–87.

59. F. W. Holden, "Foreign Government and Politics: The Prospects of English Local Government," *American Political Science Review* 40, no. 3 (1946): 533–44.

60. See the interesting section about "Municipalities overseas" in the "Villes européennes outre mer" chapter by Xavier Huetz de Lemps and Odile Goerg in Jean-Luc Pinol, ed., *Histoire de l'Europe urbaine* (Paris: Seuil, 2003), 2:152–59.

61. Traces of this cross-observation can be found in Gareth Stedman Jones, *An end to poverty? A historical debate* (London: Profile, 2004); and in Jean-Philippe Genet, and François-Joseph Ruggiu, eds., *Les idées passent-elles la Manche? Savoirs, représentations, pratiques: France-Angleterre, Xe-XXe siècles* (Paris: Presses de l'Université Paris-Sorbonne, 2007).

62. Christian Henriot, *Shanghai, 1927–1937: Municipal Power, Locality, and Modernization* (Berkeley: University of California Press, 1993); David Strand, *Rickshaw Beijing: City People and Politics in the 1920* (Berkeley: University of California Press, 1989); Bryna Goodman, *Native Place, City, and Nation: Regional Networks and Identities in Shanghai, 1853–1937* (Berkeley: University of California Press, 1995).

63. Nora Lafi, "From Europe to Tripoli via Istanbul: Municipal Reforms in an Outpost of the Ottoman Empire around 1870," in *Urbanism, Imported or Exported? Native Aspirations and Foreign Plans*, ed. Joe Nasr and Mercedes Volait (London: Wiley, 2003), 187–205.

64. See the contributions in Nora Lafi, ed., *Municipalités méditerrannéennes. Les réformes urbaines au miroir d'une histoire comparée (Moyen-Orient, Maghreb, Europe Méridionale)* (Berlin: Klaus Schwarz Verlag, 2005); see esp. Jens Hanssen, "The Origins of the Municipal Council in Beirut 1860–1908," 177–213.

65. See Le Galès, *European Cities*, chaps. 3 and 4.

66. This attitude was especially manifest during the preparation of the 1992 Earth Summit and 1996 Habitat Conference. On the environmental scene, see Bulkeley and Betsill, *Cities and Climate Change*.

67. Marjatta Hietala was the first to pay specific attention to this with her work on Finnish and Scandinavian cities. See Hietala, *Services and Urbanization*. See also her "Transfer of German and Scandinavian Administrative Knowledge: Examples from Helsinki and the Association of Finnish Cities," *Jahrbuch für*

Europäische Verwaltungsgeschichte 15 (2003): 109–30; "La diffusion des innovations: Helsinki 1875–1917," *Genèses* 10 (1993): 74–89.

68. Saunier, "La toile municipale."

69. Pierre-Yves Saunier, "*Selling the Idea of Cooperation*: The U.S. Foundations and the European Components of the Urban Internationale (1920s–1960s)," in *American Foundations and Large Scale Research: Construction and Transfer of Knowledge*, ed. Giuliana Gemelli (Bologna: Clueb, 2001), 219–46.

70. About the IULA, see Patrizia Dogliani, "European Municipalism in the First Half of the Twentieth Century: The Socialist Network," *Contemporary European History* 11, no. 4 (2002): 573–96; and Renaud Payre and Pierre-Yves Saunier, "L'internazionale municipalista: L'Union Internationale des Villes fra 1913 e 1940," *Amministrare* 30, no.1/2 (2000), 217–42. On the new municipal organizations born after 1945 and their relationship with the IULA, Oscar Gaspari, "Cities against States? Hopes, Dreams, and Shortcomings of the European Municipal Movement 1900–1960," *Contemporary European History* 11, no. 4 (2002): 529–48.

71. See the assessment of these changes and their impact in Le Galès, *European Cities*.

72. Overviews of this ongoing networks craze are available in Paolo Perulli, Fabio Rugge, and Raffaella Florio, "Reti di città: Una forma emergente di governance Europea," *Foedus: Culture Economie e Territori* 4 (2002): 53–70; and Shane Ewen and Michael Hebbert, "European Cities in a Networked World during the Long Twentieth Century," *Environment & Planning C: Government and Policy* 25, no. 3 (2007): 327–40.

Chapter 2

1. This chapter revises and expands arguments published in "'I cittadini stanno iniziando a lamentarsi.' Saperi municipali e contrattazioni intorno ai comportamenti pubblici molesti a Melbourne," in *La regola e la trasgressione*, ed. Denis Bocquet and Filipo de Pieri, special issue of *Storia Urbana* 28, no. 108 (2005): 53–66, itself developing ideas first mooted in my *Melbourne Street Life* (Melbourne: Australian Scholarly Publishing, 1998).

2. The state of Victoria separated from New South Wales in 1851, taking the name of the Empire's Queen.

3. *Australasian*, November 30, 1867.

4. The term "corporation" owed its long-term origins to the piecemeal English parliamentary procedure of "incorporation," by which urban municipal governments were granted legal status with full tax-raising powers. This process was statutorily enshrined by England's Municipal Corporations Act of 1835. The use of the specific nomenclature in this chapter reflects its everyday use during Victorian times.

5. E. G. FitzGibbon (1856–1891); John Clayton (1891–1915); Torrington George Ellery (1915–1923); William Valentine McCall (1923–1936); Harold Samuel

Wootton (1936–1955); on the role of the town clerk, see David Dunstan, *Governing the Metropolis: Politics, Technology and Social Change in a Victorian City, Melbourne 1850-1891* (Carlton, Australia: Melbourne University Press, 1984), 93–120.

6. Asa Briggs, *Victorian Cities* (London: Odhams, 1963).

7. David Cannadine, *Ornamentalism: How the British Saw Their Empire* (London: Allen Lane / Penguin, 2001).

8. See, for example, Lindsay J. Proudfoot and Michael M. Roche, eds., *(Dis)Placing Empire: Renegotiating British Colonial Geographies* (Aldershot, England: Ashgate, 2005).

9. Felix Driver and David Gilbert, eds., *Imperial Cities: Landscape, Display and Identity* (Manchester: Manchester University Press, 1999).

10. Jane M. Jacobs, *Edge of Empire: Postcolonialism and the City* (London: Routledge, 1996); Anthony D. King, *Colonial Urban Development* (London: Routledge, 1976); King, *Urbanism, Colonialism and the World Economy: Cultural and Spatial Foundations of the World Urban System* (London: Routledge, 1990).

11. Joel A. Tarr and Gabriel Dupuy, eds., *Technology and the Rise of the Networked City in Europe and America* (Philadelphia: Temple University Press, 1988); David Goodman, ed., *The European Cities and Technology Reader* (London: Routledge, 1999), Part 3.

12. David Hamer, *New Towns in the New World: Images and Perceptions of the Nineteenth-Century Urban Frontier* (New York: Columbia University Press, 1990); Driver and Gilbert, *Imperial Cities*, 3.

13. Cited in ibid., 4.

14. Albert Shaw, *Municipal Government in Great Britain* (New York: Centenary Book Company, 1895), 11.

15. On systems of municipal government, see John H. Warren, *Municipal Administration* (London: Sir Isaac Pitman & Sons, 1954; first published 1948); I. M. Barlow, *Metropolitan Government* (London: Routledge, 1991), chap. 5 on Melbourne. On municipal systems in Melbourne see Dunstan, *Governing the Metropolis*; H. E. Maiden, *The History of Local Government in New South Wales* (Sydney: Angus and Robertson, 1966).

16. Anthony S. Wohl, *Endangered Lives: Public Health in Victorian Britain* (London: J. M. Dent, 1983); James Winter, *London's Teeming Streets 1830–1914* (London: Routledge, 1993).

17. For a pertinent case-study in municipalization, see William B. Cohen, *Urban Government and the Rise of the French City: Five Municipalities in the Nineteenth Century* (New York: St Martin's, 1998), chap. 10.

18. Doreen Massey, *Space, Place and Gender* (Cambridge: Polity, 1994), chap. 6.

19. Dunstan, *Governing the Metropolis*, 93.

20. Municipal, state, and federal administrations comprise the tiers of government in Australia. For an overview of municipal government in Melbourne, see David Dunstan, "Municipal Government" in *The Encyclopedia of Melbourne*, ed. Andrew Brown-May and Shurlee Swain (Melbourne: Cambridge University

Press, 1995), 493–95; Bernard Barrett, *The Civic Frontier: The Origin of Local Communities and Local Government in Victoria* (Melbourne: Melbourne University Press, 1979).

21. Tom Stannage, "Bold, William Ernest (1873–1953)," in *Australian Dictionary of Biography* (Melbourne: Melbourne University Press, 1979), 7:335–36.

22. Peter Morton, *After Light: A History of the City of Adelaide and its Council, 1878–1928* (Kent Town, Australia: Wakefield, 1996), 253.

23. See two of the contributions to Michèle Dagenais, Irene Maver, and Pierre-Yves Saunier, eds., *Municipal Services and Employees in the Modern City: New Historic Approaches* (Aldershot, England: Ashgate, 2003): Emmanuel Bellanger, "Town Clerks in the Paris Region: The Design of a Professional Identity in the Late Nineteenth and Early Twentieth Centuries," 103–23; and Irene Maver, "A (North) British End-View: The Comparative Experience of Municipal Employees and Services in Glasgow (1800–1950)," 177–99.

24. See for example trade catalogs in the National Art Library, http://www.vam.ac.uk/collections/prints_books/trade_catalogues.

25. Public Record Office Victoria (PROV), VPRS 3181, 1915/1935.

26. PROV, Melbourne City Council, Town Clerk's Files, 1915/5407.

27. Municipal information from Carlisle, Walsall, Liverpool, Cardiff, West Ham, York, and Nottingham. Journals include the *Engineer* (1871–1913), the *Law Times* (1843–54), and *The Builder* (1872–1914).

28. A sample of the books includes: Charles Slagg, *Sanitary Works in the Smaller Towns and in Villages* (London: Crosby Lockwood and Company, 1876); Edmund W. Garrett, *The Law of Nuisances* (London: William Clowes and Sons, 1897); William H. Maxwell, *The Removal and Disposal of Town Refuse* (London: Sanitary Publishing, 1898); W. C. Popplewell, *The Prevention of Smoke* (London: Scott, Greenwood & Company, 1901); Albert E. Leach, *Food Inspection and Analysis* (New York: John Wiley & Sons, 1905); William Mayo Venable, *Garbage Cremation in America* (New York: John Wiley and Sons, 1906); George A. Soper, *Modern Methods of Street Cleansing* (New York: Engineering News Publishing, 1909); Hollis Godrey, *The Health of the City* (Boston: Houghton Mifflin, 1910); Charles Baskerville, *Municipal Chemistry* (New York: McGraw Hill 1911); Henry S. Curtis, *The Play Movement and Its Significance* (New York: Macmillan, 1917); Howard Lee McBain, *American City Progress and the Law* (New York: Columbia University Press, 1918).

29. Shaw, *Municipal Government in Great Britain*, 1–2.

30. PROV, VPRS 3181, Units 418 and 419 (Information 1862–66, 1867–72).

31. E. G. FitzGibbon, cited in Dunstan, *Governing the Metropolis*, 120.

32. Maver, "A (North) British End-View," 191–96.

33. Pierre-Yves Saunier, "Taking Up the Bet on Connections: A Municipal Contribution," in *Municipal Connections: Cooperation, Links and Transfers among European Cities in the 20th Century*, ed. Pierre-Yves Saunier, Special Issue of *Contemporary European History* 11, no. 4 (2002): 517.

34. PROV, VPRS 3181, Units 970 and 971 (Urinals 1891–1901, 1902–9).

35. PROV, VPRS 3181, Unit 822, January 6, 1862; 3181/823, August 13, 1864.

36. PROV, VPRS 54, Unit 16, Report of Street Maintenance Committee, 19/3/1866.

37. PROV, VPRS 3181, Unit 832, 1873/1334, Secretary, Val de Travers Asphalt Paving Company, London, August 5, 1873; also 3181, Unit 833, 1874/1007, March 5, 1874.

38. PROV, VPRS 3181, Unit 835, 1877/1585, James Smallpage, November 19, 1877.

39. PROV, Melbourne City Council, Town Clerk's Files, 1922/2918.

40. PROV, Melbourne City Council, Town Clerk's Files, 1915/3123; 1922/6154.

41. PROV, Melbourne City Council, Town Clerk's Files, 1915/4693; 1916/2750.

42. Andrew Brown-May and Simon Cooke, "Death, Decency and the Dead-House: The City Morgue in Colonial Melbourne," *Provenance: The Journal of Public Record Office Victoria* 3 (2004), http://www.prov.vic.gov.au/provenance/no3/DeathDecencyDeadHouse1.asp.

43. PROV, VPRS 266, Unit 284, Item 75/4301, Attorney-General's Department, Inward Registered Correspondence; *Age*, January 13, 1871.

44. Robert Freestone, "City Planning," in Brown-May and Swain, *The Encyclopedia of Melbourne*, 139–42.

45. Section XCI of the 1842 *Act to Incorporate the Inhabitants of the Town of Melbourne* (6 Vic. No. 7).

46. Christopher Hamlin, "Environmental Sensibility in Edinburgh, 1839–40: The 'Fetid Irrigation' Controversy," *Journal of Urban History* 20, no. 3 (1994): 311–39.

47. In *Melbourne Street Life*, I observed a developing corpus of regulation governing public behavior and the social use of the streets of an Australian city. Other explorations of the street as a social space, similarly inward looking—such as James Winter's *London's Teeming Streets*, or Peter C. Baldwin's *Domesticating the Street: The Reform of Public Space in Hartford, 1850–1930* (Columbus: Ohio State University Press, 1999)—while giving varying inflection to diverse reform agendas, or constructing differing narratives of continuity or decline, provide an important critical and empirical framework to pursue more global understandings of the city-making process.

48. A Central Board of Health was created in 1854 under the provisions of the Public Health Act (18 Vic. No. 13), and drawing directly on provisions of the imperial Public Health Act 1848. See Dunstan, *Governing the Metropolis*, 132–34.

49. *The Australian Woman's Sphere*, April 10, 1902, p. 159.

50. PROV, Melbourne City Council, Town Clerk's Files, 1911/164, 1912/3027, 1912/6959, 1913/2460, 1913/4285, 1914/6850, 1916/1425, 1923/4345, 1923/5005.

51. *Collingwood Mercury*, June 29, 1878, quoted in Chris McConville, "From 'Criminal Class' to 'Underworld,'" in *The Outcasts of Melbourne*, ed. Graeme Davison, David Dunstan, and Chris McConville (Sydney: Allen & Unwin, 1985), 72.

52. Norbert Elias, *The Civilising Process: The Development of Manners; Changes in the Code of Conduct and Feeling in Early Modern Times*, trans. Edmund Jephcott

(New York: Urizen Books, 1978), 156–60. See also Alain Corbin, *The Foul and the Fragrant: Odor and the French Social Imagination* (Cambridge, MA: Harvard University Press, 1986; first published in French, 1982).

53. Elmer B. Borland, "Municipal Regulation of the Spitting Habit," *Journal of the American Medical Association* (October 20, 1900): 999–1001. See also *New York Times*, January 19, May 13, and June 15, 1896.

54. *The Australian Woman's Sphere* (August 1901): 94. See also the *Age* newspaper on "The Spitting Nuisance," October 17, 1901.

55. PROV, VPRS 3181, Unit 71.

56. PROV, VPRS 3181, Unit 71, 1901/3987.

57. On accidents in the urban context see Bill Luckin, "Accidents, Disasters and Cities," *Urban History* 20, no. 2 (1993): 177–90.

58. Geoffrey Blainey, *The Tyranny of Distance: How Distance Shaped Australia's History* (Melbourne: St. Martin's, 1968).

59. Kenneth T. Jackson, editor-in-chief of the *Encyclopedia of New York City*, as quoted in the *New Yorker*, July 25, 1994.

60. Daves Rossell, comment on street lighting discussion, posted July 1, 1996, H-URBAN discussion log, http://www.h-net.org/~urban (accessed April 10, 2006).

61. Ann Curthoys, "Does Australian History Have a Future?" *Australian Historical Studies* 33, no. 118 (2002): 140–52.

62. Marilyn Silverman and P. H. Gulliver, "Historical Anthropology through Local-Level Research," in *Critical Junctions: Anthropology and History beyond the Cultural Turn*, ed. Don Kalb and Herman Tak (New York: Berghahn, 2005), 152–67.

63. Graeme Davison, "The European city in Australia," *Urban History* 27, no. 6 (2001): 791.

64. Shaw, *Municipal Government in Great Britain*, 11.

65. Saunier, "Taking Up the Bet," 508.

66. Simon J. Potter, ed., *Imperial Communication: Australia, Britain, and the British Empire c.1830–50* (London: Menzies Centre for Australian Studies, 2005).

67. Lindsay Proudfoot and Michael Roche, "Introduction: Place, Network, and the Geographies of Empire," in Proudfoot and Roche, *(Dis)Placing Empire*, 3.

Chapter 3

1. See Pierre-Yves Saunier, "La toile municipale aux XIXème et XXème siècles: Un panorama transnational vu d'Europe," *Urban History Review* (Revue d'Histoire Urbaine) 34, no. 2 (2006): 163–76.

2. Interesting from this point of view is Andrew Brown-May, "'I cittadini stanno iniziando a lamentarsi.' Saperi municipali e contrattazioni attorno a comportamenti pubblici molesti a Melbourne," in *La regola e la trasgressione*, ed. Denis Bocquet and Filippo De Pieri, Special Issue of *Storia Urbana* 108 (2005): 53–66.

3. See Nora Lafi, "Municipalités méditerranéennes: Pratique du comparatisme, lecture des changements institutionnels et analyse historique de l'evolution des pouvoirs urbain," in *Municipalités méditerranéennes. Les réformes urbaines ottomanes au miroir d'une histoire comparée*, ed. Nora Lafi (Berlin: K. Schwarz, 2005), 11–34.

4. Pierre-Yves Saunier, "Circulations, connexions et espaces transnationaux," *Genèses* 57 (2004): 110–26; Matthias Middell, ed., *Globalisierung und Weltgeschichtsschreibung* (Leipzig: Leipziger Universität Verlag, 2003); Ulrike Freitag and Achim Von Oppen, *Translokalität als ein Zugang zur Geschichte Globaler Verflechtungen*, http://hsozkult.geschichte.hu-berlin.de/forum/type=artikel&id=632&view=print.

5. Giovanni Gozzini, "Dalla *Weltgeschichte* alla *World History*: Percorsi Storiografici attorno al Concetto di Globale," *Contemporanea* 1 (2004): 3–37.

6. Paolo Capuzzo and Elisabetta Vezzosi, "Traiettorie della World History," *Contemporanea* 1 (2005): 105–33.

7. Catherine Hall, *Civilizing Subjects: Colony and Metropole in the English Imagination (1830–1867)* (Chicago: Chicago University Press, 2002); Tony Ballantyne, "Empire, Knowledge, and Culture: From Proto-Globalization to Modern Globalization," in *Globalization in World History*, ed. Anthony Hopkins (New York: Norton, 2002); Sanjay Subrahmanyam, *Explorations in Connected History* (Oxford: Oxford University Press, 2005).

8. Richard Horowitz, "International Law and State Transformation in China, Siam and the Ottoman Empire during the Nineteenth century," *Journal of World History* 15, no. 4 (2005): 445–86; Suraiya Faroqhi, *Approaching Ottoman History* (Cambridge: Cambridge University Press, 1999).

9. Youssef Choueiri, *Modern Arab Historiography. Historical Discourse and the Nation-State* (London: Routledge, 2003). The stake today is not to contest the importance of the idea of nation or of religion in societies, which is of course central, but rather to reinsert the study of so-called non-Western societies into a global history that is global not only in its geographical extent but also, and mainly, by its use of global concepts in the study of circulations.

10. Franz Rosenthal, *A History of Muslim Historiography* (Leiden: Brill, 1952). See also Marshall Hodgson, "The Role of Islam in World History," *International Journal of Middle-East Studies* 1, no. 2 (1970): 99–123.

11. Edhem Eldem, Daniel Goffman, and Bruce Masters, *The Ottoman City between East and West* (Cambridge: Cambridge University Press, 1999); see also André Raymond, *Grandes villes arabes à l'epoque ottomane* (Paris: Sinbad, 1985).

12. Ariel Salzmann, *Tocqueville in the Ottoman Empire: Rival Paths to the Modern State* (Leiden: Brill, 2004). See also Nora Lafi, *Une ville du Maghreb entre ancien régime et réformes ottomanes* (Paris: L'Harmattan, 2002).

13. Robert Mantran, ed., *Histoire de l'Empire Ottoman* (Paris: Fayard, 1989).

14. For studies on Beirut (Jens Hanssen), Jerusalem (Yasemin Avcı and Vincent Lemire), Damascus (Stefan Weber), Rhodes (Denis Bocquet), see Lafi, *Municipalités méditerranéennes*.

15. Grégoire Aristarchi Bey, *Législation ottomane ou recueil des lois, règlements, ordonnances, traits, capitulations et autres documents officiels de l'Empire Ottoman* (Constantinople: Nicolaïdes, 1873).

16. See, for example, Robert Mantran, ed., *Histoire de l'empire ottoman* (Paris: Fayard, 2003).

17. Hülya Canbakal, *Society and Politics in an Ottoman Town: 'Ayntâb in the 17th Century* (Leiden: Brill, 2007); Yücel Terzibaşoğlu, "Land Disputes and Ethno-Politics: North-Western Anatolia, 1877–1912," in *Ethno-Nationality, Property Rights in Land and Territorial Sovereignty in Historical Perspective*, ed. Stanley Engerman and Jacob Metzer (London: Routledge, 2004).

18. See, for example, Suraiya Faroqhi, Bruce McGowan, Donald Quataert, and Şevket Pamuk, *An Economic and Social History of the Ottoman Empire, Vol. II, 1600–1914* (Cambridge: Cambridge University Press, 1994).

19. Cyril Black and Carl Brown, eds., *Modernization in the Middle East* (Princeton, NJ: Darwin, 1992).

20. Ilber Ortaylı, *Tanzimat Devrinde Osmanlı Mahallî Idareleri (1840–1880)* (Ankara: Türk Tarih Kurumu, 2000). See also his *Tanzimattan Cumhuriyete Yerel Yönetim Geleneği* (Ankara: Hil Yayın, 1985); and *Osmanlı Imparatorluğu'nda Iktisadî ve sosyal değişim* (Ankara: Turhan Kitabevi, 2000).

21. Steven Rosenthal, "Foreigners and Municipal Reforms in Istanbul: 1855–1865", *International Journal of Middle East Studies* 11, no. 2 (1980): 227–25.

22. See: Osman Nuri Ergin, *Mecelle-I Umûr-ı Belediyye* (Istanbul: Istanbul Municipality, 1995; first printed, 1914–22), 1:1658–72; see also George Young, *Corps de droit ottoman* (Oxford: Clarendon, 1905–6), 1:69–84.

23. See the contributions in Lafi, *Municipalités méditérranéennes*.

24. See Denis Bocquet, "De la municipalité d'Ancien Régime à la municipalité italienne," in Lafi, *Municipalités méditérranéennes*, 51–70.

25. For example, Elisa Radovanovic, *Buenos Aires, Ciudad Moderna (1880–1910)* (Buenos Aires: Banchik, 2002).

26. Bernard Lewis, *The Muslim Discovery of Europe* (London: Weidenfeld & Nicolson, 1982), 207.

27. Ibid., 213.

28. See Vincent Lemire, "Les territoires de l'eau dans la municipalité ottomane de Jérusalem," in *Réseaux techniques et conflits de pouvoir*, ed. Denis Bocquet and Samuel Fettah (Rome: Ecole Française de Rome, 2007), 31–56; see also Vilma Hastaoglou Martinidis, "Innovative Networks: Harbour Works and City Governance in the Levant (1850–1900)," in *Mediterranean Cities Compared*, ed. Yasemin Avcı, Denis Bocquet, and Nora Lafi (forthcoming).

29. As Aristarchi, an Ottoman high-ranking government officer, of Greek identity and cosmopolitan culture, stated in his introduction to his *Législation Ottomane* (1873), his work was intended not only for the chancelleries working in the Empire, but also, in a perspective of compared law, for the public of the *Revue de droit international et de législation comparée*, or the *Zeitschrift für ausländisches Recht*.

30. Abdolomyne Ubicini, *Letters on Turkey* (London: John Murray, 1856), on municipalities see 2:182–93.

31. Laurent-Charles Féraud, *Annales tripolitaines* (Saint-Denis: Bouchène, 2005).

32. As late as 1912, for example, Italy applied the Ottoman legislation in Rhodes. Denis Bocquet, "Une municipalité ottomane face au nationalisme et à la colonisation. Rhodes en 1912," in Lafi, *Municipalités méditerranéennes*, 301–38.

33. Lafi, "Les pouvoirs urbains à Tunis à la fin de l'epoque ottomane: La persistance de l'Ancien Régime," in Lafi, *Municipalités méditerranéennes*, 229–51.

34. See Rosenthal, "Foreigners and Municipal Reforms."

35. Gabriel Baer, *Studies in the Social History of Modern Egypt* (Chicago: University of Chicago Press, 1969). See also Michael Reimer, "Urban Government and Administration in Egypt (1805–1914)," *Die Welt des Islams* 39, no. 3 (1999): 289–318.

36. Selçuk Esenbel and Inaba Chiharu, eds., *The Rising Sun and the Turkish Crescent* (Istanbul: Bogaziçi University Press, 2003).

37. Sahara Tetsuya, "Municipal Reforms in Japan and Turkey: The Belediye System of the Tanzimat and Municipal Laws in Meiji Japan," in Esenbel and Chiharu, *The Rising Sun*, 241–65. On such contacts, see also Alain Roussillon, *Identité et modernité. Voyageurs égyptiens au Japon* (Paris: Sinbad, 2005).

38. Christoph Herzog and Raoul Motika, "Orientalism 'alla Turca': Late Nineteenth/ Early Twentieth c. Ottoman Voyages into the Muslim Outback," *Die Welt des Islams* 40, no. 2 (2000): 139–95.

39. Tetsuya, "Municipal Reforms," 251.

40. All major cities of the empire were provided with a local almanac, which proved a terrific source for historians, as shown by Jens Hanssen, "The Origins of the Municipal Council in Beirut (1860–1908)," in Lafi, *Municipalités méditerranéennes*, 139–76.

41. The richness of the petition (*Şikayet*) dossier in the central archives of the Ottoman Empire (Başbakanlık Osmanlı Arşivi) in Istanbul illustrates this matter of fact.

42. See, for example, the dossier of the coordination between seventeen municipalities of the empire—including Edirne, Beirut, and Aleppo—for the equipment in the 1880s of local fire brigades with German pumps. Istanbul, Başbakanlık Osmanlı Arşivi (central archives of the Ottoman Empire), DH. ID Dossier no. 137, doc. no. 331.

43. In Istanbul: Başbakanlık Osmanlı Arşivi, Dossier Trablus al-Gharb. In Tripoli: National Libyan Archives, dossier Baladiyya.

44. A civic assembly of merchants (*jamaʿa al-balad*) with a chief of the town (*shaykh al-balad*) at its head.

45. France seized Ottoman Algeria between 1830 and 1848 and attempted the same in Ottoman Tunisia.

46. England was looking for a link between the Mediterranean, the *balad al-Sudan*, and the Indian Ocean at a time before they had seized Egypt.

47. Lafi, *Une ville du Maghreb*.

48. Lafi, "Les pouvoirs urbains à Tunis."

49. See Jens Hanssen, Thomas Philipp, and Stefan Weber, *The Empire in the City: Arab Provincial Capitals in the Late Ottoman Empire* (Beirut: Orient Institute, 2002).

50. On these issues, Joe Nasr and Mercedes Volait, eds., *Urbanism: Imported or Exported?* (Chichester: Wiley, 2003).

Chapter 4

1. Quoted in Charles A. Beard, *The Administration and Politics of Tokyo: A Survey and Opinions* (New York: Macmillan, 1923), v.

2. Ibid., 1.

3. Ibid.

4. Stephen R. Reed, *Japanese Prefectures and Policymaking* (Pittsburgh: University of Pittsburgh Press, 1986), 25.

5. Richard J. Samuels, *The Politics of Regional Policy in Japan* (Princeton, NJ: Princeton University Press, 1983), 245.

6. Jeffrey E. Hanes, *The City as Subject: Seki Hajime and the Reinvention of Modern Osaka* (Berkeley: University of California Press, 2002), 243–45.

7. Daniel T. Rodgers, *Atlantic Crossings: Social Politics in a Progressive Age* (Cambridge, MA: Harvard University Press, 1998).

8. Stefan Tanaka, *New Times in Modern Japan* (Princeton, NJ: Princeton University Press, 2004), 40.

9. Albert C. Craig, ed., *Japan: A Comparative View* (Princeton, NJ: Princeton University Press, 1979).

10. Tanaka, *New Times*, passim.

11. Edward Seidensticker, *Low City, High City: Tokyo from Edo to the Earthquake* (New York: Alfred A. Knopf, 1983), 26.

12. Fujimori Terunobu, *Meiji no Tôkyô keikaku* (Tokyo: Iwanami Shoten, 1982), 3–4.

13. David Harvey, *Paris, Capital of Modernity* (London: Routledge, 2003).

14. Mikuriya Takashi, *Shuto keikaku: keisei-ki Meiji kokka no jitsuzô* (Tokyo: Yamakawa Shuppansha, 1984), 17.

15. Fujimori, *Meiji no Tokyo keikaku*, figs. 54 and 55.

16. Jinnai Hidenobu, *Tokyo no Kûkan jinruigaku*, 224–25.

17. Seidensticker, *Low City, High City*, 29.

18. Kurt Steiner, *Local Government in Japan* (Stanford, CA: Stanford University Press, 1965), 37.

19. Quoted in ibid., 37.

20. Ibid., 47.

21. Murata Michihito, "Osaka as a Center of Regional Governance," in *Osaka: The Merchants' Capital of Early Modern Japan*, ed. James L. McClain and Wakita Osamu, trans. Kikuko Yamashita (Ithaca, NY: Cornell University Press, 1999), 259.

22. Blair A. Ruble, *Second Metropolis: Pragmatic Pluralism in the Gilded Age Chicago, Silver Age Moscow, and Meiji Osaka* (Cambridge: Woodrow Wilson Center Press, Cambridge University Press, 2001), 124.

23. On the more general tendency to project Tokyo onto other cities, see André Sorensen, *The Making of Urban Japan: Cities and Planning from Edo to the Twenty-First Century* (London: Routledge, 2002), 82.

24. Ruble, *Second Metropolis*, 124–25.

25. See Hanes, *The City as Subject*.

26. Rodgers, *Atlantic Crossings*, passim.

27. Quoted in Ibid., 12.

28. Ibid.

29. Ibid., 1–2, 33–34.

30. Ibid.

31. Ibid., 33–34, 192.

32. Ibid., 48.

33. See Shibamura Atsuki, "Taisho Showa shoki no daitoshi seido mondai," In *Yokota Kenichi Sensei Kanreki Kinen Nihonshi Ronso* (Suita: Yokota Kenichi Sensei Kanreki Kinenkai,1976).

34. Ibid.

35. Seki Hajime, "Toshi seido ron," in *Toshi seisaku no riron to jissai*, ed. Seki Hakase Ronbun Shûhenshû Iinkai (Osaka: Osaka Toshi Kyôkai, 1968), 15.

36. Ibid.

37. Ibid.

38. Carl Mosk, *Japanese Industrial History: Technology, Urbanization, and Economic Growth* (Armonk, NY: M. E. Sharpe, 2001), 233.

39. Seki, "Toshi seido," 10.

40. Ibid., 9–12.

41. Ibid., 11.

42. Reed, *Japanese Prefectures and Policymaking*, 44.

43. Seki, "Toshi seido," 9–51.

44. Ibid., 16.

45. Ibid.

46. William A. Robson, *The Development of Local Government*, rev. and enlarged 2nd ed. (London: George Allen & Unwin, 1948), 15.

47. Ibid., 52.

48. Seki, "Toshi seido," 18–19.

49. Ibid., 20–21.

50. Quoted in Seki, "Toshi seido," 24.

51. Ibid.

52. Seki Hajime, "Miezaru seifu," *Dai Osaka* 5, no. 8 (August 1929): 15–21.

53. William Bennett Munro, *The Invisible Government* (New York: Macmillan, 1928), 9.

54. Quoted in Mary Ritter Beard, *The Making of Charles A. Beard* (New York: Exposition, 1955), 53–54.

55. Ibid., 54.

56. Quoted in Ellen Nore, *Charles A. Beard: An Intellectual Biography* (Carbondale: Southern Illinois University Press, 1983), 104.

Chapter 5

1. In addition to the other chapters in this volume, see European surveys by Michael Hebbert and Shane Ewen, "European Cities into a Networked World during the Long 20th Century," *Environment and Planning C: Government and Policy* 25 (2007): 325–40; and Pierre-Yves Saunier, "La toile municipale aux XIXème et XXème siècles: Un panorama transnational vu d'Europe," *Urban History Review (Revue d'Histoire Urbaine)* 34, no. 2 (2006): 163–76.

2. It has been especially useful for us to attend intermunicipal events during the past three years, especially the Eurocities general assembly of November 2005 in Lyon.

3. On the UIV/IULA, see the special issue of *Contemporary European History* 11, no. 4 (2002), dedicated to municipal connections.

4. Patrizia Dogliani, *Un laboratorio di socialismo municipale: la Francia, 1870–1920* (Milan: Franco Angeli, 1992), chap. 2.

5. See Françoise Levie, *L'homme qui voulait classer le monde: Paul Otlet et le mundaneum* (Bruxelles: Les Impressions Nouvelles, 2006).

6. Jordi Borja, "Eurocities: A System of Major Urban Centers in Europe," *Ekistics* 352–53 (1992): 21–27.

7. Lyon Municipal Archives (now AML), 1729 WP 001, Moulinier to Borja, October 27, 1988.

8. See Javier Monclus, "The Barcelona Model: An Original Formula?" *Planning Perspectives* 18, no. 4 (2003): 399–421, and the chapter by Robin and Velut in this volume.

9. Seven such groups were established in 1989: port cities, urban renewal, culture, coordination of urban research, children in the city, universities and research, and economic development and technological cooperation.

10. It was also in 1991 that an executive committee was established, the six founding partner cities being joined by the chairs of the working groups. This scheme was tweaked to create a more democratically elected governing body during the 1990s. Practical work is accomplished though three main channels: the annual general meeting and its thematic conference, the six thematic forums and their bi- or tri-annual meetings, and the thirty-six working policy groups.

11. Commission of the European Community, Green Paper on the Urban Environment COM(1990)218 (Brussels: Commission of the European Community, 1990); Michael Parkinson, "Urban Policy in Europe. Where Have We Been and Where Are We Going?" in *European Metropolitan Governance: Cities in Europe; Europe in the Cities*, ed. Eugen Antalovsky, Jens. S Dangschat, and Michael Parkinson (2005), http://www.ljmu.ac.uk/EIUA/EIUA_Docs/cities_in_europe.pdf (accessed August 30, 2007).

12. Bruce Millan is a British socialist with a Scottish background. He was elected a Member of Parliament in 1959 and held several ministerial positions. He was European Commissioner for Regional Policy and Cohesion from 1988–95.

13. RECITE (Regions and Cities for Europe) was designed to promote knowledge exchanges among networks of local authorities. Between 1991 and 1995, the sum of 4.2 million ECU was made available to 15 European networks (Eurocities did not bid as such).

14. On URBAN, see Humbolt Study Team, "The European URBAN Experience Seen from the Academic Perspective," September 2006, http://urbact.eu/fr/projects/the-urban-experience/documents/urban-study-report.html (accessed August 30, 2007).

15. The Council of European Municipalities was created in 1951 as a step toward European federalism and expanded local self-government. It incorporated "Regions" into its title in 1984. After years of feuding and conflict between the two bodies, CEMR became the European branch of the UIV/IULA in 1990. CEMR was a patron of both the Rotterdam and Barcelona meetings and provided administrative support and lobbying connections to Eurocities until 1991. On the CEMR, see Oscar Gaspari, "Cities against States? Hopes, Dreams and Shortcomings of the European Municipal Movement 1900–1960," *Contemporary European History* 11, no. 4 (2002): 597–621.

16. In an internal memo dated October 1991, a Lyon representative captured this aspect of the ongoing discussion: "It is clear that the sooner we exist as an independent structure, the better it will be for our relations with the CEMR. This would eliminate any ambiguity" (AML, 1729 W4, memo on Eurocities steering committee, Brussels, October 7, 1991).

17. On policy windows, John D. Kingdon, *Agendas, Alternatives and Public Policies*, 2nd ed. (New York: Harper Collins, 1995); John T. S. Keeler, *Réformer: Les conditions du changement politique* (Paris: PUF, 1994).

18. See Kingdon, *Agendas*.

19. Cf. the reluctance of Scandinavian municipalities to enter into European and transatlantic municipal associations in the 1930s, as they felt able to use their own resources to harness foreign municipal experiments. See Pierre-Yves Saunier, "*Selling the Idea of Cooperation*. The U.S. Foundations and the European Components of the Urban Internationale (1920s–1960s)," in *American Foundations and Large Scale Research: Construction and Transfer of Knowledge*, ed. Giuliana Gemelli (Bologna: Clueb, 2001), 219–46.

20. Saunier, "Changing the City: Urban International Information and the Lyon Municipality, 1900–1940," *Planning Perspectives* 14, no. 1 (1999): 19–48.

21. *Exposition internationale de Lyon. Guide général* (Lyon: Editions du Guide Général, 1914), 6.

22. AML, 781 WP 005, "Exposition Universelle et Internationale de Gand 1913," report of January 10, 1913, and Herriot's letters, March 12 and 21, 1913.

23. Jacques Fauret, *Les relations internationales de la ville de Lyon*, mémoire de DEA en administration publique, IEP Lyon, 1990.

24. AML 1729W5, Mayor's letter, May 9, 1989. The council was mainly a think tank in which stakeholders discussed mechanisms for transforming Lyon into a European metropolis. The public relations aspect was especially successful, as suggested by the list of guests, among whom was European Commission President Jacques Delors, who attended a session that focused on the activities of the fledgling Eurocities network in 1991.
25. With this signature, Lyon gained its status of "organizer" of the Barcelona conference and "Eurocities founding member" label. AML, Maragall to Collomb, January 25, 1989, and Collomb to Maragall, February 24, 1989.
26. See press clippings in AML, 1729 W001.
27. Aisling Healy, "Le territoire contre la politique? L'impératif métropolitain d'un groupe d'entrepreneurs lyonnais (2001–2004)," in *Idéologies et action publique territoriale. La politique change-t-elle encore les politiques?* ed. Lionel Arnaud, Christian Le Bart, and Romain Pasquier (Rennes: Presses Universitaires de Rennes, 2006), 211–27.
28. Renaud Payre, "The Science That Never Was: Communal Science in France 1913–1949," *Contemporary European History* 11, no. 4 (2002): 529–48; Federico Lucarini, *Scienze comunali e pratiche di governo in Italia (1890–1915)* (Milan: Giuffré, 2003); Michael Frisch, "Urban Theorists, Urban Reform and American Political Culture in the Progressive Period," *Political Science Quarterly* 97, no. 2 (1982): 295–315.
29. See Saunier, "Sketches from the Urban Internationale. Voluntary Societies, International Organizations and U.S. Foundations at the City's bedside 1900–1960," *International Journal for Urban and Regional Research* 25, no. 2 (2001): 380–403.
30. See Saunier, "Changing the City," 37.
31. AML, 1114 WP 005.
32. *Conférence Internationale de Lyon* (Bruxelles: UIV, 1934), 213.
33. Louis Brownlow, *The Autobiography of Louis Brownlow. The Second Half* (Chicago: University of Chicago Press, 1958), 305.
34. Evidence is also available in Lyon's correspondence files. See, for example, the enthusiastic letter by the Mayor of Calais after his 1925 visit, AML 1112 WP 001, Léon Vincent to Edouard Herriot, October 20, 1925.
35. AML, 1112 WP 001, Vinck to Herriot January 19, 1929.
36. Herriot was twice prime minister in the 1920s and a leader of the very important Parti Radical.
37. Saunier, "Changing the City," 27–32.
38. AML, 985 WP 024, Standing Committee minutes, May 27 and 28, 1935. The committee was eventually not created, but the conference did take place amid widespread pressure from European socialists against holding a meeting in Nazi Germany, where municipal autonomy had been crushed.
39. http://www.eurocities.org/main.php (accessed June 16, 2007).
40. The "European Network for Exchange of Experience," or "URBACT" was launched in 2002. It funds working groups and studies to "exchange, capitalise

and disseminate" best practices in the field of urban policies. The whole set up shares much with Eurocities' knowledge-based rationales. The Greater Lyon Authority is currently leading the URBACT Pilot Fast Track Network: "The urban, social, economic and cultural regeneration of public housing estates in urban areas."

41. Interview with a French observer of the "urban renewal" and "urban research" working groups, March 30, 2007.

42. AML, 1729 WP 002. An internal memo issued in 1991 established that only two commissions out of a dozen were actually afloat.

43. In the case of Lyon, the Greater Lyon Authority benefited from an URBAN subsidy in 1996 (192 million francs for a program of urban renewal).

44. Such projects are long-term ones: Lyon chaired the Eurocities High Speed Trains Cities commission from 1995 to 1997, and as recently as February 2006, used the opportunity of a Eurocities' delegation meeting with the European Parliament's president to recommend the Lyon-Turin line.

45. Interview with city hall staff in charge of Eurocities at Lyon City Hall, December 8, 2005.

46. The Eurocities Awards were created in 2000 to single out "outstanding achievement by Eurocities members in the delivery of local activities or practices which improve the quality of life for citizens," http://www.eurocities.org/main.php (accessed August 8, 2007).

47. Interview with city hall staff member in charge of Eurocities, December 8, 2005.

48. The idea that the Single Market would deeply modify the European urban hierarchy became common in the 1980s. It was formalized in the 1990s with the works of Paul Krugman or Ronald Rogowski, who predicted that only a handful of European cities would still be a place on the map after fifty years of European integration. See Patrick Le Galès, *European Cities: Social Conflicts and Governance* (Oxford: Oxford University Press, 2002), 148–49, and Ewen's chapter in this collection.

49. Interview with executive secretary of an international network of municipalities, June 1, 2007.

Chapter 6

1. "Kampong" is the Bahasa Melayu word for village and is the root of the English word "compound."

2. Singapore is a single municipality with no domestic hinterland.

3. National Archives of Singapore (hereafter NAS), Lee Kuan Yew, Prime Minister's National Day Rally Speech at the Singapore Conference Hall, August 19, 1984.

4. Richard Harris's recent work on the late colonial period of British rule is especially relevant here. Harris argues the Singapore Improvement Trust (SIT) laid the groundwork for an efficient building industry despite its lack of funds and

limited legal powers, contrary to the Housing and Development Board (HDB) narrative which excoriates the SIT for its lack of productivity. Richard Harris, "Singapore in Context: The Origins and Evolution of British Colonial Housing Policy, 1930s–1962," paper presented at the Institute for Asian Research, National University of Singapore, March 13, 2002.

5. Lee Sheng Yi, "Business Elites in Singapore," in *Studies in ASEAN Sociology: Urban Society and Social Change*, ed. Peter S. J. Chen and Hans-Dieter Evers (Singapore: Chopmen Enterprises, 1978), 46.

6. NAS, HDB Box 1223, letter from N. A. Canton to J. M. Fraser, February 25, 1948.

7. NAS, HDB Box 1238, East Asian Regional Organisation for Planning and Housing Seminar in Tokyo, 1964.

8. The Colombo Plan for Cooperative Economic Development in South and Southeast Asia is not a single plan but rather the term used to indicate the collective actions of the Consultative Committee from 1950 to 1966. The committee is the major decision-making body of the plan and has representatives from all member countries. NAS, HDB Box 1227, "Extracts from the Report on Training Facilities at the Technician Level in South and Southeast Asia," February 12, 1964.

9. C. J. W.-L. Wee, "Our Island Story: Economic Development and the National Narrative in Singapore," in *New Terrains in Southeast Asian History*, ed. Abu Talib Ahmad and Tan Liok Ee (Singapore: Singapore University Press, 2003), 146–47.

10. NAS, HDB 1094, Report by the Manager of the SIT, J. M. Fraser, September 24, 1951; National University of Singapore, Malaysia, and Singapore Collections; J. M. Fraser, *The Work of the Singapore Improvement Trust* (Singapore: The Trust, 1948).

11. NAS, Microfilm NA 1169, letter from Francis Thomas, October 5, 1956.

12. United Nations, Tropical Housing Mission, *Low Cost Housing in South and Southeast Asia, Report of Mission of Experts 22 November 1950–January 23*, Document, ST/SOA/3/rev.1 (New York: United Nations, 1951), 34–35.

13. Seminar on regional planning, *Regional Planning: Seminar on Regional Planning, Tokyo, 28 July to 8 August, 1958*, ST SOA Ser. C 12 & 13 (New York: United Nations, 1958).

14. NAS, HDB Box 1239, Economic Commission for Asia and the Far East: Committee on Industry and Natural Resources, Sub-Committee on Housing, Building, and Planning, Ninth session, July 2–9, 1969.

15. NAS, HDB Box 1239, Report on International Council for Building Research, Studies, and Documentation, CIB Congress, Cambridge, September 1962.

16. International Labour Organization (ILO), *The Development of the Cooperative Movement in Asia* (Geneva: The Office, 1949); UN Report of Mission of Experts 10, no. 28.

17. NAS, HDB Box 1239, ILO Report on "Workers' Housing Problems in Asian Countries," 1954, as referenced in ECAFE Committee on Industry and Natural Resources, "Urbanization and Housing in Asia and the Far East," Seventh Session, September 25–29, 1962.

18. "Profile 4: International Labour Organization," *Population Index* 44, no. 2 (April 1978), 213–14; J. M. Fraser, "Singapore, a Problem in Population," *Town and Country Planning* 139 (November 1955) as cited in Gregory Clancey, "Toward a Spatial History of Emergency: Notes from Singapore," *Asia Research Institute Working Paper Series No. 8* (August 2003).

19. Clancey, "Toward a Spatial History," 9, 17.

20. Pierre-Yves Saunier, "Sketches from the Urban Internationale: Voluntary Societies, International Organizations, and U.S. Foundations at the City's Bedside, 1900–1960," *International Journal o f Urban and Regional Research* 25 (June 1999): 380–403.

21. Quoted in David Belloch, "Bold New Programme: A Review of United Nations Technical Assistance," *International Affairs* 33, no. 1 (January 1957): 36; C. M. Turnbull, "Regionalism and Nationalism," in *The Cambridge History of Southeast Asia*, ed. Nicholas Tarling (Cambridge: Cambridge University Press, 1992), 2:597.

22. "Resolutions of the Economic and Social Council on Technical Assistance for Economic Development of Underdeveloped Countries, August 14 and 15, 1949," *International Organization* 3, no. 4 (November 1949): 770–71; NAS, Microfilm NA 2618, "Housing in the Tropics," *UN Housing and Town and Country Planning Bulletin* 6 (1952): 83.

23. NAS, Microfilm NA 2618, J. Graham Parsons, U.S. Assistant Secretary of State for Far Eastern Affairs, "Asia and Western Policy," *Singapore American*, September 15, 1959.

24. NAS, Microfilm NA 2829, "Americans Learn More about Asia," press clippings.

25. NAS, Microfilm NA 2618, Ralph I. Straus, "Role of American Business," report to the Departments of State and Commerce as requested by Congress, February 15, 1960.

26. NAS, HDB 1227, unsigned, undated draft paper, c. 1963.

27. Cornell University, Kroch Library (hereafter CU), Charles Abrams Papers, Reel 24, letter from Otto Koenigsberger and Susume Kobe to Charles Abrams, June 17, 1963.

28. CU, Charles Abrams Papers, Reel 24, letters requesting documents from Charles Abrams to Peggy (no last name) and Hilbert Fefferman, HHFA, from Singapore, July 20, 1963.

29. Unfortunately, the transcript does not include any information on which cities Alan Choe visited, or whom he met with while in the United States. NAS, oral history of Alan Choe, Reel 4, interviewed August 1 and 29, 1997.

30. NAS, HDB Box 1244, memo from Toh Shung Pie, Acting Deputy Manager for the SIT, July 16, 1959.

31. NAS, Ministry of Culture, Broadcasting Division, "Berita Singapura," c. 1960s.
32. The mission explicitly referenced Jacobus P. Thijsse's paper in their report. CU, Charles Abrams Papers, Reel 24, Report for the Government of Singapore as prepared by an Expert Mission appointed under the UN Technical Assistance Programme, c. 1963; "Metropolitan Planning in the Netherlands" (United Nations, New York, 1959).
33. CU, Charles Abrams Papers, Reel 24, papers and reports.
34. Lee Sheng-Yi, *The Monetary and Banking Development of Singapore and Malaysia* (Singapore: Singapore University Press, 1991), 248.
35. CU, Charles Abrams Papers, Reel 24, "UN Experts' 'Go Ahead' for Big City Face-Lift," most likely *Straits Times*, c. 1963.
36. The HDB is a statutory board under the National Development Ministry. NAS, oral history of Tan Chok Kian, Reel 4, interviewed February 19, 1993.
37. Tan Chok Kian attributed the self-contained neighborhood to lingering British influences. Ibid.
38. NAS, HDB Box 1239, letter from Tan Chok Kian, for Permanent Secretary to Chief Architect of HDB, December 12, 1969; letter from Teh Cheang Wan, Chief Architect of HDB, November 27, 1969 (quote from latter.)
39. Ibid.
40. NAS, Microfilm 1238, memo from the Acting Chief Architect to the Chief Executive Officer, January 11, 1964, Microfilm 1238.
41. NAS, HDB Box 1251, Neighbourhood V, letter from S. Thiruchelvam, CEO of HDB, February 21, 1963.
42. NAS, HDB Box 1251, memos on stamp design contest, 1969.
43. Provident Funds were begun in India (1948), Malaya (1952), Iraq (1956), Ceylon (1958), and a number of African countries in the 1960s as well. Victor Gerdes, "African Provident Funds," *Industrial and Labor Relations Review* 24, no. 4 (1971): 572–87.
44. Unfortunately, the archival record for this is as yet quite slim, with key documents relating to the creation and implementation of the Homeownership Scheme still closed to researchers. At the time of this research (2004), the National Archives of Singapore had not yet released many governmental papers from 1965 onward. All archival papers must be reviewed and approved before being opened to researchers.
45. NAS, HDB Box 1263, Aide Memoire: Survey Mission on the Financing of Housing in the ECAFE Region, 1970.
46. Lim Kim San, Minister of National Development, quoted in NAS, Microfilm NA 563, "New HDB priorities," *Straits Times*, November 1, 1975.
47. "Provision of Public Housing in Singapore," Third World Network, Special Unit for South-South Cooperation, United Nations Development Programme (UNDP), n.d.
48. NAS, Microfilm NA 563, "Home Comfort," *Straits Times*, May 28, 1975.
49. Ibid.

50. Eighty-four percent of the total population lived in HDB flats in 1985, and eighty-six percent in 1995. Linda Low and T. C. Aw, *Housing a Healthy, Wealthy and Education Nation through the CPF* (Singapore: Times Academic Press, 1997), 45.

51. For one example, see NAS, Parliamentary Debates Collection: Legislative Assembly Sittings, Official Report First Session of the Second Parliament, Part I of the First Session. Columns 1 to 832. From May 6, 1968 to August 1, 1968. Vol. 27.

52. Robert Powell et al., *No Limits: Articulating William Lim* (Singapore: Select Publishing, 2002), 83–84.

53. Ibid., 74.

54. Robert Powell, Tay Kheng Soon, and Akitek Tenggara, *Line, Edge, and Shade: The Search for a Design Language in Tropical Asia* (Singapore: Page One Publishing, 1997), 15.

55. Powell et al., *No Limits*, 82–83.

56. William S. W. Lim, *Cities for People: Reflections of a Southeast Asian Architect* (Singapore: Select Books, 1990), 44.

57. Powell et al., *No Limits*, 75.

58. NAS, Microfilm 1238, Visitors' log.

59. NAS, HDB Box 1248, letter from Mr. Albert K. Ludy, U.S. Embassy, Singapore, to Mr. Howe Yoon Chong, Ministry of National Development, July 18, 1966.

60. National Library of Singapore, Legislative Assembly debates, March 14, 1974, p. 138.

61. NAS, HDB Box 1239, letter from David Wong to Lim Kim San, September 18, 1963.

62. Quoted in Low and Aw, *Housing*, 12.

63. Xavier Guillot, "Flux économiques, transferts d'expertises et production immobilière haut de gamme en Asie orientale," *Géocarrefour* 80, no. 3 (2006): 171–82.

Chapter 7

1. Michael Goldsmith, "The Europeanisation of Local Government," *Urban Studies* 30, no. 4/5 (1993): 683–99.

2. Simon Bulmer and Martin Burch, "The Europeanization of UK Government: From Quiet Revolution to Explicit Step-Change?" *Public Administration* 83, no. 4 (2005): 861–90.

3. Hank Savitch and Peter Kantor, *Cities in the International Marketplace* (Princeton, NJ: Princeton University Press, 2002).

4. R. A. W. Rhodes, *Understanding Governance: Policy Networks, Governance, Reflexivity and Accountability* (Buckingham: Open University Press, 1997), chap. 7; Michael Goldsmith and John Garrard, "Urban Governance: Some Reflections," in *Urban Governance: Britain and Beyond since 1750*, ed. Robert J. Morris and Richard H. Trainor (Aldershot, UK: Ashgate, 2000), 22–23.

5. Gerry Stoker, *Transforming Local Governance: From Thatcherism to New Labour* (Basingstoke: Palgrave Macmillan, 2004).

6. Michael P. Smith, *Transnational Urbanism: Locating Globalisation* (Oxford: Blackwell, 2001).

7. For an up-to-date literature review: Pierre-Yves Saunier, "La toile municipale aux XIXème–XXème siècles: Un panorama transnational vu d'Europe," *Urban History Review (Revue d'Histoire Urbaine)* 34, no. 2 (2006): 163–76.

8. George C. Allen, *The Industrial Development of Birmingham and the Black Country* (London: Allen and Unwin, 1929).

9. John Ralph, "The Best Governed City in the World," *Harper's New Monthly Magazine* 81 (1890): 99.

10. Quoted in Birmingham City Council, *Annual Report and Accounts* (Birmingham: Birmingham City Council, 1989), 4.

11. *The Municipal Journal & Public Works Engineer*, February 21, 1930, p. 314.

12. City of Birmingham Information Bureau, *Birmingham: The Hub of Industrial England* (Birmingham: Birmingham City Council, 1931), 2.

13. John B. Smith, "The Economic History of Birmingham," in *Birmingham: Bibliography of a City*, ed. Carl Chinn (Birmingham: University of Brimingham Press, 2004), 157–80; City of Birmingham Information Bureau, *Birmingham: Britain's Second City* (Birmingham: Birmingham City Council, 1965), 2; Anthony Sutcliffe and Roger Smith, *A History of Birmingham 1939–1970* (London: Oxford University Press, 1974), 154.

14. Phil Jones, "Historical Continuity and post-1945 Urban Redevelopment: The Example of Lee Bank, Birmingham, UK," *Planning Perspectives* 19, no. 4 (2004): 365–89.

15. Ken Spencer et al., *Crisis in the Industrial Heartlands: A Study of the West Midlands* (Oxford: Clarendon, 1986).

16. Birmingham City Council, *Birmingham's Renaissance* (Birmingham: Birmingham City Council, 2003), 1.

17. Patrick Loftman and Brendan Nevin, "Going for Growth: Prestige Projects in Three British Cities," *Urban Studies* 33, no. 6 (1996): 991–1019; Frank Webster, "Re-Inventing Place: Birmingham as an Information City?" *City* 5, no. 1 (2001): 27–46.

18. David Lister, "The Transformation of a City: Birmingham," in *Whose Cities?* ed. Mark Fisher and Ursula Owen (London: Penguin Books, 1991), 54; David Harvey, "From Managerialism to Entrepreneurialism: The Transformation of Urban Governance in Late Capitalism," *Geographiska Annaler* 71B, no. 1 (1989): 3–18.

19. Ian Latham and Mark Swenarton, *Brindleyplace: A Model for Urban Regeneration* (London: Right Angle, 1999). Alongside these prestige projects were various "booster initiatives," including the construction of Centenary Square; unsuccessful bids for the 1992 and 1996 Olympic Games; the transfer of the Sadler's Wells Royal Ballet Company and D'Oyly Opera Company from London to Birmingham; and an annual street motorcar race from 1986 to 1990.

20. Birmingham City Archives [hereafter BCA] MS2299 Box 19, Birmingham Chamber of Commerce and Industry Council Minutes [hereafter BCCI Mins], November 24, 1958, p. 70.

21. Ibid, Box 24, October 22, 1962, p. 315; Box 23, July 24, 1961, p. 190; Box 25, October 23, 1963, p. 333; Sutcliffe and Smith, *A History of Birmingham*, 159, 165.
22. BCA MS2299 Box 19, BCCI Mins, May 27, 1957, p. 47; Birmingham City Library Local Studies Section [hereafter BCLLSS] LF59.2, Anonymous, "The National Exhibition Centre Birmingham: Initial Development, Management and Financial Appraisal" (unpublished memorandum, May 8, 1970).
23. Edward Mills, *The National Exhibition Centre: A Shop Window for the World* (London: Crobsy Lockwood Staples, 1976), 15.
24. To consolidate the know-how taken from Phoenix, the Council's Chief Executive later attended a colloquium on urban development in Cleveland in April 1983, whereupon he reported favourably on the benefits of science parks to urban regeneration. This resulted in a trailblazing multi-agent partnership between the City Council, Aston University and Lloyds Bank in 1983 to develop Aston Science Park: BCLLSS [unreferenced] Birmingham City Council General Purposes Committee Minutes [hereafter GPC Mins], December 15, 1982, May 25, 1983; BCLLSS L34.3, Birmingham City Council Minutes [hereafter BCC Mins], November 5, 1985, p. 290.
25. *International Convention Centre Birmingham: Feasibility Study* (Birmingham: Birmingham City Council, 1983); GPC Mins, March 17, 1982, April 14, 1982.
26. Goldsmith and Garrard, "Urban Governance," 18–19.
27. Andrew Scott, John Peterson, and David Millar, "Subsidiarity: A 'Europe of the Regions' v. the British Constitution?" *Journal of Common Market Studies* 32, no. 1 (1994): 47–67.
28. The structural funds, as they became known in 1988, comprise the ERDF, the ESF, and the European Agricultural Guidance and Guaranteed Fund.
29. Peter John, *Local Governance in Western Europe* (London: Sage, 2001).
30. R. A. W. Rhodes, "The European Community and British Public Administration: The Case of Local Government," *Journal of Common Market Studies* 11 (1973): 265–66.
31. Ibid., 267–68.
32. BCC Mins, June 12, 1984, p. 87; Steve Martin and Graham Pearce, "The Internationalization of Local Authority Economic Development Strategies: Birmingham in the 1980s," *Regional Studies* 26, no. 5 (1992): 500.
33. BCC Mins, January 7, 1986, p. 396.
34. Ibid., April 7, 1987, p. 657.
35. Paul McAleavey and James Mitchell, "Industrial Regions and Lobbying in the Structural Funds Reform Process," *Journal of Common Market Studies* 32, no. 2 (1994): 240.
36. Funded from the ESF, Objective III status tackled long-term unemployment: ibid., 240.
37. Martin Burch and Ricardo Gomez, "The English Regions and the European Union," *Regional Studies* 36, no. 7 (2002): 770.
38. BCC Mins, April 12, 1988, pp. 681–82.

39. Patrick Loftman and Brendan Nevin, *Urban Regeneration and Social Equity: A Case Study of Birmingham 1986–1992* (Birmingham: University of Central England, 1992), 119, 138; Birmingham City Council, *Birmingham's Renaissance: How European Funding has Revitalised the City* (Birmingham: Birmingham City Council, 2003), 52.

40. BCCLSS [unreferenced], Joint European and International Policy Sub-Committee Minutes [hereafter JEIPSC Mins], April 24, 1996, p. 2.

41. This comprised a civic reception for local businesses, an economic forum, a leafleting campaign, foreign language workshops, and the launch of a Council Export Support Unit to provide advice to businesses looking to compete in the free market: BCC Mins, November 1, 1988, p. 385–87.

42. Gormley's "Iron Man" stands at the lower end of Victoria Square and was cast to represent the skills of Birmingham iron-workers. Mason's "Forward" was a statue of Birmingham people marching from its smoky industrial past into the future.

43. Geoffrey Tyack, "The Public Face," in *The English Urban Landscape*, ed. Philip Waller (Oxford: Oxford University Press, 2000), 300–302.

44. BCC Mins, December 4, 1984, p. 339.

45. *The Financial Times*, October 18, 1991, p. 22.

46. This description was from Roy Hattersley, the former deputy leader of the national Labour Party, in *The Guardian*, March 22, 2001.

47. Birmingham City Council, *An Economic Strategy for Birmingham* (Birmingham: Birmingham City Council, 1985).

48. Birmingham City Council, *City Centre Strategy* (Birmingham: Birmingham City Council, 1987).

49. Birmingham City Council, *The Highbury Initiative: Report of Proceedings* (Birmingham: Birmingham City Council, 1989), 1.

50. Ibid.

51. Francisco Javier Monclús, "The Barcelona Model: An Original Formula? From 'Reconstruction' to Strategic Urban Projects (1979–2004)," *Planning Perspectives* 18, no. 4 (2003): 399–421.

52. Birmingham City Council, *The Highbury Initiative*, 5, 7.

53. Ibid., 7.

54. Ibid., 7–9.

55. Neil Brenner, "Globalization as Reterritorialization: The Re-Scaling of Urban Governance in the European Union," *Urban Studies* 36, no. 3 (1999): 431–51.

56. Michael Hebbert, "The Vision of the European City," *Tiedepolitiikka* 30, no. 3 (2005): 27–34.

57. Charles Gachelin, "The Ambition of Eurocities," *Urbanisme*, Hors Series 10 (1998): 18–25; Commission of the European Communities, *Green Paper on the Urban Environment COM(90), 218 final* (Brussels: Commission of the European Community, 1990), 54.

58. BCC Mins, February 6, 1951, pp. 712–13.

59. BCC Mins, June 12, 1951, pp. 57–59; June 16, 1953, p. 32; July 27, 1965, p. 257; BCA MS2299 Box 19, BCCI Mins, December 18, 1951.

60. Birmingham and Frankfurt initially signed a bilateral agreement in 1954 due to their shared problems from obsolescent public housing and traffic congestion: BCC Mins, November 9, 1954, pp. 543–44.
61. BCC Mins, June 13, 1967, pp. 36–39; May 20, 1969, pp. 17–18; December 7, 1971, pp. 526–28.
62. In the spirit of detente, the geographical focus of twinning shifted toward Eastern Europe and Asia during the 1970s and 1980s, with Birmingham entering formal relations with the Soviet city of Zaporozhye in 1973 before signing friendship agreements with both Zagreb and Changchun in 1982. See Birmingham City Council, *Birmingham Town Twinning Handbook* (Birmingham: Birmingham City Council, 1983).
63. Ibid., Appendix A.
64. JEIPSC Mins, April 24, 1996, pp. 42–43.
65. Ibid., 38–39; July 18, 1996, pp. 1–6.
66. Ibid., April 24, 1996, p. 7.
67. Ibid., December 11, 1997, pp. 3–4; January 16, 1998, pp. 1–2
68. Ibid., July 10, 1998, pp. 3–5.
69. Richard Trainor, "The 'Decline' of British Urban Governance since 1850: A Reassessment," in Morris and Trainor, *Urban Governance*, 40.

Chapter 8

1. I would like to thank Richard Greenwald, Michael Hebbert, Kevin Kruse, Sarah T. Phillips, and Neal Rosendorf, among others, for their helpful comments on this article. Ed Koch, Peter J. Solomon, Gillian Sorensen, and Diane Coffey also were generous with their time and knowledge of the topic.
2. Ed Koch with William Rauch, *Mayor: An Autobiography* (New York: Simon and Schuster, 1984), 96; *New York Times*, October 6, 1977.
3. An American English word of Yiddish origin meaning insolent audacity.
4. Owen Gutfreund, interview with Jim Brigham, Columbia University Oral History Research Office (CUOHRO), May 14, 1992, p. 38. Peter J. Solomon, interview with author, November 12, 2004.
5. Jimmy Carter, *Keeping Faith* (London: Collins, 1982), 493–94.
6. Paul E. Peterson, *City Limits* (Chicago: University of Chicago Press, 1981), 3; U.S. Constitution, Article I, Section 10.
7. Saskia Sassen, *Losing Control? Sovereignty in an Age of Globalization* (New York: Columbia University Press, 1996), 28, 30.
8. See Heidi H. Hobbs, *City Hall Goes Abroad: The Foreign Policy of Local Politics* (Thousand Oaks, CA: Sage, 1994), 1.
9. Arthur Browne, Dan Collins, and Michael Goodwyn, *I, Koch: A Decidedly Unauthorized Biography of the Mayor of New York City, Ed Koch* (New York: Dodd, Mead, 1985), 266–73.
10. *New York Times*, September 26, 1983.
11. Michael H. Schuman found more than one thousand municipalities participating in some way in foreign relations and advocated expanding the field as a

way of democratizing U.S. foreign policy. Michael H. Shuman, "Dateline Main Street: Local Foreign Policies," *Foreign Policy* 65 (Winter 1986–87): 154–74, esp. 155–56. More recent structuralist and poststructuralist scholarship has focused on cities as nodes in a global network, which frequently relate to each other without the mediation of the federal government. See Paul Knox, ed., *World Cities in a World System* (Cambridge: Cambridge University Press, 1995), particularly Andrew Kirby, Sally Marston, and Kenneth Seasholes, "World Cities and Global Communities: The Municipal Foreign Policy Movement and New Roles for Cities," 267–79.

12. See Koch Manuscripts, New York City Municipal Archives (hereafter Koch MSS), NYC Commission for the United Nations and Consular Corps Annual Report 1977, Box 269, Folder 3.

13. Little Flower was one of La Guardia's many nicknames, both a translation of his first name and a reference to his short stature.

14. Brown et al., *I, Koch*, 266.

15. Ibid., 33.

16. Pat Koch Thaler, interview with author, May 23, 2001.

17. Edward I. Koch, interview with author, March 18, 2000.

18. Ibid.

19. Ibid.

20. The Uruguayan officers who made the threat were due to be assigned to Washington, DC, but the State Department "vetoed" their appointments. State Department Action Memorandum, December 13, 1976, published by the National Security Archive, http://www.gwu.edu/~nsarchiv/NSAEBB/NSAEBB112; see also Edward I. Koch with Daniel Paisner, *Citizen Koch: An Autobiography* (New York: St. Martins, 1992), 106–7.

21. Joshua B. Freeman, *Working Class New York: Life and Labor Since World War II* (New York: New Press, 2000), 257–62.

22. *New York Daily News*, October 29, 1975.

23. Felix Rohatyn, interview with author, December 1, 2003. See *New York Times*, November 18, 1975.

24. After he left the Koch administration, Solomon served as counselor to the Treasury Department, and is a member of the Council on Foreign Relations. Peter J. Solomon biography, http://www.pjsolomon.com/ourpeople/52bio.html (accessed November 14, 2005).

25. For the best exposition of this position from near the time, see Robert F. Wagner et al. and the Commission on the Year 2000, *New York Ascendant* (New York. Perennial, 1987). On the Koch administration rationale for tax abatements, see Alair Townsend, interview with author, May 23, 2006.

26. "U.S. Consular Cities Consult New York," *New York Times*, June 12, 1983.

27. "Briefing paper," Mayoral trip to Tokyo, November 13, 1985, Koch MSS 13-31-10; *Washington Post*, October 31, 1989.

28. On the David Letterman show, the announcer began: "From New York, a subsidiary of Mitsubishi, it's 'Late Night with David Letterman!'" *New York Times*, December 18, 1989.

29. Ibid.; *New York Times*, November 12, 1989.

30. *New York Times*, May 24, 1960; Harry S. Truman Presidential Library, John M. Begg interview with Richard D. McKenzie, July 11, 1975, p. 48.

31. Koch MSS 25-63-5, Robert Kaplan files. Tokyo/New York Week June 9–15, 1985, 25th Anniversary of Sister City relationship proposal, n.d. but probably early 1985.

32. Solomon, interview with author.

33. Ibid.; *New York Times*, July 7, 1985.

34. Saskia Sassen, *The Global City*, 2nd ed. (Princeton, NJ: Princeton University Press, 2001), 19, 352.

35. Sven Beckert, *The Monied Metropolis: New York City and the Consolidation of the American Bourgeoisie 1850–1896* (Cambridge: Cambridge University Press, 2001), 4.

36. Koch MSS, Box 269, Folder 3, "NYC Commission for UN and Consular Corps Annual Report 1977."

37. Gillian Sorensen, a TV producer by profession, grew up in a political family in Michigan, marrying Theodore Sorensen, one of John F. Kennedy's closest aides. A moderate Democratic activist, who worked early on for the election of Jimmy Carter and Ed Koch and also served on the board of the Committee for Public Broadcasting and as a member of the Council on Foreign Relations. Lucia Mouat, "Welcoming the World in New York," *Christian Science Monitor*, November 17, 1989.

38. Gillian Sorensen, interview with author, April 19, 2005.

39. Ibid.; Kenneth T. Jackson dubbed New York City "The Capital of Capitalism," in Anthony Sutcliffe, ed., *Metropolis 1890–1940* (Chicago: University of Chicago Press, 1984), 319–53.

40. "U.S. Consular Cities Consult New York," *New York Times*, June 12, 1983.

41. Sorensen interview with author; *New York Times*, October 13, 1979; Koch MSS Roll MN41128, Box 169, Folder 4, Sorensen to Koch September 14, 1979.

42. Koch MSS, Box 269, Folder 7, Sorensen to Leventhal, February 9, 1981.

43. Koch MSS, Box 269, Folder 4, Koch to Sorensen, July 18, 1979.

44. Koch MSS, Box 269, Folder 4, Sorensen to Koch, September 14, 1979.

45. For an update on the status of these relationships, see the Web site of the Sister City Program of the City of New York, Inc., http://www.nyc.gov/html/unccp/scp/html/about/main.shtml. The Giuliani and Bloomberg administrations have expanded the program to include Budapest, Johannesburg, Jerusalem, and Rome.

46. Sorensen interview with author. There is not space here to discuss all of Koch's numerous international trips, or the numerous relationships and visits to New York and with Mayor Koch by heads of state, foreign ministers, mayors, and other representatives from nearly every country in the world. Koch welcomed donations to the homeless from the sultan of Brunei and pleaded with the president of Italy to pardon Sophia Loren after she was convicted of tax evasion.

47. Paisner, *Citizen Koch*, 188–89.

48. Brown et al., *I, Koch*, 275.

49. Hobbs, *City Hall*, 33.

50. Ronald Smothers, "Koch Assails Jeers at Bedford Stuyvesant Meeting," *New York Times*, November 14, 1980; Clyde Haberman, "Koch Protests Policies on Blacks in Letter to South Africa Premier," *New York Times*, December 3, 1980.

51. Though Koch eventually won re-election by a large margin, his pollsters were concerned about the possibility of coalescence of an opposition coalition. Mark Penn, interview with author, January 21, 2005.

52. Moellenkopf, *A Phoenix in the Ashes*, 118, 170.

53. *Washington Post*, February 16, 1984; *New York Times*, February 16, 1984. John Sears, Ronald Reagan's former campaign manager, was senior partner. In the postapartheid era, Dumisani Kumalo became South African ambassador to the UN.

54. *New York Times*, May 31, 1984.

55. The city council president and comptroller were officials elected in city-wide elections and natural rivals to the mayor. Bellamy ran for mayor in 1985 and Goldin in 1989, though neither were strong candidates. Their main functions were to preside over the city council and audit New York's financial operations, respectively. But their real power came from their positions, along with the mayor and the five borough presidents, on a body called the Board of Estimate, which approved all city contracts, zoning, and the city budget. This body overshadowed the machine-controlled city council. Because its votes were not apportioned according to population, it was abolished in 1989 after a court declared it unconstitutional. It was replaced by a larger and more powerful city council.

56. *New York Times*, June 1, 1984.

57. Koch made the comparison between the apartheid regime and the Nazis at a memorial service for victims of the regime. See *New York Times*, October 6, 1985.

58. *New York Times*, July 14, 1984.

59. Koch MSS 29-74-20, Crotty to Mulhearn re. Banking Commission Local Law 19, August 13, 1985: Crotty to Koch, August 27, 1985.

60. *New York Times*, June 22, 1986.

61. *New York Times*, September 20, 1985; *Courier Mail* (Brisbane, Queensland), September 21, 1985; *New York Times*, October 6, 1985.

62. *New York Times*, October 29, 1989.

63. Ibid.

64. Solomon interview with author.

Chapter 9

1. John Friedmann, *The Prospect of Cities* (Minneapolis: University of Minnesota Press, 2002); Saskia Sassen, *The Global City: New York, London, Tokyo* (Princeton, NJ: Princeton University Press, 2001; first published, 1991).

2. This is the direction now taken by some researchers, as in Michael Amen, Kevin archer and Martin Bosman, eds., *Global Cities: From the Center to the Margins* (London: Rowman & Littlefield, 2006).

3. Peter J. Taylor, *World City Network: A Global Urban Analysis* (New York: Routledge, 2002).

4. The average length of an interview was approximately 60–70 minutes. Minimum editing protects interviewees' anonymity.

5. Five hundred and seven French articles of *Le Devoir* and *La Presse* between January 1985 and December 2001 were sampled through the *Biblio Branchée* database, while one hundred and eighty English articles of *The Gazette* between January 1985 and December 2001 were sampled through *Canadian Newsstand*.

6. For a historical review of transnational networks in Europe, see Pierre-Yves Saunier, ed., *Municipal Connections: Cooperation, Links and Transfers among European Cities in the 20th Century*, Special Issue of *Contemporary European History* 11, no. 4 (2002).

7. David Harvey, "From Managerialism to Entrepreneurialism: The Transformation in Urban Governance in Late Capitalism," *Geografiska Annaler* 71B, no. 1 (1989): 3–18.

8. John R. Short, *Global Metropolitan-Globalizing Cities in a Capitalist World* (New York: Routledge, 2004).

9. Charles Ruthesier, *Imagining Atlanta* (New York: Verso, 1996).

10. Robert A. Beauregard, "Theorizing the Global-Local Connection," in P. L. Knox and P. J. Taylor, eds., *World Cities in a World-System* (Cambridge: Cambridge University Press, 1995), 232–48.

11. Harvey, "From Managerialism," 352.

12. Panayotis Soldatos, "Strategic Cities Alliances: An Added Value to the Innovative Making of an International City," *Ekistics* 350 (1991): 346–50.

13. Canadian Parliament, *Evidence: Minutes of Standing Committee on Foreign Affairs and International Trade*, 1995, http://www.parl.gc.ca/committees/fore/evidence/84_95-11- 30/fore84_blk101.html (accessed October 25, 2002).

14. Interview with author, January 10, 2002. Eventually, Bombardier, the Montreal-based transportation company, won the $44 million contract to manufacture 40 coaches for the rail-link between downtown Beijing and Capital International Airport. SNC-Lavalin, an engineering company, is involved with a joint venture to construct Beijing's No. 5 subway line.

15. Interview with author, July 11, 2002.

16. Interview with author, January 10, 2002.

17. Interview with author, May 17, 2002.

18. For a full listing of Canadian-Chinese urban twinning relations, see http://www.beijing.gc.ca/beijing/en/navmain/canada/596/1958.htm (accessed December 23, 2005).

19. *The Gazette*, May 27, 1985, p. A1.

20. Fulong Wu, "(Post-) Socialist Entrepreneurial City as a State Project: Shanghai's Reglobalisation in Question," *Urban Studies* 40, no. 9 (2003): 1673–98.

21. Zhengji Fu, "The State, Capital, and Urban Restructuring in Post-reform Shanghai," in *The New Chinese City: Globalization and Market Reform*, ed. John Logan (Oxford: Blackwell, 2002), 106–20.

22. Interview with author, June 10, 2002.

23. Canadian Government, *Report of the Consultative Committee to the Ministerial Committee on the Development of the Montreal Region* (Ottawa: Minister of Supply and Services Canada, 1986).

24. William Coffey and Mario Polèse, "A Distinct Metropolis for a Distinct Society? The Economic Restructuring of Montreal in the Canadian Context," *Canadian Journal of Region Science* 22 (1999): 23–40.

25. *The Gazette*, May 14, 1985, p. A1.

26. *La Presse*, March 2, 1985, p. 7ff.; August 8, 1985, p. A1.

27. *La Presse*, January 20, 1996, p. A1.

28. *La Presse*, May 14, 1984, p. A2.

29. *Le Devoir*, October 20, 1984, p. 2; October 18, 1984, p. 4; September 29, 1984, p. 2; September 25, 1984, p. 10.

30. Pierre Bourque, *Ma Passion pour Montréal* (Montréal: Méridien, 2002).

31. Yunhua Hu, "Re: Shanghai Downtown Green Space; Choice of Design Professionals and Collaboration with the City of Montreal," attached to *Mémorandum entre la Ville de Montréal et la Ville de Shanghai Portant sur la Conception du Projet du Parc de l'échangeur* (Montreal: Montreal Municipal Government, 1999).

32. Interview with author, May 15, 2003; May 17, 2002.

33. The official twinning documents between Montreal and Shanghai were in the business-like, contractual form, which also set the tone of the relations between the two cities. I would like to thank Pierre-Yves Saunier for pointing this out after comparing Montreal-Shanghai memoranda and protocols with many other European twinning agreements.

34. Montreal Municipal Government, Mémorandum des Projets d'échanges Amicaux entre Montréal et Shanghai (2001–2003), 2001; Protocole d'Entente Portant sur la Mise sur Pied d'un Comité Conjoint des Villes de Shanghai et de Montréal sur la Gestion des Déchets Urbains, 1999; Mémorandum des Projets d'échanges Amicaux entre Montréal et Shanghai (1998–2000), 1998; Protocole d'Entente Portant sur la Coopération en Matière d'exploitation des Espaces Souterrains, de Prévention des Sinistres et de Planification des Mesures d'Urgence entre le Bureau de la Défense Civile de Shanghai et le Service de l'Urbanisme de la Ville de Montréal, 1997; Mémorandum sur le Programme D'échanges entre Montréal et Shanghai pour la Période 1988–1989, 1987, Montreal Municipal Archive.

35. *The Gazette*, May 15, 1985, p. A4.

36. *The Gazette*, May 27, 1985, p. A1.

37. Interview with author, May 17, 2003.

38. Howard Elcock, *Political Leadership* (Cheltenham: Edward Elgar, 2001), 134, 191.

39. See the Chinese official news outlet about the specific posts that Zhu had served in the Chinese government, http://english.people.com.cn/leaders/shurongji.htm (accessed December 23, 2005).

40. Interview, May 15, 2005. Qi had worked closely with Bourque since the construction of the *Chinese Garden in Montreal*.

41. Bourque, *Ma Passion*, 230, the author's translation.
42. Interview with author, May 15, 2002.
43. Ibid.
44. *The Gazette*, January 21, 2001, p. A4.
45. *The Gazette*, December 18, 2000, p. B2.
46. Interview with author, January 7, 2002.
47. Interview with author, July 11, 2002.
48. Janine Brodie, "Imagining Democratic Urban Citizenship," in *Democracy, Citizenship, and the Global City*, ed. Engin Isin (New York: Routledge, 2000), 116.
49. This type of criticism was not unique, see Jörg Dürrschmidt and Ulf Matthiesen, "Everyday Milieu and Culture of Displacement: A Comparative Investigation into Space, Place and (Non)Attachment within the German-Polish Twin City Guben/Gubin," *Canadian Journal of Urban Research* 11, no. 1 (2002): 17–46.
50. Daniel Bush, *Seattle's Cold War[m] Foreign Policy, 1957–1990: Citizen Diplomats and Grass Roots Diplomacy, Sister Cities and International Exchange* (PhD diss., Seattle: University of Washington, 1998).
51. European Commission, *Town-Twinning and the European Union* (Paris: Council of European Municipalities and Regions, 2000).
52. Interview with author, August 5, 2002.
53. Katherine A. Graham, Susan D. Phillips, and Allan M. Maslove, *Urban Governance in Canada- Representation, Resources and Restructuring* (Toronto: Harcourt Brace Canada, 1998), 109. Also see the book by a retired councilor Marcel Sévigny, *Trente Ans de Politique Municipale: Plaidoyer pour une Citoyenneté Active* (Montréal: écosociété, 2001).
54. *The Gazette*, February 14, 2001. This information was revealed by the opposing city councilor, Marvin Rotrand, through an access-to-information request. The expense was $291,141 in 1999.
55. Interview with author, January 15, 2002.
56. Interview with author, May 15, 2002.
57. Susan Clarke and Gary Gaile, *The Work of Cities* (Minneapolis: University of Minnesota Press, 1998).
58. *Falun* followers tried to meet with the mayor to express their political conviction, but the response they received was that the city could not offer them help (*The Gazette*, October 15, 2001, p. A3).
59. Saskia Sassen, *Losing Control: Sovereignty in the Age of Globalization* (New York: Columbia University Press, 1996), 38.
60. It was not until April 2006 that Mayor Tremblay visited Shanghai and renewed the twinning memorandum.

Chapter 10

1. Maria Del Huerto, "Una Aproximación Contextual y Conceptual a la Cooperación Descentralizada," in *Tejiendo Lazos entre territorios*, ed. Maria del Huerto

and Vicente Godiñez Zuñiga (Valparaiso: Municipalidad de Valparaiso/Diputacio de Barcelona, 2004), 19–52.

2. In this chapter, we use the word "model" with the meaning given by the municipal actors themselves, that is to say a more or less systematic, more or less complete set of methods that could be used and transferred from one city to another.

3. Stephen Ward, *Planning the Twentieth-Century City: The Advanced Capitalist World* (Chichester: John Wiley and Sons, 2002).

4. Roberto Böcker Zavaro, *Desarrollo, Planificación Estratégica y Corporativismo Local: el Caso de Mar de Plata, Argentina* (PhD diss., Universitat Rovira i Virgili, Tarragona, 2005).

5. Sébastien Velut, *Argentine, Des provinces à la Nation* (Paris: Presses Universitaires de France, 2002).

6. A recent discussion can be found in Sergio Boisier, "Hay Espacio para el Desarrollo Local en la Globalización?" *Revista de la CEPAL* 86 (2005): 47–62.

7. Pierre Veltz, *Mondialisation, Ville et Territoire, l'économie d'Archipel* (Paris: Presses Universitaires de France, 1997); Manuel Castells, *The Information Age* (Oxford: Blackwell, 2001).

8. In the following years Bolivia, Chile, and Peru became associated members, and, as recently as 2005, Venezuela joined the union with full membership.

9. Dieter Nohelen and Liliana De Ritz, eds., *Reforma Institucional y Cambio Político* (Buenos Aires: Legasa/Cedes, 1991). Ernesto Calvo and Juan Carlos Abal Medina, eds., *El Federalismo Electoral Argentino* (Buenos Aires: Inap/Eudeba, 2001).

10. Alicia Veneciano, *Reflexiones sobre una Reforma Orientada al Ciudadano. La Descentralización Participativa de Montevideo* (Madrid: Instituto Nacional de Administración Pública, 2005).

11. An unusual leader for the Uruguay Socialist Party, with little previous political experience, Tabaré Vázquez was professor of medicine and a successful president of the *Progreso* football club. He was invited to join the party in order to rejuvenate its leadership.

12. "Turn Barcelona into a leading center of the European macroregion; improve the quality of life and the progress of the people, make stronger industry and advanced services to the firms."

13. Carlos Vainer, "Pátria, Empresa e Mercadoria, Notas sobre a Estratégia Discursiva do Planejamento Estratégico Urbano," *Mundo Urbano* 14 (2001), http://www.mundourbano.unq.edu.ar.

14. The unusual adjective, *Iberoamericano*, is used by the Spanish diplomacy to describe the Spanish- and Portuguese-speaking countries in Latin America.

15. Tim Marshall, "Urban Planning and Governance: Is There a Barcelona Model?" *International Planning Studies* 5, no. 3 (2000): 299–319.

16. Jorda Borja, "Barcelona y su urbanismo. Exitos pasados, desafíos presentes, oportunidades futuras," *Café de las ciudades* 21 (2004), http://www.cafedelasciudades.com.ar.

17. Both became ministers in Inácio Lula's government.

18. One should remember that Liberation theology was strong in Latin America and particularly in Brazil, with participation of the high clergy, such as Bishop Leonardo Boff, and the local communities and parishes.
19. Marion Gret and Yves Sintomer, *Porto Alegre, l'espoir d'une Autre Démocratie* (Paris: La Découverte, 2002).
20. See http:// www.bestpractices.org.
21. Jackie Smith, "The World Social Forum and the Challenges of Global Democracy," *Global Networks* 4, no. 4 (2004): 413–21; Chloé Keraghel and Jai Sen, "Explorations in Open Space: The World Social Forum and Cultures of Politics," *International Social Science Journal* 182 (2004): 483–93.
22. Excerpts from the final document of the Forum of Local Authorities, World Social Forum, Porto Alegre, 2001.
23. A sociologist and urban planner, Jordi Borja I. Sebastia taught in various universities and as an elected official held many responsibilities in Barcelona's local government (responsible for the decentralization programs, vice president of the metropolitan area, director of international relations, etc.). He also worked as a private consultant in town planning.
24. Biographical details on Manuel Castells can be found in Mayté Pascual, *En qué Mundo Vivimos. Conversaciones con Manuel Castells* (Madrid: Alianza Editorial, 2006).
25. Jordi Borja, and Manuel Castells, *Local y global, la gestión de las ciudades en la era de la información* (Madrid: Taurus, 1999).
26. He was subsquently appointed to the national government, where he was responsible for coordinating relations with Uruguayans living abroad.
27. The journalist Reinaldo Gargano (Minister of Foreign Affairs) and José Díaz (Minister of the Interior).
28. For more clues, see http://www.socialistinternational.org/6Meetings/Locauth/DecAthensMayors/Athens-e.html#charter.
29. Pablo Perulli, Fabio Rugge, and Raffaela Florio, "Reti di città: una forma emergente di governance Europea," *Foedus* 4 (2002): 53–69; Le Galès Patrick, "Government e govenance urbana nelle città Europee: argumenti per la discussione," *Foedus* 4 (2002): 8–31.

Chapter 11

1. Saskia Sassen, *The Global City: New York, London, Tokyo* (Princeton, NJ: Princeton University Press, 1991); Janet L. Abu-Lughod, *New York, Chicago, Los Angeles: America's Global Cities* (Minneapolis: University of Minnesota Press, 1999); John Friedmann, *The Prospect of Cities* (Minneapolis: University of Minnesota Press, 2002).
2. Geoff Eley, "Historicizing the Global, Politicizing Capital: Giving the Present a Name," *History Workshop Journal* 63 (2007): 159; Kevin H. O'Rourke and

Jeffrey G. Williamson, *Globalization and History: The Evolution of a Nineteenth-Century Atlantic Economy* (Cambridge, MA: MIT Press, 1999).

3. Adam McKeown, "Periodizing Globalization," *History Workshop Journal* 63 (2007): 227.

4. Although it contains many useful ideas for our purpose, one such nation-centered perspective is found in Wolfram Kaiser, "Transnational Mobilization and Cultural Representation: Political Transfer in an Age of Proto-globalization, Democratization and Nationalism 1848–1914," *European Review of History* 12, no. 2 (2005): 403–24; see also Christopher A. Bayly, *The Birth of the Modern World 1780–1914: Global Connections and Comparisons* (London: Blackwell, 2004).

5. Jeffrey M. Sellers, "Re-placing the Nation: An Agenda for Comparative Urban Politics," *Urban Affairs Review* 40, no. 4 (2005): 420.

6. Neil Brenner, *New State Spaces: Urban Governance and the Rescaling of Statehood* (Oxford: Oxford University Press, 2004); Neil Brenner, "Globalization as Reterritorialization: The Re-scaling of Urban Governance in the European Union," *Urban Studies* 36, no. 3 (1999): 431–51; Mike Goldsmith and John Garrard, "Urban Governance: Some Reflections," in *Urban Governance: Britain and Beyond since 1750*, ed. R. J. Morris and Richard Trainor (Aldershot: Ashgate, 2000), 15.

7. The most inspirational study of transnational interconnectivity is undoubtedly Michael Peter Smith, *Transnational Urbanism: Locating Globalization* (London: Blackwell, 2001).

8. Michael Peter Smith, "Transnational Urbanism Revisited," *Journal of Ethnic and Migration Studies* 31, no. 2 (2005): 238.

9. Ibid.

10. Daniel T. Rodgers, *Atlantic Crossings: Social Politics in a Progressive Age* (Cambridge, MA: Belknap Press of Harvard University Press, 1998).

11. Emile Vinck, "The International Union of Local Authorities," *Local Government Administration* (June 1935): 6.

12. Antoine Vion, "Europe from the Bottom Up: Town Twinning in France during the Cold War," *Contemporary European History* 11, no. 2 (2002): 623–40.

13. Smith, "Transnational Urbanism Revisited," 239.

14. Adam Marshall, "Europeanization at the Urban Level: Local Actors, Institutions, and the Dynamics of Multi-level Interaction," *Journal of European Public Policy* 12, no. 4 (2005): 668–86.

15. Goldsmith and Garrard, "Urban Governance," 22–23; see also Peter John and Alistair Cole, "Political Leadership in the New Urban Governance: Britain and France Compared," *Local Government Studies* 25, no. 4 (1999): 98–115.

16. Lionel Martins and José Manuel Rodríguez Álvarez, "Towards Global Leadership: Taking Up the Challenge of New Local Governance in Europe?" *Environment and Planning C: Government and Policy* 25, no. 3 (2007): 406–7.

17. Sellers, "Re-placing the Nation," 423.

18. Stephen V. Ward, "Re-examining the International Diffusion of Planning," in *Urban Planning in a Changing World: The Twentieth Century Experience*, ed. Robert Freestone (London: E. & F. N. Spon, 2000), 40–60.

19. Christian Lefèvre and Ernesto d'Albergo, "Why Cities Are Looking Abroad and How They Go about It," *Environment and Planning C: Government and Policy* 25, no. 3 (2007): 319.

20. Pierre-Yves Saunier, "Taking Up the Bet on Connections: A Municipal Contribution," *Contemporary European History* 11, no. 2 (2002): 507–27.

21. This phrase is borrowed from Robert Putnam, *Bowling Alone: The Collapse and Revival of American Community* (New York: Simon & Schuster, 2000).

22. Marjatta Hietala, *Services and Urbanization at the Turn of the Century: The Diffusion of Innovations* (Helsinki: Suomen Historiallinen Seura, 1987).

23. Hank V. Savitch and Paul Kantor, *Cities in the International Marketplace* (Princeton, NJ: Oxford University Press, 2002); Patrick Le Galès, *European Cities* (Oxford: Oxford University Press, 2002).

Epilogue

1. On competitiveness today, see *Competitive Cities in the Global Economy*, Organisation for Economic Cooperation and Development (OECD) Territorial Reviews (Paris: OECD, 2006), 55.

2. Ibid., 85–153.

3. These clusters are classified into four categories: competitive clusters, visibility clusters, emerging technology clusters, and manufacturing clusters; ibid., 110.

4. Policies in the Habitat Programme of the United Nations and Eco-efficient Cities of Council for Local Environmental Initiatives, http://www.iclei.org.

5. *OECD Territorial Reviews. Seoul Korea. Policy Brief* (Paris: OECD, 2006).

6. Charles Landry, *The Creative City: A Toolkit for Urban Innovators* (London: Earthscan, 2000), 87–90.

7. Paul Edwards, "Infrastructure and Modernity: Force, Time, and Social Organization in the History of Sociotechnical Systems," in *Modernity and Technology*, ed. Thomas J. Misa, Philip Brey, and Andrew Feenberg (Cambridge, MA: MIT Press, 2003), 185–91.

8. Mercer Human Resource Consulting Worldwide Quality of Living Survey 2007, http://www.mercerhr.com.

9. Saskia Sassen, ed., *Global Networks, Linked Cities* (New York: Routledge, 2002), 71–115.

10. Marjatta Hietala, *Services and Urbanization at the turn of the century. The diffusion of innovations* (Helsinki: Suomen Historiallinen Seura, 1987), 361–95.

11. Anthony Sutcliffe, *Towards the Planned City: Germany, Britain, the United States and France 1780–1914* (Oxford: Blackwell, 1981), 163–66, 176. It is estimated that from 1886 to the end of the century there were 853 international congresses, and 2,271 conferences in 1900 and 1914: E. P. Hennock, *British Social Reform and German Precedents: The Case of Social Insurance, 1880–1914*

(Oxford: Oxford University Press, 1987). A recent bibliography on international exhibitions from 1851 to 1951 includes one hundred exhibitions held in more than twenty countries: Alexander C. T. Geppert, Jean Coffey, and Tammy Lau, *International Exhibitions, Expositions Universelles and World's Fairs, 1851-2005: A Bibliography*, http://www.tu-cottbus.de/BTU/Fak2/TheoArch/Wolke/eng/Bibliography/ExpoBibliography3ed.pdf.

12. Hietala, *Services and Urbanization*, 23–25.

13. IULA Newsletter. Monthly review of the International Union of Local Authorities (The Hague 1967–1979).

14. Figures taken from http://www.cities-localgovernments.org/uclg/index.asp.

15. Marjatta Hietala, *Tietoa, taitoa, asiantuntemusta. Helsinki eurooppalaisessa kehityksessä 1875–1917. 1: Innovaatioiden ja kansainvälistymisen vuosikymmenet* (Helsinki: Suomen Historiallinen Seura, 1992), 276–79; Hietala-Bell, *Helsinki: The Innovative City; Historical Perspectives* (Helsinki: Finnish Literature Society/City of Helsinki Urban Facts, 2002), 127–29.

16. Hietala, *Services and Urbanization*, 203–20, 239–58.

17. Hietala, *Tietoa, taitoa*, 269–76.

18. Hietala–Bell, *Helsinki*, 183–200.

19. Mike Davis, *Planet of Slums* (London: Verso, 2006), 1–49.

20. Lawrence J. Vale and Thomas J. Campanella, eds., *The Resilient City: How Modern Cities Recover from Disaster* (New York; Oxford University Press, 2005).

21. William J. Mitchell and Anthony M. Townsend, "Cyborg Agonistes: Disaster and Reconstruction in the Digital Electronic Era," in ibid, 313–34.

22. James K. Mitchell, ed., Crucibles of Hazard: Megacities and Disasters in Transition (Tokyo: United Nations University Press, 1999), 15–47.

23. The UN-HABITAT's resolution on human settlements was originally discussed at its Habitat I conference in Vancouver in 1976 but was not made official policy until the Habitat II meeting in Istanbul in 1996. Later resolutions tightened the body's resolution to eradicate urban poverty. See Resolution adopted by the General Assembly, session 6, Agenda item 102, February 26, 2002. On the genesis of UN-HABITAT, see Richard Harris, "A Double Irony: The Originality and Influence of John F. C. Turner," *Habitat International* 27 (2003): 245–69.

24. On the Mega-Cities Project, see Akhtar A Badshah and Janice E. Perlman, "Mega-Cities and the Urban Future: A Model for Replicating Best Practices," in *The Blackwell City Reader*, ed. Gary Bridge and Sophie Watson (Oxford: Blackwell, 2002).

Index

The authors wish to acknowledge the financial support of the School of Cultural Studies, Leeds Metropolitan University, in the production of this index. They also thank Rebecca Francescatti for creating the index.